First in the field

A Century of The Camping and Caravanning Club

Hazel Constance

Hazel Constance has been a Club member since 1960 and has held a number of offices in the Association of Lightweight Campers. After a varied career in library work, nursing and teaching, she wrote a series of articles on making camping equipment for *Practical Camper* magazine. This was followed by further features on camping and touring for other journals. In 1979 Hazel wrote her first book. More books followed co-authored with her husband Pat. Always interested in the Club's history, Hazel was appointed Honorary Club Archivist in 1996. She has been able to collect some historic equipment, pennons, badges, etc to add to the Archive, as well as photographs and documents. She was commissioned in 1999 to write the history of the Club's first one hundred years.

Author's acknowledgement
I would like to thank the Executive Committee of The Camping and Caravanning Club for commissioning me to write the Club's history. It has been a time-consuming task, at times frustrating, but a task which I have enjoyed.

I wish to thank the many people who have, perhaps unknowingly, helped with the writing of this book. In particular, thanks are due to the many Club members, past and present, who have supplied photographs, information and archive material from which we have been able to draw.

Special thanks to Miss Stephanie Hilhouse for allowing us to use many of her father's photographs, and to Mrs Pauline Godsall, a descendant of Thomas Hiram Holding, for her assistance with the Holding family history.

Thanks to David Welsford and the staff at Greenfields House for their forbearance, and especially to Peter Frost for his advice and assistance.

Last, but by no means least, I must thank my husband Pat for his help with the research and for his long-suffering patience and understanding, especially at those times when the book had to take priority over the housework.

Published in 2001 by
The Camping and Caravanning Club
Greenfields House
Westwood Way
Coventry
CV4 8JH

British Library Cataloguing in Publication Data
A catalogue record for this book is available from the British Library
ISBN 0-9541659-0-X

Typeset in Didot and ITC Officina Sans
Design and origination by Paul Samat
Repro and printing by GreenShires Ltd

First in the field

A Century of The Camping and Caravanning Club

The Centenary of the founding of the world's first club for campers is an appropriate moment for the publication of an official history of what eventually became The Camping and Caravanning Club. The founders were indeed "first in the field" and, had they been alive today, they would have found it hard to believe just how big the Club has grown and what an impact it has had on camping and caravanning in Britain and all over the world.

Life is never easy for pioneers, but there is strength in numbers and this is important in two respects. Membership of any club involves abiding by rules and a big membership gives the club a status within society, which enables it to influence public opinion as well as legislation and regulation. It is also an invaluable asset when it comes to negotiating with landowners and local authorities for sites and other facilities; something which individual campers would find very difficult to achieve on their own. It is also a guarantee that agreements will be respected by all members and that any infringements will be handled by the Club. I can speak from experience since we have had a very successful Club site at Sandringham for over ten years.

I have had the pleasure of being Patron for the Club for 49 years – almost half its life! I am therefore very pleased to have this opportunity to congratulate all the members, committees, volunteers and staff on achieving this anniversary and to wish them and all future members even greater success in the next hundred years.

H.R.H. The Prince Philip, Duke of Edinburgh K.G., K.T., O.M.
Patron of The Camping and Caravanning Club

My great grandfather, the original Lord Baden-Powell, was proud to be the President of The Camping Club from 1919–1940.

He had a justifiably high opinion of the Club. Indeed, he wrote in his famous book, *Scouting for Boys*: "The members of The Camping Club are wonderful in leaving no trace behind them that there has been a camp. I have even seen them brushing the grass with a clothes brush to make it stand up again where they had been lying."

In the last ten years, I have also been proud to follow in his footsteps and I have an equally high view of the members of, what is today, The Camping and Caravanning Club. It is a tremendously influential organisation in all sorts of ways but, most importantly, it has brought much pleasure and enjoyment to thousands of people, giving them a chance to explore and enjoy the wonders of the countryside at home and abroad over the last one hundred years.

This book tells that story.

Bade Powen

The Lord Baden-Powell
President of The Camping and Caravanning Club

Contents

Thomas Hiram Holding. (Club Archive)

First in the field A Century of The Camping and Caravanning Club

Thomas Hiram Holding – the man who started it all

Born on 29 December 1844, in Prees, Shropshire, Thomas was the eldest son of Daniel and Sarah Holding. They belonged to the Mormon church and in 1853 they emigrated to Salt Lake City with their four children. Twins were born shortly after their arrival in New Orleans in March, but they and another child died during the 1,200-mile journey across the prairies.

Word reached them at Salt Lake City that Thomas's grandfather had died and the family made another long trek, this time through the Rockies, to return home. Thomas remained in England and, at 13, was apprenticed to the tailoring trade.

After some years travelling around the country – during which time he married, inspired the founding of the Cyclists' Touring Club and became an expert canoeist and canoe-camper – he arrived in London to work for The Tailor and Cutter magazine. He later became the Editor of The London Tailor. At the same time he built on his own successful tailoring business, taught many students and wrote more than 30 books.

At the age of 56 he founded the Association of Cycle Campers (A.C.C.) and is rightly described as the father of lightweight camping. He not only had very

lightweight fabrics made for tents but also designed other items of lightweight kit, which were made for him; thus, he added camping equipment to his tailoring business.

A man of outstanding personality and character, he inspired loyalty in his friends, making him an excellent companion in camp when things went wrong. However, he had a stubborn streak which could make him enemies, and which led to his resignation from the A.C.C.

A fine raconteur, he could speak on many subjects, including church architecture, although he was by inclination and upbringing a non-conformist.

At the age of 79 he cycled from Fulham to Brixham, Devon – a distance of 212 miles, and was asked to preach at a local church. "Impossible, sir," he said, "I have no sermon, and besides, only a flannel suit of light grey." The curt reply was "It's not your clothes, but your counsel we want."

How did he manage to find the time to found the Club? It seems that the old adage 'Ask a busy person if you want something done' could have been relevant. In this case the busy person thought up the ideas himself.

How the Club began
and the first five years

The founder of the Club, Thomas Hiram Holding, was a great outdoorsman, interested in all things involving the outdoor life. He was a keen cyclist, and as such was the man behind the founding of the Cyclists' Touring Club (C.T.C.) in 1878. He was also a very keen and able canoeist, and spent many holidays on Irish loughs and rivers with his own self-built sailing canoe. He always camped on these trips, and had been for many years trying to work out how camping kit could be carried on a bicycle.

In July 1897, a chance meeting with his friend 'H' (possibly Frederick Horsfield), who was planning a camping holiday with his wife on their tandem, led him to design an outfit suitable for carrying on a cycle. Holding was a high-class bespoke tailor and, as such, was able to use his skills to help his friend.

"Within eight days two complete outfits were made – made in four towns by seven separate people at a cost of about three guineas each – either lot weighing when in bulk some 14lbs, and so easily carried on a tandem or on two Safeties, and practically carriable with almost equal ease on *one* machine."

One of these outfits was taken with Holding when he, his son Frank, and two friends made a trip to Ireland. Not only was this kit taken, but also a small sailing yawl and sailing canoe, two heavier tents and equipment, and four cycles! The intention was to try cycle-camping as part of their

Left: Long before he founded the Club T.H. Holding used to camp when on boating and canoeing holidays. This photograph was taken in 1878 when on his cruise in the canoe Ospray. *(Club Archive)*

T.H. Holding took this photograph of (front, left to right) Rev. E.C. Pitt-Johnson, Francis Penn, (back, left to right) G.W. Penn, Tom Penn and T.W. Lowther, who joined him for the first camp of the newly-formed Association of Cycle Campers at Wantage, 1901. (Club Archive)

holiday: "We vainly believed we were the pioneers of it," writes Holding.

Their experiences were later described by Holding in a book entitled *Cycle and Camp in Connemara*, published in 1898. It has to be remembered that at that time those who were able to afford a holiday mostly spent their time in a hotel – Holding, however, preferred to camp.

"Personally, I like the camp so much better than the hotel – which I could afford – that, apart from the economy of camping, it is a real luxury in its freedom, and with one or two campers incontestably jollier.

"It is clear that the poor clerk or workman who wishes to see fresh countries at home or abroad may gratify his whim and have a fine holiday on the weekly expenditure of his pocket money and be independent of weather, distance or, to him, the prohibitive tariff of hotels. Let these tariffs no longer stop the poorer cycle man from his rightful feast of fresh air and the grandest scenery his country affords.

"Two men camping with their cycles could nohow spend more than four shillings per day for the pair or, to do it luxuriously, say 30 shillings a week for both. Thus the cost of the camp is saved, and, say 50 shillings besides towards next year's mount out of ONE week's holiday to each man. All this will be proved later on, much, I hope, to the promotion of Touring-by-Cycle-Camp.

"Who can question the advantages of camping? Only those who have never tried camping. All the horrors which outsiders fear and with which they threaten us we neither meet nor find. But it is not a lazy life – far

First in the field A Century of The Camping and Caravanning Club

from it. The camp affords exercise without fatigue; fresh air night and day, and sufficient excitement to create interest."

In his book, Holding not only describes the benefits of camping and the tour itself, but also the equipment and the problems incurred with two of the cycles – these were Bantams propelled by pedals directly attached to the front axle and with no chain. They must have been very uncomfortable to ride for any distance and also presented difficulties when it came to carrying camping kit on them. Nevertheless, four men between them carried a tent and other kit, including four sets of waterproofs.

It has to be said that most of their provisions were obtained from the farms on which they camped and, in addition, it was the usual practice to hire a blanket or two from the farmer – these, however, were not always used.

The importance of keeping dry was emphasised, even though "dry feet are the exception rather than the rule". The steep sloping sides of the 'A' cycle-tent were designed to shed water easily, but it must have been quite a difficult job for four men to keep dry in a tent measuring just 6ft long, 5ft 9ins wide and 5ft 9ins high, with no flysheet.

B.F. Fletcher with his "record kit" near Dursley, Gloucestershire, 1905.
Note the Japanese baskets in which the kit was packed.
(Club Archive)

Dry clothing was essential and needed to be kept so. Waterproofs were necessary, and Holding did not approve of cycle capes. These, he said, only kept the wearer dry above the knees, and the legs needed protection as well as the body. Capes were also inconvenient when pitching a tent in the rain, and a coat was therefore to be preferred.

At the end of the book, *Cycle and Camp in Connemara*, Holding describes the equipment in detail and invites readers to contact him if they have any difficulty with equipment. This resulted in a great deal of correspondence from people "starting to question me and make tents".

Because of the social conditions prevailing at the end of the 19th century, many of the poorer people were unable to read or write, and would certainly not have had the money to purchase Holding's book. Therefore,

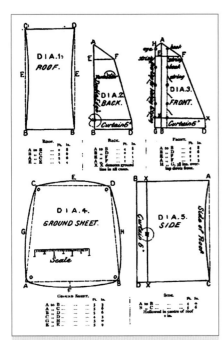

Instructions for making a new-style tent, The Gipsy, were published in the C.T.C. Gazette, February 1902. It was not long before they were to be seen at Association of Cycle Campers' events. (C.T.C. Archive)

most of those who wrote to him are likely to have been from the middle or upper-middle classes. This is later borne out by the first Club membership lists, where the addresses of the members at the time confirm this fact.

There is also the question of holidays. Under the Bank Holidays Act of 1861, Bank Holidays became statutory, non-religious days off. A few enlightened employers offered improved working hours and better pay, which led to some of the less well-off being able to have a long weekend away from work.

By 1880, a few employers were giving their workers paid holidays, and the introduction of Wakes Weeks for mill workers and Trip Weeks for miners meant that more people were able to take some kind of holiday.

Even so, very few poor people would have been able to afford a holiday of any description at the turn of the century, and the cost of a bicycle would have been beyond the reach of many. It would be a long time before the Holidays with Pay Act was passed in 1938, and a week's paid holiday became the right of every working man and woman.

Holding had some 20 names and addresses of those who had written to him after reading *Cycle and Camp in Connemara*. All the letters were carefully kept, but he "found one person more interested than any other". This was E.C. Pitt-Johnson, whom Holding visited in his rooms at Oxford, where they discussed the idea of forming an Association of Cycle Campers (A.C.C.). He elected Pitt-Johnson as Secretary and Holding was elected President by Pitt-Johnson. It appears that the persons mentioned by Holding were contacted by post; twelve replied and were enrolled as members of the new Association.

Although Holding describes Pitt-Johnson as "M.A., of New College, Oxford", according to an early membership list and Crockford's Clerical Directory he was, at that time, a B.A. He was at Exeter College and Wycliffe Hall, and was not ordained until 1903. The original notice of the first camp gives Pitt-Johnson's address at Surbiton, amended to a new address in Bath as from 29 July 1901.

Japanese baskets

These are woven boxes which nest together. One would form the lid of the next size down, and they were strapped to the cycle to carry equipment. Members often covered them with waterproof fabric and they made useful tent tidies.

At about the same time as Holding met Pitt-Johnson, a gentleman named Exeter described, in the correspondence column of the *C.T.C. Gazette*, May 1901, a trip he and his wife had made the previous year, having seen some articles in *The Exchange and Mart* which led him to believe it would be possible. He had also been loaned a copy of Holding's *Cycle and Camp in Connemara*, and he set to work and made a tent and collected "the various apparatus necessary". The couple cycled from Shrewsbury to Llangollen, taking eight days for the trip which, by all accounts, was a very enjoyable experience. Exeter received so many letters that he gave more detailed descriptions of his equipment in the June issue of the *Gazette*, giving his full name as the Rev. Hubert Kingdon. He later became one of the first members of the A.C.C.

Further correspondence followed in the *C.T.C. Gazette*, including a letter from Holding and in July, Pitt-Johnson wrote to say that an Association of Cycle Campers was being formed and he would be pleased to give more information to those who were interested. Notice of the first camp was published in the August 1901 issue of the *Gazette*. Tucked away at the bottom of page 330, it reads: "CYCLE CAMPING – Mr E.C. Pitt-Johnson, of 4 Lambridge, Bath, the Honorary Secretary of

---

ASSOCIATION OF CYCLE CAMPERS.

August Bank Holiday Fixed Cycle Camp,
AT WANTAGE (BERKS).
FRIDAY, AUGUST 2ND TO MONDAY, AUGUST 5TH.

ENFIELD HOUSE,
SURBITON.
July 29°
On and after 3rd. August my address will be 4 LAMBRIDGE, BATH.

DEAR SIR,

The President has paid a special visit to Wantage, and reports as follows:—

" HAZELDEAN,"
FULHAM, S.W.

"I have been to Wantage purposely to fix up a camp. Had great difficulties, but think all were overcome. Have selected for site Mr. Haily's meadow, Eagleton Road, now in occupation of Mr. Paul Whitley. Whilst near town it is secluded and sheltered, and affords the following: Deep mill dam for bathing, spring water, a shed for cycles, and hay for pillows and beds. Mrs. Sheppard (whose cottage is close at hand in Eagleton Road) will receive parcels and render necessary attentions. If blankets are needed, better write to her in advance.

Wantage is a town of 4,000 inhabitants, and is the birthplace of Alfred the Great.

The Parish Church is extremely fine and interesting, with special architectural features.

King Alfred's bath is near camp.

The White Horse Hill is seven miles distant. This vast outline is pre-historic.

The town is situated in the Vale of the White Horse, and is surrounded by fine stretches of rolling downs, bisected by Roman sunk-ways.

The valley of the camp is beautiful, well-watered and shady.

Wantage is about 12 miles (of an average) from Swindon, Newbury, Oxford and Didcot, on the Great Western main line.

There is a steam tram from Wantage Road to the centre of the town.

I propose riding, on the Saturday, from Reading at 3 o'clock and invite others to join this run.

Roads undulating and excellent. The ride from Reading (24 miles) is one of the finest in Great Britain.
T. H. HOLDING."

SECRETARIAL.—

It is hoped campers will come as if on tour, i.e., in flying form. Each camper must cater for himself. I shall pitch early on the Friday.

Things to bring:—Tent poles, ground sheet, pegs, thin pillows to stuff, thin woollen ground blanket, candles and holders, cameras, cycle cape, long leggings, and card bearing name of tent: instance, President's will be " Presidency," my own will be " Treasury " and so on.

A meeting will be held on Saturday at 8-30 p.m., to confirm officers and rules, and to consider suggestions, and to receive members.

The Rectory grounds will be kindly opened to our inspection, per courtesy of the Vicar.

The campers will be taken round the church after morning services on Sunday.

Lunch will be provided for the whole camp at 1-30 on Sunday.

The demesne of R. Croker, Esq., will be visited on Sunday afternoon.

A spin to the White Horse on Monday morning and a lunch, in company, at King Alfred's Head, at 1-30.

The President will procure for members any camping appliances they may not be able to make or otherwise get.

Yours very faithfully,
E. C. PITT-JOHNSON.

CYCLE CONVENIENCES: A. J. Belcher, Market Place.
HOTEL: " King Alfred's Head."

" CYCLE AND CAMP " 1/3, post free, from De Vere & Co., Church Passage, Shaftesbury Avenue, London, W.C., or any Booksellers.

---

the Association of Cycle Campers desires to say that a Cycle Camp will be held at Wantage during the coming Bank Holiday. Each camper must bring his own paraphernalia."

The notice sent by post in July to the original twelve members was more detailed. Holding stated that the site was in Eagleton Road but we now know, from research carried out by Capt. Frazer-Allen during the 1950s and 1960s, that it was in Ickleton Road. Old maps prove this, and it is probably the local dialect that led to Holding's error.

Six persons, including Holding himself, camped at Wantage from 2–5 August 1901. The other five were E.C. Pitt-Johnson, T.W. Lowther from Birmingham, and three brothers, Francis, Tom and G.W. Penn from Lambeth.

A prospectus entitled *Cycle Camping Association* was published later that year with a photograph of Lowther and Pitt-Johnson in a tent at

H.P. MITCHELL, in 1951, became the only Club member to have reached 50 years of membership aged 85. He first camped at Hillhead, after which, he cycled with T.H. Holding to London before travelling home to Manchester. He was later involved in the formation of the Lancs, Cheshire and North Wales District Association.

Wantage on the cover. It contained a list of 35 members including the Rev. Hubert Kingdon and H.P. Mitchell, both of whom had described their experiences of cycle-camping in the *C.T.C. Gazette* before the Association of Cycle Campers was formed. Also included in the prospectus was a list of appliances available from Holding's tailoring premises in Maddox Street.

The second Annual Camp at Haversham, Whitsun 1902. Back, left to right: Austin Binning, Fred Binning, Eric Thornley, Clare Fry, Peyton Baily. Front, left to right: Graves, T.H. Holding, Mrs Horsfield, Fred Horsfield and 'Little Billy', one of the four cyclists recorded in Cycle and Camp in Connemara. *(Stephen Hilhouse, Club Archive)*

Visitors and campers at the Coronation Camp, Hillhead, Hampshire, July 1902. The Coronation was postponed but the camp went ahead. T.H. Holding is in the centre of the middle row. (Stephen Hilhouse, Club Archive)

It was originally suggested that the Association should become a branch of the C.T.C., but Holding, "as originator of the C.T.C. would be slow to propose, suggest or start anything that should oppose that Club's aim, but those interested in camping will know, perhaps, that it is best for the Association to work independently on its own lines".

The first Annual General Meeting (A.G.M.) of the Association was held during the Annual Supper on 7 February 1902. This seems to have consisted of Holding talking about the pleasures of cycle-camping and demonstrating some new equipment. Thirty-three people attended and a Committee was appointed, although we have no knowledge of the members of that Committee.

It was also agreed that a typed magazine be started, under the Editorship of J.H. Skilton. This, unfortunately, only appeared sporadically and we have no other record of it and no copies have survived. Members relied on the *C.T.C. Gazette* to keep themselves informed, although notices of some of the camps appear to have been sent out by post to members.

By 1902 over 100 members had been enrolled. The *C.T.C. Gazette* continued to publish news of the Association and notices of camps, and Holding wrote a series of articles – describing camping equipment and how to make it – published throughout 1902. These included detailed instructions for making the Gipsy tent, which was later to become very popular. In 1902 Stephen Hilhouse was in a restaurant reading one of

these articles when he was approached by Frederick Horsfield, who told him about the new Association, and persuaded him to join – this was the start of a lifelong friendship.

Eighteen members attended a Whitsun Camp, described as "The Second Annual Camp" at Haversham, near Wolverton, Buckinghamshire. Forty-three members attended a Coronation Camp at Hillhead, near Fareham, Hampshire (a figure which would not be exceeded until Easter 1906). The site is now part of the Titchfield Haven nature reserve and was described as "a snug and sheltered corner behind the keeper's house, and but 100yds from the sea".

According to Stephen Hilhouse's reminiscences, the inaugural meeting for the Association was held towards the end of 1902. Rules for the Association were drawn up, Frederick Horsfield was appointed Honorary Secretary, and Hilhouse himself became

Honorary Treasurer. E.C. Pitt-Johnson, by now a curate in Bath and unable to continue as Honorary Secretary, was appointed a Vice-President. Hilhouse tells us that when someone proposed him as Treasurer, Holding asked him to stand up. When he did so, Holding said: "Oh, 6ft 6ins, he will do," and that's how it was that he became the Honorary Treasurer.

The nine members of the Committee elected at that time included Alex [Papps] Moeller and Mrs Horsfield, who had the distinction of being the first lady ever to camp with the Association – the rules stated that any lady or gentleman could apply for membership but an official application form had to be obtained from the Honorary Secretary; those not known to a member were required to provide a reference. Most of the rules drawn up in 1902 are very similar to the current Club Constitution, so they were obviously a good base on which to build.

The subscription at that time was 2s 6d per annum, payable in

The Binning Brothers and Fred and Margaret Horsfield with their Gipsy tents at Elstree, 1903. (Club Archive)

advance. Lists of members were produced periodically and this practice continued until 1910 when, presumably, the membership became too large for this to be done.

In the first edition of the *Handbook* for 1903 there was a request for "Town Members" to "look for and report upon a nice spot, 15 miles or so from town, which we may secure as an A.C.C. Camp Ground". The second edition showed a slight change to Committee membership and also included a list of new members.

The following Easter, despite freezing conditions, 21 members camped at Aldenham Lake, including Greevz Fisher and his son who rode from Leeds, camping twice on the way.

At Whitsun, the camp was held at Dorchester-on-Thames in glorious weather. Holding camped in his new crimson silk Gipsy tent, and five of the 33 campers present were ladies. Despite severe thunderstorms on the Saturday night, every tent withstood the test.

This photograph shows T.H. Holding with his lightweight kit in his garden in Fulham, 1908. (Club Archive)

In June 1903 the first tent-pitching competition was held in Holding's garden in Fulham, and members of the public and the press were invited to view the proceedings. *The Daily Graphic* produced a superb sketch of the event, which was later reproduced in an appendix to *Cycle and Camp in Connemara*, by then re-issued by a new publisher.

This booklet appears to be a miniature handbook giving an inventory of camp essentials and including instructions for making a mummy-shaped sleeping bag and two different designs of tents, the 'A' tent and Gipsy.

The list of essentials, compiled by Holding based on a single-handed expedition to Donegal, makes interesting reading: "Tent, poles, pegs, ground sheet, ground blanket, cooking apparatus of three or four parts to fold one in the other, five little bags for tea, coffee, sugar, oatmeal, and bread, marmalade or jam tin, combined knife and fork, one spoon, ½ pint spirit tin, bit of soap ¼in thick by 2ins square, small toilet tackle and razor, spare under-vest, gossamer pillow to stuff with hay, etc, pair of spare thin stockings, leg overalls, special cycling cover coat*, candelabra, candles, matches, two spare flannel collars, a pair of knit slippers with thin leather soles, maps, bathing drawers, towel. *N.B:- Capes are bad to pitch a tent in, in the wet, and I have adopted the coat."

The Mersey Cuisine

A slow-burning methylated spirit stove used by early Club members. Two wicks soaked up the spirit and, when lit, the stove burned rather like a modern gas stove. Heat output could be controlled by adding water to a special compartment in the fuel container. A gauze windshield sat on top of the container, and the whole thing packed into a pan with fry-pan lid.

By the end of 1903 there were 143 members, including two from overseas and 13 ladies, two of whom were members of the Committee. A lady needed to be very strong-minded to be seen cycling in public and take no notice of remarks about it being unseemly, and only those who could afford to ignore such comments were really able to stand firm and carry on cycling. For a single lady to embark on the sport of cycle-camping was even more daring. If, for example, her employers heard of her exploits she could well lose her job.

For this reason, yet again, it was the middle and upper-middle classes who took part in such activities

Typical garments worn by gentlemen campers in 1903.

because many of the ladies involved would have had a private income and were unworried by such constraints. Married ladies, of course, had the support of their husbands, themselves involved in cycle-camping, and for them the difficulties were not so great.

The Secretary remarked that if all who enjoyed the benefits of the Association would support it by joining, the membership would go up by leaps and bounds. This was shown by the large amount of correspondence received and by the prominence given to the doings of the Association in cycling and other papers.

The year 1904 started off with a Camp Fire, held in Chelsea, when "no less than 200 assembled to watch the preparation of meals by the campers, and were greatly interested in the proceedings". The President, Holding, arranged some tableaux of camp life and Alex Moeller gave a lantern slide lecture on cycle-camping in the Ardennes.

Sixteen members attended the Easter Camp held at Ley Hill, Chesham, in very cold weather. The other camps that year were well attended, culminating with 42 members at the Autumn camp, again held at Ley Hill. A second tent-pitching competition was again held and included a display of new tents, including a Motor Gipsy.

The 1904 *Handbook* was more comprehensive than that of the previous year and, as well as the Annual Report and a list of members, it included a list of seven sites available to members: in effect, this was the first *Sites List*. The fees were set by the Association at one shilling a night, or half-a-crown a week for each tent. Official camp regulations were printed and more detailed information on tents was given, plus suggestions for camp kit. Two pages were devoted to a list of appliances designed and supplied by Holding, and included motor tents.

For the first time, an advertisement appeared in the *Handbook*. This was for the Jupiter oil stove, "the latest development of the wickless or Vapour oil stove". Two types were available in two sizes, priced

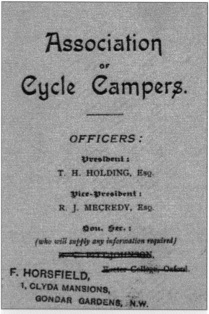

Original Association of Cycle Campers membership card belonging to George Spyer, dated 22 April 1904. Note the change of Secretary. (Club Archive)

From the Club magazine

May 1906 *On selecting camp kit: "Recruits to this sport of sports cannot be too strongly warned against attempting to get together a cheap kit. That the best is the cheapest in the long run is shown in camping appliances as in everything else."*

July 1906 *A summer pest (advice for the prevention of mosquito bites): "The camper will be able to resist their onslaught by rubbing the face and hands with the following mixture: six parts sweet oil, one part creosote, and one part pennyroyal. If this is too much bother, oil of eucalyptus or oil of lavender are said to be good preventives." (Just imagine the consequences of applying this concoction to the skin.)*

from 9s 6d–14s 6d. The collapsible versions were recommended for cyclists, travellers and yachtsmen. Holding's list includes both these stoves, described as Primus pattern, and the genuine Primus stove. The price was much the same but the Jupiter stoves were made in England by the Wilson Engineering Company of High Holborn, London – the Primus stoves originated in Sweden.

Curiously they are both described as using petroleum, but we are 99 per cent certain that they used what we know as paraffin because in the 1905–6 *Handbook* the Primus stoves are listed as paraffin stoves. (Paraffin is still known as petroleum in certain European countries, notably Holland.) The Jupiter stove could apparently boil a quart of water in two-and-a-half minutes at a cost of 1/96th part of a penny!

Prior to the development of these stoves most members used a Mersey cuisine made from beaten copper with a methylated spirit burner. The design was such that the spirit vapourised and burned as a gas and it was, for its time, a very efficient stove.

The fourth A.G.M. of the Association was held at 7 Maddox Street, London, Holding's tailoring premises, on 3 November 1904. This was the first formal A.G.M. of the Association which was not held at the same time as the Annual Dinner, and very few people attended.

Earlier in 1904 there had been some correspondence in the *C.T.C. Gazette* concerning the use of aluminium for camp kit. In the November issue, Holding in his notes stated: "I am sorry to say that so

Ley Hill, Chesham, was a popular venue for the Association of Cycle Campers in the first years of the Association. 'Little Billy' is seated on the left, Stephen Hilhouse is in the striped shirt on the right. (Stephen Hilhouse, Club Archive)

First in the field A Century of The Camping and Caravanning Club

Holding's Handle Touring Bag

A semi-rigid bag, fixed behind the handlebars with straps, appeared to get in the way of the rider's knees but apparently this was not the case. It was said to have no effect on the steering, and could be removed in an instant.

far as my tests are concerned – though I do not expect everyone to agree with me – aluminium is little more than a fetish.

"It failed in the cycle trade. I consider it a complete failure in regard to tent pegs, which when made to be nearly twice the size of the small iron ones they bend almost with a touch. As for cooking utensils they require a lot of attention. As for a salt cellar you may get the lid on but it will not come off. As for spoons they require a great deal of keeping up. They are light, and I stop at that. There are many things it is useful for, but for the necessities of camp life it is really unsuitable."

He must have changed his mind the following year because he lists aluminium pans (So-soon) in his appliance list in the 1905–6 *Handbook*, into which the new Baby Primus could be packed. A number of members strongly disagreed with his remarks and had sent their comments to the Committee rather than to the *C.T.C. Gazette*. Holding, as President, had always taken the chair at Committee meetings until a motor-cycle accident in November, in which he broke his leg, prevented him from attending.

When he was next able to attend in March 1905, he was amazed to hear that there were letters censuring him for his remarks in the *Gazette*. As Chairman, he ruled that the correspondence was nothing to do with the Association and the Committee should not read out the letters but should instruct the members to send their comments to the *C.T.C. Gazette*. A motion was carried to this effect but Holding seems to have upset certain members of the Committee. The motion was rescinded and the letters were read.

Later, in 1905, the Committee decided that it would be "in the interests of the Association" that Rule 9 should be amended to read: "The Association shall be governed by a Committee consisting of the Honorary Treasurer and Honorary Secretary of the Association and twelve other members who shall be elected annually at the General Meeting to be held in February." Holding was not at all happy at this

The All-England Series

CAMPING OUT

By A.A. MACDONELL.

PRICE TWO SHILLINGS

Thomas Hiram Holding's cycle with kit, 1904. (Club Archive)

decision, which he saw as an effort to dethrone him, but it was put
before the A.G.M. in February 1906 and was carried. At that meeting
he was elected President.

Early in March, a meeting of the new Committee was held and both
Holding and Hilhouse were proposed as Chairman. Hilhouse was elected
with a three vote majority and Holding immediately resigned from the
Association he had founded. He was very bitter about what had happened,
believing he had the right, as Founder and President, to chair the
Committee meetings. According to other sources, Holding had already
indicated, privately, to a number of older members that he would like to
stand down as President as he felt the Association had grown large
enough to stand on its own feet.

There was nothing in the rules concerning the election of a Chairman
of Committee and so, having in view the contemplated resignation of
the President, the Committee thought that it would be undesirable if a
figurehead with no real interest in camping were to be elected as President
and then hold the position of Chairman as of right. It was, therefore, put to
the A.G.M. and Holding was in the chair when the resolution was passed.

As President he was considered to be an *ex officio* member of the
Committee and, as such, was eligible for election as Chairman. However,
he felt insulted that anyone should stand against him. Committee members

made several attempts to try and placate him but, on 29 March 1906, Holding circularised members informing them that he had severed his connection with the Association.

After his resignation, Holding sent out another circular calling on certain members of the A.C.C. to resign stating that a "new and stronger body" was being formed. Some 19 members did resign and the National Cycle-Camping Club (N.C.C.C.) was formed at an inaugural meeting on 26 April 1906.

Holding did not waste any time. A notice in the May *C.T.C. Gazette* stated that he had "withdrawn from the Association which I founded a few years ago, but that fact will have no bearing on my continued efforts in the interests of camping and touring by cycle. That a new Association has been founded is sufficient evidence that the movement will continue to be fostered". Twenty-seven A.C.C. members joined the new Club, although some of these still remained members of the A.C.C. In July 1906, R.B. Searle, later to play a very important role in the life of the Camping Club, first joined the N.C.C.C.

The first printed copy of *Cycle Camping* was issued free to members of the A.C.C. in March 1906. It is with this four-page leaflet that the volume numbers of the Club magazine commence.

Members were "cordially invited" to send in accounts of their tours, novel and practical ideas on camp kit, and particulars and localities of camp sites. No mention was made in the magazine, however,

Christmas Camp at Ley Hill, 1904. Miss Elsie Wallace is in the centre of the photograph. (Stephen Hilhouse, Club Archive)

of Holding's resignation. One of the first contributors was a Miss Wallace who, in an article entitled *Method or Muddle?*, gave some hints on being tidy in camp. Some of the comments she makes could easily apply today.

Notice of the 1906 Easter Camp, again to be held at Ley Hill, was included, and it was stated that the Stewards' tents (one for gentlemen, one for ladies) would be distinguished by a special flag. (The camps were always divided into bachelors' quarters, married quarters and ladies' quarters – a married lady was always appointed to chaperone the single ladies.)

It was also noted that the Association had badges in stock and that "small flags, swallow-tailed in shape, in green and red with black lettering" were available for 1s 3d each. A correspondence column would also be available to members.

In the same year a camp display and exhibition of kit and appliances opened on 21 April at the Crystal Palace. Each Wednesday and Saturday, tents of different patterns were erected and kits displayed in detail. Arrangements had been made whereby a large quantity of aluminium goods, Sirram cooking sets, eiderdowns, sleeping bags, stoves, etc, were on view.

Despite appeals from the Committee very little help from ordinary members was forthcoming, and "had it not been for the splendid energy of these few" the whole exhibition would have been a lamentable failure.

A 1905 Christmas card, sent to Stephen Hilhouse from Mr and Mrs Horsfield. (Club Archive)

We're having a RIPPING TIME — and hope that YOU are!

Weybridge July 8 06

The only known photograph of a camp on the Club's first official site at Weybridge, Surrey. Stephen Hilhouse is demonstrating a new sleeping bag. (Club Archive)

Fortunately, however, because of their efforts and those of the Committee, it was a great success. The camp was visited by many thousands of people, with the result that many new members joined. New campers were able to see what kit to get, what to avoid and how to set to work generally, and many new ideas were exchanged. Each weekend the exhibitors camped in the grounds amid large clusters of azaleas, rhododendrons and lilacs in full bloom, with a view of the Surrey Hills between the large cedar trees in front.

The competitions for members proved to be popular, with prizes given for the most complete kit, a tent-pitching competition, and a Primus-lighting competition. Miss Wallace won the most complete kit competition with everything, including utensils for two people, weighing less than 23lbs – that included the weight of the straps and baskets in which the equipment was carried. It would be extremely difficult to beat today, even with modern materials. It has to be said that although the kit included bags in which to store bread, oats, sugar and ground rice, the food itself was not included; neither was any spare clothing!

On 1 June an official camp was held at Hamhaugh Island, Weybridge. This site was rented by the Association as an experiment and became the first permanent site of the Club. (It is later referred to as Dunton's Island.) Fees were 6d per night per member or married couple using the same tent, non-members paid double fees. An official tent was pitched on the site, and members could leave kit, if neatly packed, in the tent from time to time at their own risk. The tent was not available for sleeping in except in an emergency.

In the July 1906 issue of *Cycle Camping* the Honorary Secretary requested members to send in the total number of nights they had camped, together with a list of places visited, plus photos of tents, sites, etc "for the album". This information was requested as it was desired "that this Association should have as members *practical campers only* as nearly as may be". Requests were also made for hints and suggestions for the new *Handbook*.

A small, but very important paragraph appeared in that July issue, viz: "A new association titled The Camping Club has been inaugurated to promote all forms of camping not provided for by the A.C.C. Much information is already available and those interested should write to the Honorary Secretary (*pro. tem.*) T. Wharton Robertson, 97 Chapter Road, Willesden Green."

This is the very first mention of The Camping Club. Many felt that with the improvement of motor-car travel, plus the interest in canoe, boat and pedestrian-camping, such a body would be useful in widening the appeal of camping – motor-cyclists were already catered for in the A.C.C. Clearly, the development of the internal combustion engine was going to make a lot of difference to camping, although it took many years for motor-camping to become more popular than cycle-camping.

H. BIDEN-STEELE was Honorary Secretary in 1906 and was probably responsible for Holding's resignation from the Club. He proposed that the Chairman should be elected from the Committee members and thought it undemocratic for the President to hold the office of Chairman as of right.

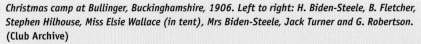

Christmas camp at Bullinger, Buckinghamshire, 1906. Left to right: H. Biden-Steele, B. Fletcher, Stephen Hilhouse, Miss Elsie Wallace (in tent), Mrs Biden-Steele, Jack Turner and G. Robertson. (Club Archive)

In the next issue of *Cycle Camping*, it was suggested that the Association should consider limiting membership because of the amount of work being borne by Committee members, all of whom were volunteers and enthusiasts, but all had their daily work to do. The membership had grown to over 300 and the administration and supply of kit had greatly increased. It was difficult to find members with sufficient time to devote to the work. In some ways, the Association had made a rod for its own back. Holding had always, when asked, stated that the Association itself did not supply kit to members, quoting the amount of time that was needed to do the job.

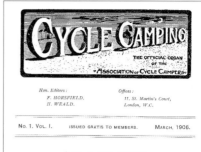

After Holding resigned some members had difficulty in obtaining suitable items of equipment, so the Committee arranged to supply certain items at advantageous prices. We do not know if Holding refused to supply A.C.C. members after his resignation but he made it clear that he wanted nothing more to do with it. Administrative work was also becoming a burden, the vast majority of A.C.C. members being professional people who did not have sufficient leisure time to spare. However, the thought of utilising paid secretarial services, the Committee felt, would introduce a commercial element to what had been a purely social organisation.

All this would be discussed before the A.G.M. in the ensuing year but, meanwhile, an advertisement appeared at the end of the November issue: "Wanted: A gentleman with intellectual ability, high administrative capacity, and with an aptitude for hard work, to act as Honorary Secretary to the A.C.C. To one who is willing and able to maintain the high standard of efficiency set by the present holder of the office, an excellent opportunity is afforded of earning the gratitude and good will of some of the Members. Preference will be given to one who has filled a similar position. Address – The Offices of this Journal, 11 St Martin's Court, London." Prior to March 1906 all important notices and matters concerning the A.C.C. were regularly published in the *C.T.C. Gazette*, and indeed such matters continued to be published in that publication until 1910 and beyond.

We must be thankful that the C.T.C. was such a strong body and continued to grow. If it were not for that organisation, The Camping and Caravanning Club would have lost the first five years of its history.

Early days of canvas by Hazel Constance

The use of tents for leisure purposes began in the 19th century and in the hundred years following the Club's foundation there have been radical changes in tent development. But is everything modern a new idea?

T.H. Holding pioneered lightweight tent design with the 'A' tent – it had a steep sloping roof and no walls – and he described how to make it in *Cycle and Camp*. Similar tents were used at the first Association of Cycle Campers meet at Wantage in 1901.

Finding that the 'A' did not give enough elbow room, Holding used a spreader across the poles, thus the Gypsy tent was made. Instructions for this tent were published in the *C.T.C. Gazette* in 1902. Holding's favourite was a small silk 'A' tent called the Wigwam, which packed into a coat pocket, weighed 11oz, but had very heavy steel pegs. Walking stick poles were sometimes used for this tent, which he used for demonstrations when he packed all his kit in his coat pockets.

Stephen Hilhouse did not find either tent roomy enough so he designed the first Cottage tent in 1903 to suit his rather large frame. The Cottage in its various weights and sizes remained a favourite for many years and was a common sight until well into the 1960s. The Gipsy design was re-used for toilet tents!

In 1907 a Dr. Bartholomew designed a tent "to render a health-giving pastime still more healthy, pleasant and invigorating". A simple ridge tent, it had net-covered ventilators under the eaves and in the doors "to allow for the exit of respired air" and was intended for fixed camping. The Club's Supplies Department made mostly lightweight equipment but other companies such as C. Nielson and Son, and Piggot Brothers, began to cater for the standing camp market. Established manufacturers of military and expedition tents, Thomas Black and Benjamin Edgington, also made tents for the leisure market.

Many members made their own tents with some degree of success, and designs were often published in *Camping* for others to copy. Many of these appeared during World War One, the most revolutionary being the Itisa single-pole tent. Designed by J.H. Wood in 1916 for a kit competition that failed to materialise because of the war, it was first seen at a Club meet in

Derbyshire in August that year. R.B. Searle modified the design to give better protection over the doorway and the plans were published in September 1917. Further modifications in later years gave better floor space and peg-out doors. Larger models to sleep three or four persons were later devised, some having extended flysheets.

Camp and Sports Co-operators succeeded the Supplies Department in 1920 and became independent of the Club. Its tents, bearing the trade mark Camtors were made from top quality materials and built on a framework of linen tape. They were known as the Rolls-Royces of the camping world. Imitation being the greatest form of flattery, other suppliers such as Benjamin Edgington, John Edgington and Blacks soon brought out their own versions of single pole tents. Perhaps the nearest to the quality and build of the original Itisa was the Midge from John Edgington, which was awarded a Club Certificate of Merit.

A radical new idea in the 1930s was the Igloo inflatable tent introduced by the Pneumatic Tent Company, and new continental-style ridge tents with down-to-earth flysheets and extended living areas became available through Pindisports in 1950. Made by Marechal of France they were quite popular and some British manufacturers introduced their own versions.

The biggest design change came when the first British frame tents were introduced by Benjamin Edgington and Blacks of Greenock in 1955. Simple square models with a zip-up door that acted as an awning, they were somewhat reminiscent of scenes from Olivier's film *Henry V*. Once the French-style tents, with standing headroom and a separate living area with kitchen space, were introduced, many manufacturers jumped on the bandwagon and a huge choice became available from both mainland Europe and the U.K. Although roomy, frame tents were also very heavy, and campers soon realised their cars were being overloaded so a trailer was necessary.

Frame tents gradually lost their popularity and by the mid-1970s several well-known brands began to disappear. At the same time there was an upsurge in lightweight camping, with new names like Robert Saunders and Ultimate entering the arena. Saunders' Lite Hike tent weighed only 3lbs – a revolution at the time.

The advent of nylon fabrics and polyurethane proofings meant that tents soon became much lighter for the amount of space offered.

1907–1913: The Club takes huge strides forward

T he next seven years saw huge strides in the development of the Club, during which a tremendous amount of work was done by volunteers, in particular Alex Moeller, a bachelor who literally "lived for the Club" all his life.

A milestone in the Club's history was 9 February 1907, when Club rules were changed, replacing the Committee by a Council and allowing the creation of District Associations (D.A.s). Alex Moeller was elected as Honorary General Secretary, Biden-Steele having resigned because of the increasing pressure of his professional commitments, and an Honorary Supplies Secretary was appointed for the first time to assist in the supply of quality equipment to members. At the start of 1907 there were 365 members, increasing to over 800 by 1910.

By June 1910 a new king – George V – was on the throne. Sir Edmund Verney, Club President from 1906–1909, had died and obituaries for both Edward VII and Sir Edmund were published. Special Kit Insurance for Club members first became available, following a suggestion made eight years previously. A new Honorary Secretary was appointed in 1911, when H. Winton Wood took over the reins from Alex Moeller. The Council, in recording "their great appreciation of the whole-hearted service which Mr Moeller has so enthusiastically given to the Club's affairs for many years", made a presentation to him.

In the wider world

Women clash with police: Suffragettes agitating for equal voting rights for women saw 57 of their number arrested following a struggle with police outside the House of Commons. A mass rally in Hyde Park supported by huge crowds was followed by increasingly violent protests, without apparent effect on Government policy.

A nation in mourning: After just over nine years, once more the nation has lost its King, as Edward VII died of pneumonia. The Coronation of George V as King and Emperor, in Westminster Abbey in June 1911, began a reign which was to see many changes at home and world wide.

Engineering triumphs and tragedies: Mass-production of Ford's Model-T car revolutionised manufacture. A bill sanctioning a railway tunnel under the English Channel was withdrawn, fearing threats to national defence, while Blériot flew across the Channel in 43 minutes. The sinking of the "unsinkable" liner *Titanic* with the loss of more than 1,500 lives horrified the world.

At a meeting of the Council in July 1911 it was agreed that the Ladies' Committee should be supplied with agendas and receive Council minutes. In addition, reasonable out-of-pocket expenses in connection with the work of all D.A.s would be met. The Council was also prepared to consider applications for exceptional expenditure in connection with increased propaganda work.

After the establishment of the separate Supplies Department and the introduction of the increased subscription, the sporting interests of the Club were freed from financial dependence on the Supplies Department. The Council hoped, when the guarantee fund for that Department had been released, that there would be a large increase in propaganda work which, for lack of funds, had had to take a secondary place. Finally, the year 1913 saw another change of Honorary Secretary when H. Winton Wood was appointed to be General Manager of the Supplies Department. The new Honorary Secretary was A.F. Skinner.

When Sir Edmund Verney stood down after three years as President of the Association of Cycle Campers (A.C.C.) in 1909, Capt. Robert Falcon Scott – Scott of the Antarctic – was elected President. He chaired the Annual Supper later in that year and in his speech said he hoped he would find the A.C.C. a "much bigger thing" on his return from his next venture. On being offered a Club pennon to take with him he suggested that it should be "light and portable", promising to carry it with him, and he hoped to plant it at the Pole. Mrs Gill and Miss Wallace presented Scott with an embroidered silk Club pennon that compressed into a tiny roll weighing just ¼oz.

SIR EDMUND VERNEY was a retired naval captain and owner of Clayden House in Buckinghamshire. A keen cyclist, he joined the Club in 1903 and invited members to camp on his estate. He was elected Club President when T.H. Holding severed his connection with the Club in 1907, and died in 1910.

Baby Primus and So-Soon pans

Holding had this Primus specially made for cycle-campers, as the first paraffin pressure stoves were too heavy for the purpose. He then had a set of two pans plus a lid made, into which the stove fitted for carrying. The handles fitted into holes, not slots, so there were no projecting pieces.

At the Club's Annual General Meeting (A.G.M.) Scott was elected President for a second term of three years in 1912, and at the 12th Annual Supper the following November, Mr Gill said that all members "hoped to welcome him home before long". Sadly, no one knew that he had already died in his tent with his companions, having written his last message just two weeks after the previous A.G.M. Archie Handford, a Club member and well-known photographer, wrote to the Editor of *Camping* in March 1913, pointing out that a film of Scott's last expedition was being shown at

Right: Captain Scott, famous for his Antarctic exploration, was Club President from 1909–1912. (Club Archive)

continued on page 42

The Terra Nova *in Antarctic Ice.*
(Photo Club Archive)

First in the field A Century of The Camping and Caravanning Club

Robert Falcon Scott – Scott of the Antarctic

Robert Falcon Scott was born in Devonport in 1868. He entered the Royal Navy in 1882.

In 1899 Sir Clements Markham, President of the Royal Geographical Society, was looking for a naval officer to command the proposed National Antarctic Expedition and wanted a young man, a good sailor with experience of sailing ships and with a scientific turn of mind. He needed to be enthusiastic and imaginative, with a cool temperament and be calm but quick and decisive in action. Ideally he would also be resourceful, tactful and sympathetic.

Markham recognised Scott's potential leadership qualities when he had first encountered him some twelve years earlier, and asked his current commanding officer for his opinion.

Captain Egerton wrote of Scott: "Lt. Scott is in my opinion a very worthy candidate for the Command of the Antarctic Expedition and I am at a loss to name any officer who is likely to be more suitable. Lt. Scott is an officer of great capabilities and possesses a large amount of tact and common sense, he is of strong physique and robust health – a scientist and an expert in electricity, very keen, zealous, of a cheerful disposition full of resource and a first rate comrade. He has had considerable experience in square rigged ships and

writes a clear and concise report. I therefore have much pleasure in recommending him."

Scott also had a deep and reverend attitude towards nature and hated having to kill seals for food. He had a charming manner and pleasant smile, and was a great reader, although sometimes prone to moodiness he was always concerned for the welfare of his men.

Scott was appointed Commander of the National Antarctic Expedition in June 1900 and was promoted to the rank of Commander, Royal Navy. Before he sailed for New Zealand in July 1901, King Edward VII invested Scott with the Victorian Order. By the beginning of 1903 Scott, together with Lt. Ernest Shackleton and Dr. Edward Wilson, had travelled further south than any man in history.

Returning home in 1904, Scott was promoted to Captain, was given honorary doctorates in Science at both Cambridge and Manchester universities in 1905, and was awarded the Gold Medal of the Royal Geographical Society.

In 1910 he left for a second expedition to Antarctica, from where he never returned. His body, and those of his companions, were found in February 1913, almost a year after they had perished.

continued from
page 38

cinemas, and suggested that members should make every attempt to see it.

According to the new rules at the Camp Fire in March 1907, on the written request of six local members, the Metropolitan D.A. was formed, to include Essex, Kent, Middlesex and Surrey. Later in the same month, the Council sanctioned the formation of the Birmingham D.A., covering Shropshire, Staffordshire, Warwickshire and Worcestershire.

The work of the D.A.s continued to thrive, and a North Midlands D.A. covering Derby, Leicester, Lincoln, Nottingham and Rutland was formed in March 1908, with an inaugural camp near Loughborough. By 1909 Glasgow and the West of Scotland D.A. was in being, and suggestions were coming in for Liverpool, Manchester and Yorkshire. At the same time D.A.s were empowered to send a Representative, with full voting rights, to Council meetings.

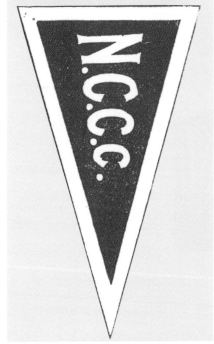

The pennon of the National Cycle-Camping Club founded in 1906, when T.H. Holding severed his connections with the Association of Cycle Campers. The name was later changed to the National Camping Club. (Club Archive)

At the 1910 A.G.M. the Council proposed that the London (formerly Metropolitan) D.A. should be disbanded and that in future the Council should promote and manage all official camps in the Home Counties, due to "considerable duplication and waste of money in the partial dual control". The motion was carried with only one opponent. The Council also sanctioned the division of the North Midlands D.A. into Nottingham D.A. and East Midlands D.A., and the formation of the Northumberland and Durham D.A.

By July 1911 both the Manchester (later to be re-named Lancashire and Cheshire D.A.) and Yorkshire D.A.s had been established, and a short list of District Representatives was printed in *Camping*, mostly for areas where there was no D.A.

In January 1913 D.A.s were asked to ensure that their meets covered their expenses. They were meant to be self-governing, in the hope that some good "missionary work" might be done in the provinces. At the end of 1913 a suggestion was made in a letter to the magazine that an Edinburgh and East of Scotland D.A. be formed.

The D.A.s were an essential part of Club organisation because the burden of administration could be spread over a much wider area. Some fell by the wayside, but others grew rapidly and proved a real asset to the Club.

The National Cycle-Camping Club (N.C.C.C.) – later to become the National Camping Club (N.C.C.) – had also inaugurated provincial centres that appeared to be similar to A.C.C. District Associations, and were probably based on them.

Various changes to the rules were necessary during the next few years to allow for changes in the make-up of the Club and for the large growth in membership. It was again suggested that membership should be restricted as the work involved was becoming so time-consuming for the voluntary officers of the Club.

A giant Gipsy tent being used as the official tent at an early National Cycle-Camping Club Meet. (Club Archive)

The first rule change was made in 1907 to provide for the payment of an entrance fee by new members in addition to the annual subscription. This helped pay for the extra costs involved in sending out membership papers and other information. Members of other camping organisations were exempt from the entrance fee. For 1908 members of the Cyclists' Touring Club (C.T.C.) were also exempt from these fees. A.C.C. subscriptions, originally half-a-crown, were increased to five shillings at the same time, although existing members would not have to pay the increased rate.

Down quilts

Light enough to be carried on a cycle, they were better than blankets which were too heavy to carry. One down quilt spread over three men – "we sleep in our clothes of course" – would keep them warm and, to prevent the quilt being pulled off, a 12ins valance was sewn all round, which had tapes attached to tie to the tent pegs.

In November 1910 a new standard subscription was introduced, abolishing the lower rate for those who had joined in the very beginning of the A.C.C. That meeting also endorsed the Council's negotiations with the N.C.C. The rules of the Club were changed slightly to incorporate some of the N.C.C. rules, but there were no radical changes.

The 1912 A.G.M. approved a new rule that no officer of the Club or member of the Council should engage in any occupation, business or profession connected with camping for pecuniary gain, and that any member trading, or attempting to trade in articles of kit at camp fires, official camps or camp sites should cease to be a member of the Club.

Camp rules also had to be formulated, and among the most interesting were some of the bye-laws published by the N.C.C. in the first issue of the *Campers' Quarterly* in 1909: "Camp Bye-Laws: Ladies' Quarters – A separate site will be set apart for ladies and married couples, near to the general camp.

"Official Tent – The official tent will be erected at all chief camps. Those campers not having tents and who wish to join experimentally may use this for one shilling per 24 hours, but on the closing day it must be cleared by 10.30am." Nothing is said about any problems arising if a lady wished to use it!

"Hours of Pitching – No tent shall be pitched after 10pm on the official site so as to avoid disturbing those already encamped.

"Sites – Promiscuous pitching is prohibited at official camps. The Camp Steward will assign all pitches.

"Obstructions – No camper shall peg out guy lines in such a manner as to cause any obstruction to neighbouring tents, or gangways.

"Co-operation – As no paid help is supplied, the Camp Steward may call upon members to fetch water, remove rubbish, and perform other acts for the well-being of the whole camp.

"Quietness – Silence must be observed between the hours of 11pm and 6.30am."

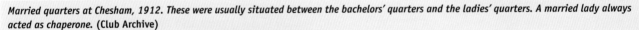

Married quarters at Chesham, 1912. These were usually situated between the bachelors' quarters and the ladies' quarters. A married lady always acted as chaperone. (Club Archive)

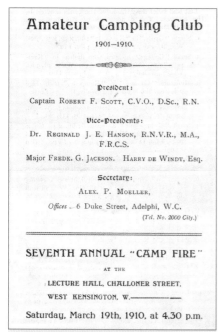

Camp Fires were indoor meetings for members to show their camping kit to others. Tea was served and lectures on camping topics and other entertainment were included. Non-members were invited and these occasions generated excellent publicity for the Club. (Club Archive)

A.C.C. rules for camping were less formal but very strict concerning the disposal of rubbish, particularly as some unauthorised burning nearly caused a serious fire at one of the official camps. On another occasion, the Editors of *Camping* chided a member for driving his motor-cycle across the camp late at night and disturbing members. Unfortunately, it transpired the culprit was not a member and the Editors resigned.

The A.C.C. and The Camping Club encouraged co-operation between the two organisations, and the A.C.C. offered Camping Club members the chance to buy supplies from them. At a meeting at the Travel Exhibition in 1907, in order that greater contact between the two clubs could be maintained, Henry Gilbertson-Smith suggested the formation of a Camping Union.

Camping Club members were not the only ones to benefit from the A.C.C.'s expertise. J. Harris Stone, M.A., one of the promoters of the Travel Exhibition, had invited members of the Council to inspect the caravan that Alfred Priestly, of Bradford, was exhibiting at the show.

Mr Stone expressed his desire to form a club for caravanners and the A.C.C. offered to help. Alex Moeller and Henry Gilbertson-Smith, representing the A.C.C., attended a meeting at Mr Stone's home and were able to assist in the formation of The Caravan Club.

In February 1909 D.B.L. Hopkins hoped that something might be done towards establishing closer relations between the various light camping bodies, possibly by an interchange of camp sites and a combined camp once a year. His remarks were well received and later bore fruit far beyond his expectations.

A Special General Meeting was held in May to consider extending the scope of the A.C.C.'s activities. So many enquiries, in particular for kit, had been received from non-cyclists that it was felt that membership should be extended. A suggestion was made that the name be changed to the Amateur Camping Club, thus keeping the well-known initials A.C.C. The Camping Club expressed a willingness to be incorporated into the A.C.C. and this was agreed. At the same time the title of the magazine was changed to *Camping*.

D.B.L. HOPKINS, R.N., joined the Club at the Travel Exhibition in 1907. He edited Camping *for eight years and was the founder of the National Feast of Lanterns. Many of his ideas for camping gadgets were published in* Camping, *including the idea of folding legs for a Primus stove – which was later adopted by the manufacturers.*

Following D.B.L. Hopkins's suggestion, Holding, together with members of the Council of the N.C.C., was invited to the A.C.C. Camp Fire in March 1910. At the Camp Fire "Mr Hopkins made sympathetic reference to the pioneer of the cycle-camping movement, and his remarks were very cordially received". Members of the N.C.C. were also invited to a joint Annual Supper and A.C.C. members were invited to their Camp Fire.

In 1910 the N.C.C., whose purpose was to "unite lovers of camping by cycle, motor, van, or boat", and which had just under 300 members – less than half the membership of the A.C.C. – was incorporated with the Amateur Camping Club. It was hoped that "all members, both old and new, will feel that they are no longer divided, but are members of one body with one hope – that of increasing by every legitimate means their Club's influence in the camping world".

On 12 August 1907 the Club opened its first office at 6 Duke Street, London – this was shared by The Camping Club and The Caravan Club, which had also joined the Camping Union. The need for a single address where members and other enquirers could seek information without making appointments to see members in their own homes was obvious.

Fred Horsfield taking his daughter, Peggy, for a ride in a trailer made from a baby carriage. **(Club Archive)**

Council meetings could be held there, and tents and other kit could be displayed on the premises. The Honorary Secretary was in the office daily from 11am–1.30pm and from 3pm–5pm, (until 8pm on Wednesdays). These hours show the amount of time that Alex Moeller put into the running of the Club in its early days. Despite all his other commitments he then took on the work of Honorary Editor of the magazine, and almost immediately agreed to act as Honorary Supplies Secretary as well.

Mrs Lowther and H. Townley at a camp near Dodderhill Common organised by Birmingham District Association, September 1907. (Club Archive)

Membership of the A.C.C. doubled during 1907 despite the appalling Summer weather and the question of paid assistance had to be considered by the Council, although there was some reluctance to do this in case the Club lost its amateur status. The A.G.M. in February 1908 granted the Council permission to appoint a paid Secretary. Alex Moeller was appointed, carrying on the work which he had previously done in a voluntary capacity. The post of Editor and Supplies Secretary was incorporated into the full-time post.

A telephone was installed at the office and "proved of the greatest service in keeping in touch with and expanding the work of the A.C.C. Kits for distant members have been delivered within a few hours of the receipt of the telephone order". G.W. Penn, one of the original six campers at Wantage in 1901, was elected Treasurer at that A.G.M.

By this time, the office was rapidly growing out of its accommodation and a new suite of rooms in the same building was acquired which, it was hoped, would prove to be more adequate.

In January 1911 the Club moved into new premises at 4 New Union Street, near Moorgate Station, and as well as providing office accommodation for the Club there was also space for an entirely separate Supplies Department.

The Secretarial Office, although in the same building, was distinct from the Supplies Department and dealt solely with the sporting interest

From the Club magazine

June 1911 *Sound advice for Alpine touring: "Never take anything you* might *want."*

August 1913 *About equipment: "If some misguided genius should invent a camping equipment that no one could find fault with, half our pleasure in life would be swept away."*

of the Club. The duties of the Secretary were therefore much reduced and Alex Moeller resigned from the post.

An advertisement appeared in *Camping* for the position of Honorary Secretary to the Club, which would carry an Honorarium of 25 guineas per annum to cover clerical assistance and personal out-of-pocket expenses. At the same time as this reorganisation, The Caravan Club decided to secure its own premises, and the Camping Union was amicably dissolved.

With the increase in the popularity of camping it was almost inevitable that controls would come. In 1908 anti-camping legislation first appeared when the Moveable Dwellings Bill was introduced in the House of Lords by Lord Clifford of Chudleigh: "This measure, vigorously attacked by Earl Russell, is not likely to be placed on the Statute Book. There is no need for such an Act so far as camping for pleasure is concerned; our case is entirely different to that of professional showmen and gipsies. The Council is alive to the possibilities of the measure, and will take such action, in conjunction with our kindred clubs, as the situation may warrant." From the very first it was obvious that all the Clubs were at least going to pull together against punitive legislation.

In November 1909 the Moveable Dwellings Bill reared its ugly head again with the possibility of subjecting amateur campers and

National Camping Club Meet, near Iver, 1909. Standing in the punt (right) is R.B. Searle who was to be the linchpin of the Club in the next few years. (Club Archive)

T.H. Holding and friends at a National Cycle-Camping Club camp, around 1908–09. (Club Archive)

caravanners "to many vexatious regulations", and although it was unlikely to reach the House of Commons during the current session, the Council again reassured members that they would keep a careful watch for its reappearance in the Spring.

In August 1910 the Moveable Dwellings Bill appeared again with the publication of a White Paper. Referring to tents, the Report reads: "Registration for any purpose would be inapplicable to ephemeral dwellings of this description, and conditions of cubit space applied to shelters which check the free air of heaven almost as little as does an umbrella are altogether incongruous.

"Local authorities might provide camping grounds, but these would not apply to amateur campers and caravannists, who would continue to use private sites with the permission of the owners, provided that such owners had received no prohibition from the local authorities."

In 1907 around 70 members camped at the official camps, including those run by the new D.A.s, during the August Bank Holiday weekend.

The Campers' Quarterly, magazine of the National Camping Club, first appeared in March 1909. Only four issues were published before the National Camping Club was absorbed into the Amateur Camping Club. (Club Archive)

In May the following year The Caravan Club held its first camp at Ockham, Surrey, the first organised meet of pleasure caravans ever held: "A cordial invitation comes from their Honorary Secretary to the members of the A.C.C. to visit the meet and to camp if they so desire," although tickets for entry had to be obtained from the office.

The N.C.C., started by Holding as the National Cycle-Camping Club in 1906, continued to hold its own camps, publicised in the *C.T.C. Gazette*. Many of the events and fixtures in 1907 followed the same format as those of the A.C.C.; they even used some of the same camp sites, notably Claydon House, home of Sir Edmund Verney, then President of the A.C.C.

The Club published its own *Sites Lists* and set the fees that members had to pay on all listed sites. After 1913 children under 16 were no longer charged site fees at official camps.

Coronation Camps were held at Portsmouth and at Neasden, London in June 1911. Some 60 campers attended the Portsmouth camp, but only eight tents, mostly belonging to provincial members were pitched at Neasden. A sad reflection on this camp was the note from the Chief Camp Steward: "Will those members who were responsible for the many broken bottles found afterwards on the site kindly note that by such carelessness they lay their Club open to serious liability in the event of injury to livestock on the farm."

In May 1912 the Council reported that they had secured a new permanent riverside site at Iver, Buckinghamshire, and a weekend camp was later held there. Unfortunately a loss was made, and members were urged to patronise the site to justify the heavy expenditure incurred in securing it for exclusive use. At the same time, all D.A.s and individuals not resident in a D.A. area were invited to send particulars of sites they found to the Honorary Secretary.

In May 1913 a new permanent site for Club members was opened at Field Common Farm, near Esher – Walton Club Site, the oldest site owned by the Club. Originally leased by the Club, it was purchased in 1946.

The Camping-Out Caravan

A one-horse caravan, weighing about 11cwt, was designed by Thomas Holding. Plans were published in The Campers' Handbook *in 1908, but it is not known if the 'van was ever built.*

Left: Walton Club Site was first opened in 1913, chosen for its convenient location and close proximity to water (for bathing). Over the years the site has changed due to flood relief schemes and gravel extraction. You can no longer bathe in the river and it is now one of the Club's few minimum facility sites. (Club Archive)

Following the success of the Crystal Palace demonstrations in 1906, the Club took a stand at the Travel Exhibition at the Royal Horticultural Hall in Westminster in 1907. Some 30,000 people visited the Club stand, where members of the Council and others were in attendance throughout the entire three weeks of the exhibition. It was noted that "such enthusiasm is to be found in but few clubs". The A.C.C. was awarded a Diploma of Merit for its cycle-camping outfits and for demonstrations of efficiency.

The Summer of 1908 was one of the best since the A.C.C.'s formation. Members had toured extensively, both at home and abroad, and many had spent long periods in camp, cycling to and from business daily. The Camping Club held its first demonstration in July, which included heavier tents and equipment as well as lightweight A.C.C. tents. The display was effective and better things were promised for the future.

The A.C.C. exhibited at the Ideal Home Exhibition at Olympia in October and at the Stanley Show (an important annual cycling exhibition) in November – both attracted a large number of visitors. The future of cycle-camping now seemed assured as a sport, with great interest being shown both by visitors to, and organisers of, those exhibitions. The A.C.C. had contributed to this in no small measure. Improvements were constantly being made to camping kit, and the A.C.C. was making every effort to

Goodbye Rotterdam – members of the Netherlands Club of Tourist Campers on the quayside bid goodbye to Club members on the first official tour overseas to Holland in 1913. **(Club Archive)**

First in the field A Century of The Camping and Caravanning Club

H. Winton Wood (centre) and James H. Wood (right) visited by their sisters in camp about 1908. Both men later played a leading role in the Club. (David Wood, Club Archive)

increase the value and utility of its literature. Members were being kept informed of new developments through the medium of *Cycle Camping*.

The Travel Exhibition at Olympia, in May 1909, was again a great success, with eight tents and a caravan belonging to members on show.

Camp Fires were held each year during the Winter months, to which members and their friends were invited. Competitions were held for useful gadgets and interesting items of kit, with small prizes offered, and these proved to be popular.

At the Camp Fire in March 1912, seven tents were erected, but only two were of standard pattern from the Supplies Department. It seems that members knew what they wanted from their own tents and were very inventive. After this Camp Fire, the following notice appeared in *Camping*: "Wanted. The yellow silk sou'wester removed by some wandering camper from the recent Camp Fire at South Kensington. Will the borrower kindly return it to the Supplies Dept?"

From its very beginning the Club had a small number of overseas members, who naturally took the sport back to their own countries. As a direct result, several European clubs were founded, based on the same principles of the A.C.C.

In 1909 Monsieur Morot, an N.C.C. member in Dijon, France, wrote that he had successfully launched the first camping club in France.

In July 1910 an A.C.C. member, Francis Young, wrote a letter (in French) to *Camping*. A rough translation reads: "I am happy to tell you that we are going to form Le Camping Club Français, and we dare to hope that you will assist us from your experience. The aim of our society is to create a movement in France to foster the camp life so in favour in neighbouring countries, and especially in England." We do not know whether this is the same club mentioned the previous year in the *Campers' Quarterly*, but we do know that the Camping Club de France celebrated its 90th birthday in the year 2000. The Secretary of Le Camping Club Français was elected an Honorary member of the A.C.C. and a similar courtesy had been extended by Le Camping Club Français to the Secretary of the A.C.C.

The Netherlands Association of Cyclists' weekly journal, *De Kampioen*, also carried an article on camping by Wouter Cool, an A.C.C. member. Interest aroused in these foreign journals "is astonishing and is demonstrated by the steady growth of the colonial and foreign membership of the A.C.C.".

In 1912 an official of the Dutch tourist board, having read of the Club's interest in a Dutch tour, wrote to the Editor of *Camping* saying it was difficult to find a camp site in Holland.

CARL DENIG, a Dutchman studying in London in 1911, read about the Club in a cycling magazine. He joined and, after meeting a number of Club members, made his own tent. On returning to Holland in 1912, he founded the Nederlandse Toeristen Kampeer Club and later started his own camping business, which still exists.

In the next issue Carl Denig, a Club member now returned to his native home, wrote in reply, suggesting suitable areas, and asking members who wished to know more to write to him. He signed himself "Honorary Secretary of the Nederlandse Toeristen Kampeer Club [N.T.K.C.]". This Club had been formed by Carl Denig and his sister Louise on 5 May 1912. The N.T.K.C. has, since that time, had long-standing links with the British club, and in later years particularly with the Association of Lightweight Campers. Besides Carl Denig, two of the original members of the N.T.K.C. Committee were members of the A.C.C.

In March 1913 it was announced that the N.T.K.C. was offering A.C.C. members the opportunity of purchasing goods from its supplies department on the same terms as its own members – the A.C.C reciprocated this offer. A Belgian camping club was also established during these years, but the exact date of its foundation is not known.

In January 1909 A.W. Robbins put forward a proposal in the magazine for official A.C.C. tours, possibly starting with a tour to Switzerland in the following July. His letter ends: "There need be no difficulty about chaperonage if ladies wished to join, as there would sure to be some married members with their wives in the party" – matters of great importance in 1909.

The Swiss tour went ahead (although it was not an official tour) with Mr Zuber, a member living in Switzerland, finding sites for the party and acting as guide and friend during the tour. The cost was seven guineas for 16 days, with second class rail travel on the continent and allowing 15 shillings a week for food.

In November, the Editor of *Camping* proposed that a portfolio of touring information should be started, as an aid to members planning tours, and members were invited to co-operate with the idea and make it a success.

In 1912 a Miss Beattie described a canoe-camping tour made in Pennsylvania in *Camping*, and mentioned an offer received from the United States of America of particulars for a canoe tour. Miss Beattie remarked that, apart from the voyage across the "Herring Pond", there would be very little expense.

In July 1912 five Club members toured Holland for three weeks at the N.T.K.C.'s invitation. The account of the tour by Miss Wallace, Secretary of the Ladies' Committee and a frequent contributor of *Ladies' Notes*, makes very interesting reading. Some of her remarks concerning the friendliness and the welcome, with offers to ride with them and show the way, could well apply today: on their first tour of Holland in 1976, the author and her family experienced the same hospitality.

ELSIE WALLACE did much to make camping practicable and popular for ladies. The first secretary of the Ladies' Committee, she had a passion for mothering camping debutantes. Her notes in Camping gave hints on keeping down weight, including using the skirt as a blanket, and a tent designed for ladies.

In the summer of 1912 four Club members embarked on a tour of Switzerland, using both mountain huts and camping – it was a real mountaineering tour. A note at the end of the account said: "The trip is impossible for cycles".

In July 1913 the first official Club tour took place, when 32 members toured Holland at the invitation of the N.T.K.C., and had a wonderful time. "Now that the Club has broken the ice, it is very sincerely to be hoped that this kind of tour, namely a continental one, will become an annual event at least."

It was decided to separate the Supplies Department from the Club administration at the end of 1911, and it had been hoped to transfer the whole of the Supplies Department to "some firm or individual", but no satisfactory solution could be found.

A.W. Robbins was appointed General Manager of the new department and, together with three managing trustees (George Gill, Stephen Hilhouse, and R.B. Searle), would have control of supplies. A loan of £200 had to be raised to secure capital for the reorganisation and an appeal was issued for members to give small loans, although sufficient capital had been guaranteed by individual members of the Council to enable a start to be made. Members responded to the appeal and the required amount was soon raised.

The Supplies Department reminded members that all orders had to be paid for in full, in advance, and later made tents available for hire, especially for the convenience of novices. The first full year's working amply justified its existence, and R.B. Searle, the Club Chairman, was thanked for his work in general for the Club in that year, which had resulted in the Club's very satisfactory position. It was R.B. Searle who suggested separating general Club business from that of the Supplies Department.

Some Club members had assumed that the kit the Club supplied was made by an outside manufacturer. This was not the case, as all the kit was made at headquarters, under the supervision of the Manager of the Supplies Department. All the people involved were Club members and did the work voluntarily in their own time. The workmanship was always first class, and the best materials were always used – one can imagine what would have been said about unpaid work if unions had been in existence.

Although the A.C.C. had launched its own gazette in 1906, information

The official Handbook described the 'A' tent as "a good model for one camper" – it depends on the size of the camper!

Another idyllic camping scene from those peaceful days before World War One. This picture of H. Winton Wood and J.H. Wood probably dates from around 1910. (Club Archive)

about the Club and its activities continued to appear in the *C.T.C. Gazette*. In addition to this, the N.C.C.C., founded by T.H. Holding in the previous year, publicised its activities in the same magazine. Holding also published many useful articles on camping equipment in the *C.T.C. Gazette*.

At the beginning of May 1907 the fifth edition of the A.C.C. *Handbook* was published on a scale never before attempted by the Association. Its 109 pages contained detailed information on equipment, including making it, plus a list of camp sites and a full list of members. There were hints and tips on cookery and first aid, and a comprehensive price list of goods obtainable through the Supplies Secretary. At about the same time, the Camping Club published its first newsletter, a typed leaflet entitled *Camping*.

Holding's new *Campers' Handbook* was finally published in March 1908, the *Daily News* calling it The Camper's Koran, it having been written by such an authority on the subject. Full of information, it included chapters on camping by boat and by caravan, in addition to cycle- and pedestrian-camping.

March 1909 saw the beginning of volume four of *Cycle Camping*, which appeared in a very smart green cover. The issue ran to 16 pages and was the biggest so far produced.

The *Camper's Quarterly* magazine of the N.C.C. also appeared in March. In this first issue, the Chairman, Holding, said that the magazine was issued at his suggestion and asked for designs for the cover for future issues, having provided the cover of the first issue at his own expense.

A new *Handbook*, much of which was compiled by D.B.L. Hopkins, Chairman of the Council, was produced in 1910, but he had temporarily to retire from active participation in Club work due to ill health. During his Chairmanship, separate price lists for supplies were introduced.

Apart from containing official notices and general Club information, the magazine was also a useful means of communicating ideas to others. Miss Wallace wrote in May 1909 that ladies had been complaining the standard A.C.C. kit was too heavy for them to carry on their cycles, so they could not take up cycle-camping. She was therefore designing "a small tent which will afford head room for the necessary coiffure and average comfort under all weather conditions", intended for "pedestrian work" but light enough for any cyclist.

"It is absolutely necessary, if one goes in for light kit, to dispense with some of the luxuries of life, and a clean sweep must be made of all the superfluous pots and dishes, carrying just the bare necessities and adopting the simple life without reserve. The sleeping kit might be reduced – a light eiderdown quilt must suffice, with the aid of the much-abused skirt, or a very light and compact sleeping bag. During the Summer months it is really not necessary to carry much covering, as the nights should not be cold."

That same month a member sent in an idea for pedestrians, suggesting that: "two canes should be fixed lengthways along the bottom of the rucksack and two others, quite short, secured across these and fitted into a belt. This throws the weight upon the hips, relieving the shoulders and allowing airspace between the rucksack and the pedestrian's back, keeping him remarkably cool." The idea of a hip-belt which transferred the weight of the sack from the shoulders to the hips was not adopted commercially in the U.K. until the 1960s, when Karrimor introduced its Totem frames and hip-belts.

Yet another idea, from D.B.L. Hopkins, was one for modifying the feet on a Primus stove to provide fold-out legs to give better stability. Like so many Club members' ideas, this was another which was later adopted by the manufacturers.

In June 1912 Mr Strugnell described a handcart he had made for use when family camping, and Miss Wallace made no apology for writing again about pedestrian kit. T.W.L. Casperz tells of taking his cycle and camp kit on board his ship, so that he can go camping when he has a 48 hour leave. Later he was to take his motor-cycle on board!

In July 1913 the magazine published plans for a "cycle-car caravan", reproduced from *The Irish Cyclist* magazine. This was, in fact, what we now know as a trailer tent, which unfolded from the trailer base. The cycle-car is also described having a water-cooled engine but light in every other respect.

The Club's magazine continued to provide a wealth of information for members, and provided the distant members with a link to those in more populated areas where the D.A.s were more active.

This design is probably the first ever recorded trailer tent. The car, itself, was very lightweight and had a water-cooled engine. (Club Archive)

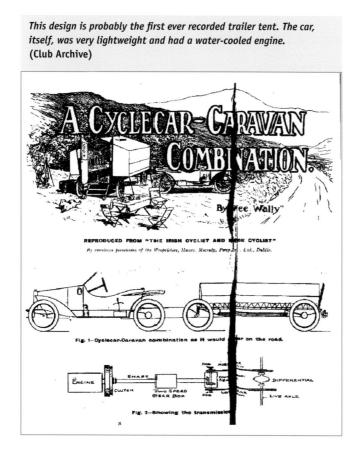

Pioneer caravans by Andrew Jenkinson

Early 1930s Raven caravan, still looking as though it is from the previous decade.

Gentleman Gypsies, as they were called, were the first caravan users for leisure, but with the advent of the internal combustion engine it wouldn't be long before both users and early builders took a fresh approach to the new leisure caravan. The advent of World War One saw trailers being used and showed how easily cars could pull them. After the war several early caravan manufacturers were founded due to their experiences in the war with trailers.

Early pioneers such as Bertram Hutchings (Winchester) and Bill Riley (Eccles) persevered with trailer caravans, built very much in the vogue of their horse-drawn ancestors – very rectangular in profile and featuring the entrance door at the rear. With caravans being a rich man's hobby the price, up to a point, didn't matter, and some early caravans were lavishly equipped and built using the finest craftsmen.

By the 1920s it was obvious that caravans needed to be sold to a wider audience. Caravans had to be designed and built to make them more affordable as well as to tow better and be lighter. Eccles was the first to go into full caravan production and heavily promoted this new hobby. Owners sent the company letters on how well their Eccles caravan had performed. Sales grew steadily and other makers such as Raven and Car Cruiser established themselves to become market leaders.

The 1920s also saw caravan manufacturers head into aerodynamics, such as Car Cruiser and its fast rake back, which was said to improve stability at speed – probably around 40mph max! Paraffin was used for cooking and heating in the early caravans. Eccles developed the caravan awning, calling it a lean-to tent – which is what it really was. Among the extras was a toilet tent plus spade!

The 1930s though saw caravanning expand at a great rate of knots. New makers sprang up with super streamlined profiles, gas lamps, radios, 12V lighting, ball couplings, steel chassis and baths, no less. Airlite caravans had plastic moulded corner units on the front and rear panels – a first for caravans. Winchester produced super luxury caravans that were well known

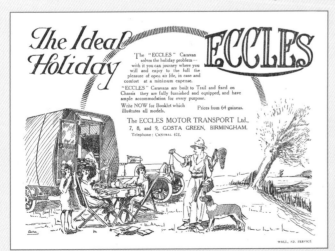

for quality, design and superior equipment levels. As caravanning grew in the 1930s many early caravanners built their own 'vans; some models were very poor but others were excellent and the builders became manufacturers.

However, the advent of World War Two stopped virtually all caravan production in its tracks. Many manufacturers made ambulances and did other war work. After the war materials were in short supply and most caravan makers ceased production. Some new names, though, were about to emerge. In the late 1940s one man, Sam Alper, saw that caravans had a big future – if they were light and cheap to buy but of good quality. His first designs utilised wartime surplus materials and proved cumbersome.

The first Streamlites (later Sprites) came about, and Alper showed just how good his 'vans were by taking them on endurance tests. Sales proved a great success, pushing the Sprite name to the forefront of caravan ownership. Other new makers though were up and coming in the 1950s as wartime had seen the introduction of new tools, materials and glues that would revolutionise the caravan industry. Paladin, Berkeley, Willerby, Bluebird and Bailey were all out to make their mark and quickly gained acceptance, although luxury makers such as Burlingham and Siddall along with Carlight still tempted caravanners to spend over £1,000 for the privilege of luxury tourer ownership.

At the end of the 1950s caravan manufacturing in the U.K. reached a high level of production. Aluminium was replacing hardboard for caravan exterior walls while the roof construction of stretched canvas was also to be replaced by aluminium. Glass fibre moulding took on a new role in tourer design with makers such as Willerby, Berkeley and Freeman using it to its best.

Other developments saw a few makers try amphibious 'vans, double deckers, extending units and tourers such as the Berkeley Messenger with fold down end wall, which came complete with a sun canopy. The next decades were to see further development in tourer design.

Interior picture of a 1958 Sprite Ariel.

1914–1919: The devastation of the Great War

The Club had been growing apace, with the amalgamation of several clubs into one strong group, and a membership exceeding 800. The magazine was thriving and included in its pages were many good ideas regarding kit for camping that members could copy. The Supplies Department was also very busy, and the Club had its first permanent camp site at Walton – 1914 had begun well.

In the January issue of *Camping*, the editorial contained the following: "We certainly had not much to complain of in the year just passed, except, perhaps, that it had a 13 in it; but, as true joy lies in anticipation, we look forward to even better things in 1914. Light hearts, bright days, and good fellowship."

After the successful tour of Holland the previous year, a Touring Committee was set up as one of the Club's working committees to arrange both home and overseas tours. Members would be able to meet each other in advance at an official camp in England before going overseas, appropriate maps for the country concerned would be available to participants, and a camping phrase book would be prepared in Dutch, French and German.

Invitations were received from the Belgian, Dutch and French clubs to camp with them at various locations, and the Club invited members of the Nederlandse Toeristen Kampeer Club (N.T.K.C.) to camp in England – a return visit after the previous year's tour. An additional tour to France in September was suggested.

Left: No-one would describe the privations of World War One mud as any kind of holiday. But, ironically for some men, it showed them how life under canvas could be a comfortable leisuretime activity. It also took thousands beyond their native shores for the first time – something they would repeat as peacetime adventures with the Club. These bell tents are pitched in a mine crater, near Arras, in the Summer of 1917. (Imperial War Museum, Q2555)

In the wider world

Balkans powder-keg explodes: The assassination at Sarajevo of the Austro-Hungarian Archduke Franz Ferdinand by a Serbian student increased tension in Europe. Germany invaded Belgium, leading to war between the Austro-German alliance and Britain, France and Russia, spreading beyond Europe to dominate world affairs for the next five years.

Stonehenge knocked down: One of the world's most famous ancient monuments was sold at auction for a rock-bottom price. Stonehenge and 30 acres of surrounding downland was sold as Lot 15 of the Amesbury Estate for only £6,600 to a Mr C.H. Chubb.

Women get the vote: Influenced by the increasing part played by women in the war effort, the Representation of the People Act in 1918 gave married women over 30 the vote. The following year Nancy Astor became the first woman M.P. to take her seat in the Commons.

A new *Sites List*, combined with a *Club Yearbook* was produced which, for the first time, included details of a permanent official site at Walton. The list included overseas sites available to members, among them two sites used by the N.T.K.C. in locations where it still has sites today.

The 11 o'clock rule was in force even in 1914. In this same year a separate *Price List* (in reality an illustrated catalogue) was produced, as was a new *Handbook* which, unlike its predecessor produced in 1907, was devoted purely to the technicalities of camping. As well as suggestions for model kits (intended for cycle-campers), instructions for making several tents, together with hints for proofing groundsheets, choosing tent lighting, and making all kinds of little gadgets were included.

Hints on kitchen equipment and cooking, carrying kit, site selection and tent pitching, fixed-camping and boat-camping, pedestrian-camping and camping with a handcart are all to be found within. For the first time in a *Handbook* reference is made to caravan-camping, with an illustration of the interior of a Bertram Hutchings caravan. Notes for "the Fair Sex", hints on photography and first aid were also included.

Folding candle sconce

Candles were regularly used by Club members, and this candle sconce, designed for attachment to the tent pole was first illustrated in the 1914 Supplies Department catalogue. Having an integral windshield it was safer than others and is identical to those available in Holland in 1999.

The magazines for the year contained more useful hints and a kit competition was announced with entries shown at the Camp Fire. The winning design would become the property of the Club, to be used for the benefit of members. That year's winning gadget was a device in the shape of a hinged brass clip which, when sewn into the tent, would enable it to be pitched or taken down without disturbing the flysheet – a novel idea that could still be of use today.

The Club accepted an offer of space at The Simple Life and Open Air Exhibition to display kit and distribute Club literature. By all accounts it was a great success, although *The Guardian* newspaper was highly critical of the sophisticated caravans and tinned foods on display.

One Club member commented that should *The Guardian* have observed the Club exhibits a little closer they would have seen the simple kit that the cycle camper carried. The only complaint of Club members manning the stand was that of hoarseness at the end of the day.

July 1916 *A sad re-proof: "I must be one of the greatest blockheads that ever walked on two legs. Last year I re-proofed my tent with linseed oil and it was perfectly water tight. The other day I fetched it out and it tore into pieces as if made of cobwebs. I buried it."*

September 1918 *A sign of the times: "The Honorary Secretary is now engaged upon War Work elsewhere and consequently can only give occasional and irregular attention to Club affairs."*

A record recruitment of 61 new members in July – 183 since January – was almost certainly due to the efforts of members at that exhibition, together with appreciative reviews of the new Club *Handbook* in the press. More general causes were thought to be the rediscovery of England, made easier by the popularity of the motor-car and motor-cycle, with a rapid increase in motor-camping. The Honorary Secretary, in his notes for July, said: "The future is full of promise for the camping movement, and we look to every member to do his or her best to maintain or increase the present rate of progress."

Camping meets and Club tours, especially the Irish tour, were a great success but the French tour was cancelled due to lack of support – in the circumstances perhaps it was just as well. The first part of an article entitled *France Revisited*, by Oliver Wade, was published in the September magazine. Perhaps it was prophetic, for by the time the magazine was published Britain was at war and before very long many of our young members would be in France.

Strangely, the only reference to the war in the September issue of *Camping* came from the Secretary of the N.T.K.C who, in his letter of 20 August, said: "At present the members of the N.T.K.C. do not camp much. A great deal of them get under arms, for the whole Dutch Army and Navy have been mobilised to maintain our neutrality. The whole world fixes its eyes upon Belgium, where soon the greatest battle may take place that was ever fought. Who will be the conqueror?

"Holland will remain neutral in every respect, but this does not prevent us from wishing Germany's defeat. Germany crushed the Law of Nations under foot; with this infamous deed Germany incurred the whole world's horror. We wish your Army and famous Navy a great success!" Holland remained neutral and communications with the N.T.K.C. were maintained throughout the war.

OLIVER WADE joined the Club when still at school and while still only 16 wrote a short series entitled **By Heath and Hedgerow,** *under the name Roland de Bois. His mature style and beautiful illustrations belied the fact that they were the work of a schoolboy.*

He also wrote an account of a trip to France in 1914, including a superb photograph of the Rose Window in Amiens cathedral taken by him the previous year with an exposure time of half an hour.

In February 1915 he was elected as the youngest ever member of the Council, and agreed to write more articles, but he joined an Officer Training Corps, and no more were written. He resigned from the Council in June to take a commission and was sent to Egypt, then joined the Royal Flying Corps and returned to England to train as a pilot.

On 15 October 1915 he flew to France, dropping a cheery message in the field at Cudham, source of inspiration for his Heath and Hedgerow *articles. Described as a most capable and fearless pilot, he was reported missing over the German lines ten days later. His death was confirmed.*

He was a great asset to the Club and but for the war might well have finished up as Chairman. A brilliant scholar, gifted naturalist and photographer, he had won an open scholarship to Kings College Cambridge, but preferred to serve his country – just one of the young men who gave their lives in what was cruelly called "the war to end all wars".

AMATEUR CAMPING CLUB.

HEADQUARTERS:
4. NEW UNION STREET,
MOORFIELDS,
LONDON. E.C.

URGENT AND IMPORTANT.

In view of the fact that practically the whole coast line of the British Isles and the districts surrounding garrison towns and naval bases are "declared military areas," members are earnestly warned against attempting to camp in any place where their presence might invite suspicion or add to the difficulties of the authorities.

No illuminant should be used, nor should campers roam about after dark in any neighbourhood where sentries are posted.

In a matter of such importance as this the Council feel that they can rely upon the co-operation and discretion of individual members in preventing difficulties arising during the present crisis.

LIGHTING RESTRICTIONS.

During the continuance of the present lighting restrictions, the Council strongly urge campers not to use artificial light of any sort for the illumination of their tents.

This rule will be strictly observed at all camps officially arranged by the Club and the Council appeal to all campers, when camping elsewhere than at officially arranged camps, to loyally support it in this request.

IMPORTANT WARNING.

Campers are earnestly urged to bear in mind the importance of closing and fastening all gates on Farms after passing through them. Neglect of this duty laid a member open to a heavy claim for damage to growing crops owing to cattle straying through a gate left open.

Members are reminded that they are personally responsible for the good conduct in this and all other respects of friends whom they invite to join them at any Official Camp.

Notice to members concerning wartime restrictions on camping, and about lighting up after dark. It was strictly forbidden to use artificial light on Club-approved sites and members were asked to respect this ruling elsewhere. (Club Archive)

An amusing story is told by a member who had been camping with friends near Land's End at the outbreak of war. Their original pitch was near the Atlantic Cable Telegraph Station, so the group had to move to the other side of the village when war broke out. This time their pitch was near the Coastguard Station and, during the night, the party was rudely woken by two officers, two soldiers with rifles and fixed bayonets and two policemen who wanted to see "the foreign-looking gentleman".

The ladies were somewhat alarmed and the gentleman concerned – W.F. Skinner from Redditch – had very few papers with him since he "did not dream of having to prove his nationality when he left home", but managed to find sufficient Club membership cards and correspondence to prevent his being arrested as a German spy.

One of the policemen spotted a name on his trunk 'Granit Fibre' and suggested that was his real name. One of the officers, however, informed the policeman that Granit Fibre was the material from which the trunk was made. The conversation was stated to be "an absolute fact".

By November a very large number of Club members had "joined the colours" and were asked for their full regimental addresses so that the Club could keep in touch with them.

Members were asked to send extracts of interesting letters received from the Front to the Editor for possible publication. Social evenings and the Annual Supper went ahead in order to try and be as normal as possible, profits from these evenings being sent to the Prince of Wales' Relief Fund. Members of H.M. Forces and recognised Scout patrols were authorised to obtain kit from the Supplies Department.

Early in 1915 the Club faced serious difficulties in both the Secretarial and Supplies departments. The position of Secretary at that time was a voluntary one and the Supplies Department was also managed by volunteers. A temporary Secretary had been appointed in the previous September, pending changes in the Secretarial Department, but it was clear that a more permanent arrangement was needed.

R.B. Searle had lost his assistant in the Supplies Department to the Forces and felt that, owing to the war's effect on his own business, he could not continue with the large amount of voluntary service needed to keep the Supplies Department viable. The Club offered him the combined post of Secretary and Supervising Trustee of the Supplies Department, with an Honorarium dependant on the number of Club members and the profits of the Supplies Department. In doing this, the Club hoped it would then be able to function properly for the duration of the war. Since R.B. Searle was at that time the Chairman of the Council, he resigned from the Council and his place as Chairman was taken by G.J. Gill.

The November 1915 supplement to the Supplies Department price-list contained useful items suitable as Christmas gifts for members of the forces, including a metal mirror in a canvas case, a cutlery set and a folding candle lantern. (Club Archive)

Amateur Camping Club.

SUPPLIES DEPARTMENT,

4, NEW UNION STREET,
MOORGATE STREET, LONDON, E.C.

NOVEMBER, 1915.
SPECIAL NOTICE.

POSTAGE.—In view of the proposed postal alterations it may be necessary to revise the present rate of postage on goods, if and when any new Regulations come into force.

ADDED TO LIST.

	Price s. d.	Weight lbs. ozs.	Post d.
Pennon Carrier as described on page 32 of the Handbook, but with several minor improvements ... ... each (pennon not included)	2 0	1¾	1
Mirror (metal), best quality; size 4⅝ x 2⅝ ins., in Willesden Canvas Case, drab colour (*lined with "Selvyt."*) each	1 6	0 2	1

"With Gill on the bridge, and Searle at the helm, we can confidently face the future," said the Editor D.B.L. Hopkins.

The support of every member, and as many new ones as possible, was sought in order to keep the Club going. So many members were serving at the Front that unless all others retained their membership, "the usefulness of the Club might very well be curtailed".

R.B. Searle's assistant, Charles Payne, one of the first Club members to volunteer for military service, wrote describing life as a private in the trenches: "Can you imagine a trip of three days and three nights with no shelter and living like rabbits in a wet clay soil? No wash, no shave, clothes never off, and always on the alert. Oh! it tries your nerves. When we do return to our base for rest, you should see the poor fellows – wrecks – of which I must add myself for I have found each trench tour has made me feel absolutely dead; but a rest soon pulls one round, and although not feeling in the pink of condition, I am able to keep free of the hospital. We have lost a good few of our fellows, which depresses one, but what plays more havoc with one's comrades is the exposure."

Because of his camping activities he may well have been fitter than many of his comrades and was able to fight the problems of exposure.

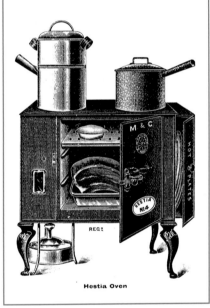

Hestia oven

This oven was made specially for outdoor use and was heated by a large Primus stove. It was ideal for families and fixed campers and you could cook a joint in the oven and boil pans on the hob at the same time. Heavyweight equipment such as this first appeared in the Supplies Department Catalogue in 1914.

Hestia Oven

Another member wrote that after a night attack he was glad to get back without a twisted ankle. He also complained that the cooks could not light their fire in pouring rain, and "why on earth don't the Army take up the Primus?". Other quotes include: "My full kit weighs 35lbs (actual weight, as weighed on the butcher's balance – none of your Holding guess-work)" and "Wouldn't I like one of those really good meals we used to have in camp now? Most of our one shilling a day is spent in the canteen on extra food."

A letter from the Rev. T.W.L. Caspersz, M.A., a Chaplain in the Home Fleet, tells of having his Amateur Camping Club (A.C.C.) pennon attached to his cabin wall. He also had his down quilt on board, and regarded it as a friend as it was so useful during the cold nights.

He describes sighting the periscope of a German submarine close to the ship and its bubbles going right beneath them. There was no explosion and he wondered what had saved them. "All I know was that the following Sunday all hands put a lot more into the General Thanksgiving than they have ever put before! And so the old ship is still one of Britain's sure shields and, please God, will be till her Sky Pilot takes down the A.C.C. pennon from his cabin wall and rolls up his quilt."

Club members were still active in England, and "two novices" wrote of their experiences pedestrian-camping in Sussex.

They had joined the Club after visiting the Simple Life Exhibition, and toured for a fortnight with a complete outfit from the Supplies

Department. This consisted of a small 'A' tent, "the usual sleeping kit" (which included a "wonderfully warm" quilt), a pocket Primus, light aluminium canteen, bucket and basin, a few other necessities and two rucksacks to carry it all in – all for £6. They seem to have had a wonderful time, despite some mixed weather, and thought that the kit supplied by the Club to be thoroughly reliable, and had no doubt this contributed very largely to their comfort.

District Association's (D.A.s) were busy, although Birmingham was looking for a new Secretary, and Northumberland and Durham D.A. cancelled its annual meeting because only a few members could attend due to the war. Lancashire, Cheshire and North Wales D.A. had its first meeting, and opened the season with a social in Liverpool. The Camp Fire in London was an even greater success than before, 340 persons attending as against a maximum of 200 in previous years.

A special offer of a Comet oven (without the stove) at a cost of 10s 6d was made by the Supplies Department. Stock, once sold, would not be repeatable at that price. A suitable stove to use with the oven cost 13s 6d. (Club Archive)

AMATEUR CAMPING CLUB.

SUPPLIES DEPARTMENT,

4, New Union Street, Moorfields, London, E.C.

STOVES, ETC.

INCREASED PRICES.

"PRIMUS" STOVES. (See Price List, 1916 Edition, pages 18 and 19), ... **Add ten per cent.**

SPECIAL OFFERS.

The prices of all Air-pressure Paraffin Stoves having advanced considerably, the attention of Members is specially drawn to the following Stoves, etc.; the prices will be found to be the lowest on the Market; the Stock is strictly limited, and cannot be replaced at the present time.

"COMET" OVEN, including kettle, saucepan, steamer, and baking-pan, but no stove. *(Carriage forward)*. *Price,* **10s. 6d.** *Weight,* 20 lbs.

"COMET" STOVE No. 1, for use with the "Comet" Oven and otherwise. (See illustration of oven). *Capacity about 2½ pints.* (These Stoves have been refitted with "Roarer" burners of the "Primus" type, and are now quite satisfactory in use). Iron stand 9 in. by 9 in. *Price.* **13s. 6d.** *Weight,* 4¾ lbs.

P.T.O.

On a slightly more sombre note, the Honorary Secretary reported: "On several occasions recently, envelopes which should have contained *Camping* or other communications from headquarters have been delivered by the postal authorities with their contents missing." Members were asked to report the matter and return the envelopes to the Honorary Secretary. Someone was heard to remark that the Post Office staff found the contents so interesting they were reluctant to part with them!

The May 1915 issue of *Camping* had reports of tours, camps and reminiscences, including a portrait of Holding and an article by Frederick Horsfield. Clearly it was intended to boost morale when news from France was not good.

Congratulations were offered to Charles Payne, who had been gazetted a First Lieutenant. This "special Spring Number" attracted some favourable comment from the press, but an insert warning campers not to show lights, not to camp in any place where their presence might invite suspicion, and a strong warning about closing and fastening all farm gates attracted some rather unfortunate comment from *The Star* newspaper. In the next issue of *Camping* its comments, referring to the insert, were printed: "It seems to us that the very best place for them to pitch their tents is the nearest military camp. The King's shilling awaits them."

The Club replied: "It is quite obvious to us that *The Star* does not know the stuff that campers are made of, as practically all the eligible young men in the Club have already taken the King's shilling. We are preparing a list, and hope to publish it at an early date." Unfortunately, this list was not published in the magazine, and the Club has no other records from that time, so we shall never know exactly how many Club members served. In this same issue, the first notified Club fatality was reported from France— Lt. Bainbridge of Newcastle-upon-Tyne having been killed in action.

In an effort to interest more of the general public in the Club, a number of copies of the *Handbook* were placed in public libraries and institutes. A limited number of copies of *Camping* would be placed at the disposal of librarians who would undertake to place them in their reading rooms.

It had been thought that the Walton Club Site might not be able to open in 1915 because of the war conditions, but open it did with the only wartime requirement that every camper was required to sign the Register kept by the Camp Steward. The site had been considerably enlarged and additional trees planted "for members' exclusive benefit". J.H. Wood, who

JAMES H. WOOD (brother of H. Winton Wood, Honorary Secretary in 1911 and later in charge of the Supplies Department) designed the original Itisa tent in 1916, as well as a number of other camping gadgets, including a home-made pressure stove. He was Chief Camp Steward at Walton during World War One.

was then Chief Camp Steward, said it was impossible to spend a dull hour at Walton and, indeed, the site proved to be very popular with members. The season was a record in more ways than one, not only because of a record number of campers, but also a record number of wasps!

The impossibility of having the usual Club tours meant that a series of eleven holiday camps, mostly arranged by the various D.A.s, was held. The camps were all self-supporting, and any surplus was given to the host D.A.

Amateur Camping Club Meet, somewhere in England, 1914–15. (Club Archive)

With the exception of one camp, members travelled from all parts of the country and several asked that the camps could be made a permanent feature of Club events, even when the tours could be resumed. Since the camps generated great interest among the general public, and many new members were gained, the Council agreed to repeat the arrangements in the following year.

Participation in ordinary D.A. camps and social events was increasing, which was a great encouragement to all. An amusing story is told of a camp near Keswick: "We found that a half-gallon tin of castor oil was both the cheapest and best insurance against wet feet. This supply, however, ran out by the Friday of the first week, and I volunteered to cycle into Keswick to replenish the indispensable oil.

"Naturally, I sought the chemist who had provided the first tin and asked him for another. The poor man looked very perturbed, and regretted he had no more tins in stock – after all, one was sufficient supply for six months normally. Anxious to help, he retreated to his little desk, and making one or two calculations on a scrap of paper, glanced at his stock with satisfaction. 'I can do you Beecham's Pills,' he said cheerfully – 'a party of 50, you said, didn't you, and the tin has not quite lasted a week?' – and he checked his calculations.

"Disguising my laughter as best I could, I said I thought that would not do and took my leave. Before I had mounted my cycle he had come out after me, sympathising and offering the local doctor's address. I ended the evening by running all the Keswick butchers out of dripping – true, a little dearer, but more to my wants than Beecham's Pills!"

More families with children were camping lightweight and members with experience of family-camping were asked to pass on their knowledge. A suggestion was made that the *Handbook* should include some advice on the subject. The closing camp of the year, at the end of September, of Lancashire, Cheshire and North Wales D.A. attracted a record number of 28 campers, including six children.

Members were still very interested in camp kit, the more so because of the difficulty in obtaining some supplies. A letter from George Gill in November 1915 offered prizes for a pedestrian kit competition to be held during the Autumn camp in 1916. Prizes were offered for a complete single pedestrian kit, a complete double kit, and an appliance for pedestrian-camping. Those competing for the first two prizes had to arrive carrying their complete kit, including sufficient food for at least one day, properly packed for carrying.

By the beginning of 1916 most of the few remaining young men in the Club were being called up and women were beginning to take their places as officials of the Club. The first of these was the Secretary of Birmingham D.A., and indeed their Committee consisted of more ladies than men. This was to be followed by an even more significant event

Young women enjoying a quiet weekend during World War One. Their Chalet tent was made by the Club's Supplies Department. **(Club Archive)**

First in the field A Century of The Camping and Caravanning Club

when Mrs Lynn was elected as Chairman of the Council; she took the chair for the first time on 8 March.

The Supplies Department issued a warning that certain items, mostly those made from aluminium, could not be replaced once stocks were sold because of Ministry of Munitions' restrictions. Most other stock would be available reasonably promptly during the season, but members wanting specially designed tents and other articles were warned to give as much notice as possible of their requirements.

The annual Camp Fire in 1916 was a quiet one, intended for the London members to keep in touch with each other during the war. There was, however, "a sense of widening the circle", for two provincial members sent slides of the Summer camps held in the north of England the previous year, and a Scottish member travelled to London to give a much-appreciated lantern lecture.

In the magazine, an elderly camper suggested the use of an air bed as being ideal for camping with a motor, and "the operation of inflation is good exercise for the lungs, and a source of interest and amusement to fellow campers". However, at 4lbs in weight he thought it too heavy for a lightweight camper.

Enamel mug with folding handle

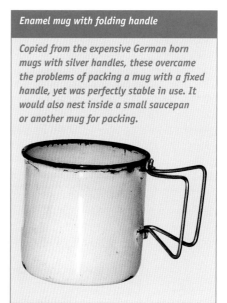

Copied from the expensive German horn mugs with silver handles, these overcame the problems of packing a mug with a fixed handle, yet was perfectly stable in use. It would also nest inside a small saucepan or another mug for packing.

The Irish Cyclist and Motor-Cyclist magazine allowed the Club to reproduce an article on making a tent cot, which could be carried on a motor-cycle and obviated the use of a tent. Later in the same month its offices were burned to the ground in the Dublin uprising and everything, apart from documents in the safe, was lost.

Sir Martin Conway, Vice-President of the Club, invited a limited number of members to camp on his estate at Allington Castle, Kent. The military authorities refused permission for the Walton Club Site to be used that year; however, holiday camps would be organised by the D.A.s.

In 1916 there were several new designs for tents published in the magazine, plus an article on fixed-camping with two families, including six children, by Frederick Horsfield. "In view of the number of children, and the tender ages of the youngest, our maids accompanied us, enabling our wives to take more rest than they otherwise would have been able to do."

They also took five tents with them, including a striped kitchen shelter and a bell tent. All the kit was sent by train and delivered to the site by lorry. Another article describes a tour by a couple using a second-hand ice-cream cart for carrying their kit. The railway booking clerk could not decide if it was a pram or a cycle, decided it was a hybrid and let it go for the cheaper rate.

Colin Gill, one of the three sons of George Gill who were all serving in the Forces, wrote of his experiences, both in the trenches and in the observer's seat of a plane "all in connection with my work". He describes being able to see the trenches and a big bombardment, despite his face being covered with leaking oil during a steep dive, and of knowing every house in the villages taken from the enemy as he had been observing them all through Winter.

Despite the war, a 48-page price list (actually an illustrated catalogue) was produced by the Supplies Department in 1916. (Club Archive)

Colin had attended the Slade School of Art and became the first winner of the Rome Scholarship in 1913. He served as a camouflage officer. Among his duties he often had to make detailed drawings of a tree in the front line, and then have it reproduced in metal. The real tree would then be removed during the night and the metal replica set up in its place and used as an observation post.

He was invalided out of the army, suffering from gas poisoning, and in 1918 he became the official war artist for the Canadian government – some of his work is in the Imperial War Museum. He later became famous for his murals and portraits, and painted the first portrait of Queen Elizabeth (now the Queen Mother) after her accession. He was, by all accounts, a very quiet and modest man, and died after a very short illness in South Africa in 1940.

In the last magazine of the year there are reports of the Summer camps, including a description and photograph of the first Itisa tent seen at the camp in Hope, Derbyshire, organised jointly by Lancashire, Cheshire and North Wales and Nottingham and East Midlands D.A.s – this was the best attended of the camps, with a total of 30 campers present. The Tours Secretary reported that all the camps were favoured by ideal weather, were self-supporting and in the exceptional circumstances "may be regarded as very satisfactory and as justifying the arrangements made".

January 1917 began with a report that the number of members at the end of 1916 stood at 820 as compared with 900 at the end of the previous year, and once again members were asked to continue their support.

Despite the fact that so many Club members were on service for their country, it was still possible to do some propaganda work on behalf of the Club, and the Secretary asked members to distribute copies of the prospectus where it might do some good. The Editor wrote: "The Royal Flying Corps seems to have an attraction for our younger members. Perhaps it is the life in the free and open air which appeals to them." Sadly, he then reports that one of them, Oliver Wade, had been reported missing.

Another article appears on family-camping, in which W.F. Skinner describes his tent, made by the Supplies Department, measuring 22ft long and 11ft high. It was designed for fixed-camping, had a solid floor and furnished with beds, a chest of drawers, folding iron washstand, provisions cupboard, meatsafe and bookshelves, plus folding table, forms and chairs. "If any of my readers say this is not lightweight camping, I can say it is as light as it is comfortable, and the whole of the kit – remember it is for eight of us and two cats – goes in a four-wheel covered spring cart."

The tent and equipment was used for a month in the Spring and a month in the Autumn. At the other extreme, information is given about a camping tent/bed annexe attached to the side of a light car (and we thought the Caranex was a relatively modern invention).

In February a ballot was taken at the Council meeting for a new Chairman. Mrs Lynn had last chaired a meeting in the previous October and there is no mention of her thereafter, so we do not know what happened to her (Mr Lynn remained on the Council). Alex Moeller had by this time changed his name to

A good programme of entertainment was arranged for the Camp Fire of March 1915 – a talk on lightweight camping, a lantern lecture on camping in the Highlands, as well as refreshments. (Club Archive)

ALEX PAPPS – advised to drop his German name of Moeller during World War One and take his mother's name – spent most of his early life in artistic studies, and was a Professor of Elocution at the age of 20. He was also a pianist, singer and actor, but became increasingly interested in sport, especially cycling and camping.

He joined the Club in 1902 at the age of 30 and was a member of the first Committee. Appointed Honorary Secretary to the new Council in 1907, he was also the first Honorary Secretary of the original Camping Club.

He supervised the establishment of the first official Headquarters in Duke Street and from 1908–1911 was the first paid Secretary, incorporating the position of Supplies Secretary and Editor of Cycle-Camping. *In 1909 he steered the Association of Cycle-Campers, the Camping Club and the National Camping Club into the Amateur Camping Club, and also saw the change of title of the magazine from* Cycle-Camping *to* Camping. *He was Honorary Editor of* Camping *for over 30 years in total – from 1907–1910 and 1919–1945.*

Known as the camp jester in the early days, he had a fine voice and regularly entertained members at Camp Fires. He devoted his whole life to the Club and continued working on its behalf, holding the post of Honorary Librarian until a few months before his death, in 1960, at the age of 88.

"No one will know just how much the Club owes to him," said Club President J.A.C. Champion at the time.

Papps, his mother's name, and was appointed Club Press and Propaganda Secretary. Club subscription renewals were "not up to last year" and members were urged not to let the Club break down "just when there is a hope before many months that normal times may return".

That hope was, sadly, not to be realised. Because of the exceptional conditions it was impossible to arrange Summer camps for 1917, and there was an appeal to caravanners within the Club to give or loan a caravan to the Imperial Association to assist officers disabled by shell-shock to return to a more normal life.

Members wishing to attend a D.A. camp in Wales over the Whitsun weekend were asked to bear in mind the food restrictions and bring most of their provisions with them – especially sugar – and members were exhorted to "eat less bread". Petrol was in very short supply and strictly rationed. The Club Roll of Honour was growing longer, with several well-known Club members losing their lives.

One bright spot in 1917 was the publication of the plans to make a modified version of the Itisa tent, first seen in 1916. The planned kit competition, for which it was designed, had been abandoned due to the war, but it was thought that the design would be of great interest to members. Another car-camping idea, this time with a tent attached to the boot, was published.

Stephen Hilhouse, on service in East Africa, wrote of his experiences in lion country, and told how "all the native boys were up the nearest tree in a jiffy" as soon as a lion was seen. At the end of the year the membership had dropped to 740.

There was a change of Editor in 1918 when Alex Papps took on the job which he had done very early on in the life of the magazine. The Supplies Department announced that it would have to suspend its hire services until after the war ended, and also that repairs using metal or leather were difficult to execute due to the shortage of raw materials. Special orders were also becoming increasingly difficult to fulfil.

In May the new Military Service Act required all men aged up to 50, and in some cases up to 56, to enlist for war work. Such was the price being paid by our young men. The Club was very hard hit by this new Act, with the Honorary Secretary being among those called up. Doubts were expressed as to the possibility of keeping the Club going, even on a small scale. A temporary Secretary was sought, but could not be found, so R.B. Searle continued to do this job, despite his war work. Special appointments to see

Pedestrian campers – Dutch style. Messrs Boers (left) and Van Dunne (right), members of the Nederlandse Toeristen Kampeer Club, carry their kit on back and front. **(Club Archive)**

him could be made for after 7.30pm on Mondays–Fridays only, such was his dedication to the Club.

The Supplies Department continued working on a very restricted base, and for the second year running it was not possible to organise the holiday camps – Walton Club Site was still barred to members.

Articles on making kit still appeared regularly in the magazine and even included instructions on making an oil vapour stove by J.H. Wood, the original designer of the Itisa tent.

In addition to all his duties, R.B. Searle found time to write about the possible future of the Club, in a series of articles in the magazine.

Throughout the war years many of the Club's veteran members submitted articles to the magazine, reminiscing on their experiences. Others submitted regular features about camps and tours, virtually all of them penned under a pseudonym. Many were written under the general title *The Lone Star* by Pajaro Raro. It later transpired that this was Topham Steele, of Lancs, Cheshire and North Wales D.A. All of these features told of specific areas of interest in places where he had camped and made interesting reading.

January 1919 saw the first post-war issue of *Camping*, although the Treaty of Versailles had not yet been signed. Membership had reached 755 at the end of 1918, and H.J. Lewis, Club Chairman, wrote: "Everything points to the necessity of building up a strong and efficient organisation, one which will enable us to secure the fullest possible measure of benefits from our pastime, an organisation which will be looked upon by all as *the* authority on camping and all matters connected with it."

At the Annual General Meeting in February, Lt.-General Sir Robert Baden-Powell was elected President, filling the gap left by the death of Capt. Scott in 1912. R.B. Searle resigned as Honorary Secretary, and applications were invited for the position of Secretary (paid) to the Club.

It was considered desirable to incorporate the Club and to change the name to one which would convey the idea of its far-reaching activities. An alternative to the word 'Amateur' was sought.

After much discussion, the Supplies Department was taken over by a Co-operative Society formed by R.B. Searle for the benefit of members, and a Peace Camp was held at Cudham in September.

Finally, on 1 November 1919, the Amateur Camping Club became

The Camping Club of Great Britain and Ireland and new rules were drawn up. Mr Maddock, the Club Chairman, wrote: "A brand new groundsheet was laid down on 1 November 1919, and we express the hope that over that groundplan a new super-structure shall arise, staunch, well-set and weatherly, capable of withstanding all the storms that blow, but flexible and adaptable to its surroundings, as all good tents should be, and above all expressing the life of joy in the open-air. And long may the pennon of the Camping Club float at its summit."

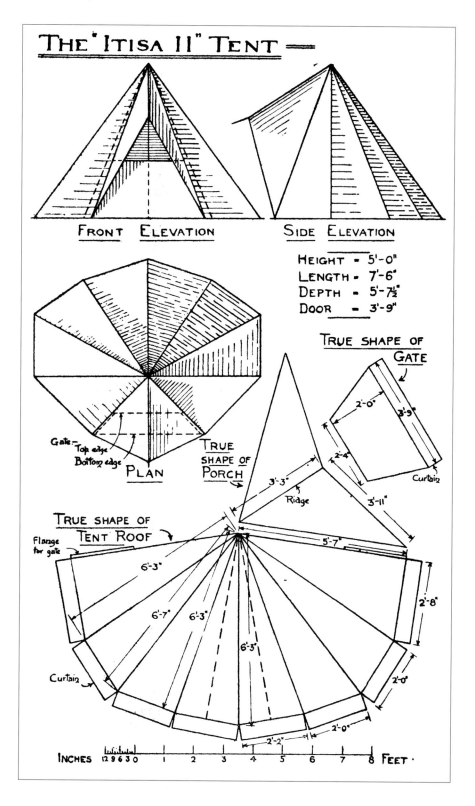

Motor caravans – the early pioneers by Chris Burlace

A 1905 Cadillac, with a body fitted years later by Bertram Hutchings.

The first really practical motor caravan in Britain was almost certainly that belonging to Mr J.B. Mallalieu. Built in 1906 by the Belsize Motor Co. on its new 40hp chassis, it provided a living room/bedroom, kitchen and washroom with W.C. The 21½-footer weighed 3¼ tons unladen and was equipped with an oil stove and 50-gallon water tank. It cost over £1,000 and could average 9mph.

Between 1906 and 1914, probably no more than about a dozen motor caravans were built. Featured at the 1909 Motor Show was a 40hp Austin built for a Mr Du Cros with dining/bedroom to seat six and sleep two, kitchen and dressing/toilet room. It cost £2,000, boasted electric lighting and provided two foldaway, canopied beds on the roof for the chauffeur and the chef. Another palatial outfit had seats on the roof, affording its passengers "fleeting glimpses of the scenery... as they whizzed by".

More modest motorhomes included Mrs Paton's 16/20hp Halley,

A 1913 Ford Model T with Baico chassis extension carries this body, probably made by Bertram Hutchings after World War One, and it's still ready for the road.

The Tortoise – with two compartments for the caravanners and the more usual cab quarters for her driver, and Mr Appleton's two-berth on a 35hp Bristol.

The *English Mechanic,* incidentally, finally came out with a report of a practical motor caravan in 1913. Based on a White steamer, a top speed of 25mph and an 18mph average was claimed for it.

Still rallying is this 1930 Eccles Chevrolet. At one time it had been converted to a fish and chip van.

The year 1913 also brought the promise of affordable motor caravans. W.A.J. Riley and his son, W.A., built a small body on a 1909 Talbot. World War One froze development but afterwards it was the Rileys who set up Eccles, the foremost caravan manufacturers in the 1920s and 1930s.

Several other post-war entrepreneurs, such as C. Fleming-Williams (Car Cruiser) and N. Wilkinson-Cox (Raven) quickly switched from motor

A 1929 Ford AA with a caravan body fitted in 1940. Still rallied, it tows a 1930s Eccles.

caravans to making almost exclusively trailer caravans. Bertram Hutchins (Winchester) built both but with the emphasis on trailers. His motor caravans appear to have been mainly one-offs and often on used chassis – after 1918 there were plenty of ex-military Ford Ts and Daimlers.

Already, in 1921, the Rileys were exhibiting at the Motor Show and looking to appoint agents. Quick to publicise their Eccles caravans the Rileys ensured news of their models reached *The Autocar* and *The Motor* magazines. Later their caravan adverts made front covers. The Rileys were pioneers in mechanisation and first with a purpose-built factory for caravan manufacture.

Bodies and layouts were developed to suit bases from a Ford TT or Morris up to a Leyland Lioness bus chassis. By the late 1920s there were well over a dozen variants at prices – excluding the chassis – from £175 to £600 plus options. Mod cons such as hot and cold running water, baths or showers and chemical toilets were available. Melville Hart, a naval architect, was in the caravan business from 1923 until 1934. He called his creations 'Flatavans' and specialised in luxury motorhomes for the super rich – some for Indian princes had a train of towed units for their retinues.

The 1930s saw the first motor caravan-only rallies. The first was at Minehead in 1932 and, of 91 units, less than half-a-dozen were motorised. At Cheltenham in 1933, only three of the 68 that attended were motorised. Motor caravans had for a decade been overtaken by their towed cousins. Interest in ordinary motor caravans plummeted in the 1930s, but some specials were still built.

Motor caravan on a 1936 Pontiac specially built for a disabled owner by Russells of Bexhill. Inside shows the passenger's wheelchair.

In 1933, by coincidence, two double-deckers were built: one in Scotland on a Bedford WLB and one by Thomas Harrington at Hove. Other reports record that in 1938 the wife of the Chairman of Peek Freen & Co. took delivery of a motorhome and planned to travel to India. Did actor/comedian Claude Damper get to enjoy his Bedford M-Type, with body by Carlight boasting a slide-out side extension, before war and petrol rationing wiped out private motoring?

1920–1929:
The Club at the crossways

The 1920s were remarkable years for the Club. The decade began with a fresh start. It had a new name, an improved larger magazine and a new badge that would remain unchanged for 60 years. The promise of a Co-operative Society, run in conjunction with the Club and primarily for the benefit of the members for the supply of camp kit, became an accomplished fact.

It was an era of new ideas, new contacts leading to an increased interest in foreign touring, and new District Associations (D.A.s) were established. The Club celebrated its coming of age. By the end of the decade membership would be more than quadrupled and the Club would have bought its first freehold site.

On the other hand, the Club had to fight yet more attempts to restrict camping by local authorities and co-operated with other organisations in order to do so. The country's economic problems also caused difficulties for the Club. There were some quite serious disagreements among members that had to be resolved.

Seven issues of *Camping* were produced in 1920 but by 1929 there was an issue each month. Members were asked to submit articles to improve the standard of *Camping*. Miss Wallace, well known in the early days for her lightweight kit, wrote from Rome: "For we distant members the magazine should be more than a list of happenings and accounts of meetings. It should be a live wire which holds us all together and makes our Club one great family of enthusiasts."

In the wider world

Petrol price rise sparks concern: A fourpence-halfpenny rise in pump prices led to fears of an end to the motoring boom. Petrol cost around two shillings a gallon and the A.A. said this would deter many from buying new well-priced small cars.

England win Test in Australia at last: England's cricketers ended a drought of nearly 13 years with victory in the fourth Test by an innings and 29 runs – a return to a quality of English cricket not seen since the Great War.

General strike: The first general strike in English history began on 4 May 1926, followed by a declaration of a state of emergency. Volunteers undertook to drive public transport and, lacking newspapers, the B.B.C.'s news broadcasts provided almost the only source of information.

Left: This photo by Mr A. Holt is entitled "The Happy Pair" – Mr and Mrs Callander, believed to be from Lancashire and Cheshire District Association, may have been recently married. (Club Archive)

It proved to be a useful vehicle for members to debate thorny problems, and many interesting travellers' tales were published. Technical articles, hints and tips, and notices of coming events were included. The Council was able to let members know of the risks to campers of proposed anti-camping legislation and inform them of what was being done to counter such proposals. In 1927 the magazine celebrated its coming of age. Alex Papps had been Editor for more than half its 21 years.

Camp and Sports Co-operators became established in February 1920, and some Club members were not happy to see the Supplies Department disappear from the Club's control. The Committee of the Society was made up of well-known Club members, and they hoped that other members would support the new venture as it would help retain control by the Club.

ROBERT BRUCE SEARLE *was a keen boat-camper who joined the National Cycle-Camping Club in 1907. He was its Chairman when it merged with with the Amateur Camping Club. He soon became Club Chairman, and was responsible for the separation of the Supplies Department from the sporting side of the Club.*

During World War One he acted both as Club Honorary Secretary and Supplies Manager and without his untiring efforts the Club would have ceased to exist.

He suggested the formation of a co-operative society to manufacture and supply camping equipment (Camp and Sports Co-operators, later known as Camtors) in 1919 and was very disappointed at the lack of Club members' support for the Society.

At the same time as being the paid manager of the Society he was also Honorary Secretary of the Club and Joint Editor of the magazine. This was the cause of much conflict because at the time Camp and Sports Co-operators was also being paid to do the Club's clerical work.

He spared neither cash nor labour in his efforts to help the Society, always insisting on top quality materials and workmanship, the Camtors trade-mark representing the Rolls-Royce of camping equipment.

He remained General Manager of Camtors until 1946, when Thomas Black and Sons acquired a controlling interest in the company. He died in 1955 aged 84.

R.B. Searle, who was very much involved with the setting up of Camp and Sports Co-operators, agreed to become Honorary Secretary to the Club again, owing to the resignation of C.K. Cullen for health reasons.

Reciprocal working arrangements between the Club and the Society were made as both shared the same premises in New Union Street. This meant that the affairs of the Club and the Society were inextricably linked.

At a stormy Club Annual General Meeting (A.G.M.) in 1922 members discussed the relationship of the Club with Camp and Sports Co-operators. It was suggested that the Club should not share the same premises and that the Club "should be officered by persons who are uncommitted to trade interests in connection with the sport". Despite the fact that the Club had played a very large part in the development of camping kit, many considered there should be no connection between the Club and "the trade". The high cost of postage, office accommodation, etc, made it essential that the Club should share work with Camp and Sports Co-operators, and even making savings in this way they still had to raise the subscriptions substantially over two years.

A reform group was started by dissidents, including two members of

The favourite lightweight tent of many
Club members because it was so simple
to erect and only required one guyline.
It weighed only 1lb 13oz (but pole, pegs,
groundsheet, etc were extra) and was
ideal for solo campers, but two could
sleep in it at a pinch.

(2.) Closed   (3.) With fly-sheet.

the Council who, naturally, had to resign. Because
of the concerns expressed, a sub-committee was
established to consider Club Policy and Housing. Many
letters were received supporting R.B. Searle and his
work for the Club and Camp and Sports Co-operators.
As Secretary he often visited D.A.s and a Manchester
member wrote: "I have never heard a single complaint
of 'shop' after any one of his visits."

A disastrous fire at 4 New Union Street in June
1922 destroyed most of Camp and Sports Co-operators' stock, and the Club
records, housed in the same building, were badly damaged by water. Some
records, unfortunately, were damaged beyond repair. It was possible for Club
work to continue on the premises, and Camp and Sports Co-operators was
also soon able to start work again, although some delays were inevitable.

The year 1922 ended with the Club's Coming of Age Supper attended
by more than 200, including the President and Lady Baden-Powell, and
Vice-Presidents T.H. Holding and Sir Martin Conway, as well as guests from
overseas clubs and organisations and the Cyclists' Touring Club (C.T.C.).
In his speech, Lord Baden-Powell pleaded for unity within the Club
expressing hope that it would not become divided over the question of

Camp furniture

Used for fixed camping on Club sites but was listed in the Camp and Sports Co-operators' first
catalogue. Folding camp beds, wash-stands and chairs became available, many of the designs
originating from officers' furniture used during World War One.

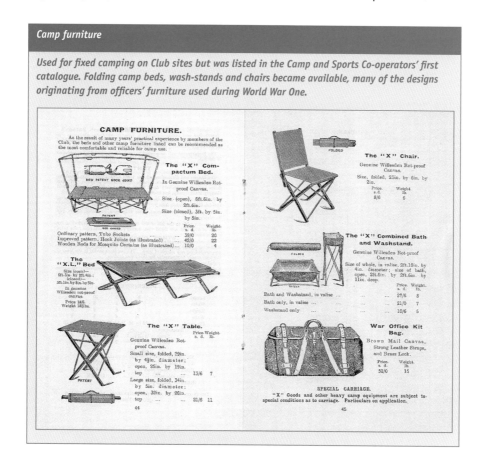

arrangements between itself and its shop.

By the end of the year, the Club had appointed a paid Assistant Secretary and a shorthand-typist to work exclusively for the Club. The office remained at New Union Street but the Club would not commit itself to a tenancy of more than twelve months as it was actively looking for new premises.

R.B. Searle was due to retire as Honorary Secretary to the Club at the end of 1923. The Council had to reconsider the organisation of secretarial work. A full-time Secretary was appointed but R.B. Searle was asked by the Council to accept the new post of Honorary Organising Secretary as his experience was too valuable to lose. The Club at last found suitable premises for offices, away from Camp and Sports Co-operators, in Princeton Street, not far from Holborn.

The clerical work previously done by the various Honorary Secretaries – tours, sites, etc – was taken over by Headquarters staff, thus taking some of the burden from those busy volunteers.

The Council tried to persuade Camp and Sports Co-operators to allow members to purchase equipment on an instalment plan but the Society refused to consider the proposition so it was not pursued.

The Society felt that members were already getting a good deal by receiving a discount – which would be greatly increased if a member bought shares in the Society – and that the equipment was the very best on offer, therefore members would buy it. Unfortunately, other companies – some of whom were also making good quality equipment – were offering easy terms to their customers, and the Society must have lost trade and some goodwill by its refusal.

Another move, this time to Greville Street, Hatton Garden, took place early in 1928, when once again the Club shared a building with Camp and Sports

From the Club magazine

June 1923 *Description of the new zip fastener: "It is a most ingenious device, but is a little difficult to describe. Imagine a row of metal paper fasteners on either edge of the tent door with a cord running through them and a clip which, when pulled downwards, rapidly and smoothly closes the opening and vice-versa, and you have it. A fascinating and novel invention which completely took us by surprise."*

July 1928 *Club Library: "Will the member who may have borrowed the bound volume of* Camping *for 1925 kindly return same as soon as possible?"*

Co-operators. As well as office space there was a club room for meetings, but the management and staffing of both organisations was kept entirely separate. The A.G.M. was informed that larger premises were necessary because of the huge increase in the membership, but that the Greville Street offices should serve the Club for some considerable time.

At about the same time, the Council was reorganised, scaling down the number of meetings and passing the bulk of the essential work of the Club to various committees. A Finance and General Purposes Committee and seven other committees were established. These committees and Club officers would produce monthly reports for the Council. The Council would in future be elected by means of a postal ballot and proxy voting would be retained for voting on motions before all general meetings.

While the Club was sorting out its problems of accommodation, etc, all other work had to continue. It was essential to have good publicity, and the Camp Fire, which used to be an annual fixture during the Winter, was revived.

Membership increased to 1,500 by the end of 1920 but apart from a drop in 1923 – almost certainly due to the depression and the sharp rise in Club subscriptions – the membership continued to rise in leaps and bounds so that, by the end of 1929, the membership of the Club was over 4,500.

These increases were largely as a result of the success of the new Camp Fires, which were mostly held in prestige premises and attracted large

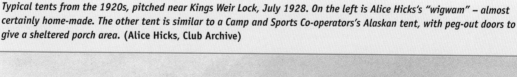

Typical tents from the 1920s, pitched near Kings Weir Lock, July 1928. On the left is Alice Hicks's "wigwam" – almost certainly home-made. The other tent is similar to a Camp and Sports Co-operators's Alaskan tent, with peg-out doors to give a sheltered porch area. (Alice Hicks, Club Archive)

crowds. Some were organised by the D.A.s, but the most successful was organised by the Club in 1927 when over 2,500 people visited the event with the resulting applications for membership far exceeding expectations. Every D.A. and permanent site had a stand, and there were displays of kit, talks, lantern lectures and entertainment by Club members.

In addition to Camp Fires, a Holidays, Sports and Pastimes exhibition took place at the Royal Agricultural Hall in 1925, which lasted three weeks. Many were attracted to the Club stand by the backcloth of an enlarged magazine cover, complete with two stuffed rabbits! This backcloth, and that of the adjoining Camp and Sports Co-operators stand, was designed and painted by M.P. 'Percy' Lindsey. Yet again, many new members were recruited.

M.P. 'Percy' LINDSEY. Prior to joining the Club in 1920, he had already made his own tent in which he and a friend went camping. Their poles were unfinished, so they used camera tripods, which were badly damaged in an overnight storm. This never deterred him from designing and making more tents, the plans of which were published in Camping *for others to use. His Little Gem tent was particularly popular.*

Elected a National Councillor in 1921, he immediately took on the job of Honorary Art Editor, Social Secretary in 1923 and Tours Secretary in 1926. He kept these positions until his sudden death in 1956. He was the Club's delegate to the Saxenheim Rally, Holland, in 1932, when the International Federation of Camping and Caravanning (F.I.C.C.) was formed. He held the post of Chairman of the Club, from 1941–1948, and steered the Club through the war years.

He never owned any motorised transport and travelled on foot, cycle or public transport, carrying much of his kit in his roomy jacket pockets. He camped in most European countries, Africa and North America, and even pitched his tent on the deck of the Queen Mary *when travelling home from the United States of America.*

His efforts led to the increasing popularity of Club tours where he often went on reconnaissance visits at his own expense. He was also Master of Ceremonies at many Club dinners and led the singing at Feasts of Lanterns. It was also due to his efforts that the Youth section of the Club was started, and the Association of Cycle Campers became a Section in its own right.

He was a talented artist who prepared the backcloth for the Club's stand at many camping exhibitions and drew the maps for foreign tours, N.F.O.L.s and Club sites. He was also a brilliant cartoonist and keen photographer, and was Chairman of both the Artists' Group and Photo Group of the Club.

There was great excitement in 1925 when H.J. Lewis, a former Tours Secretary and member of the Council, gave two broadcast talks about camping from *2LO*, the B.B.C.'s first radio station in London. Alex Papps described how he listened to the broadcast with his mother, who had been born during the reign of William IV – it was a novelty for many younger people in 1925, but one wonders what she must have thought about it.

Following complaints in

H.J. LEWIS was Chairman of the Council from 1917–1919, and became Tours Secretary in 1920. He organised the first post-war tour of Holland in 1921. Always a lightweight camper, he was the first to broadcast on the subject in 1925, resulting in many enquiries about Club membership.

the magazine that the Club was not promoting lightweight camping – the purpose for which it had been founded – it was pointed out that times had changed since 1901 and, according to the new rules passed when the Club was re-named, it had to cater for all classes of campers.

One of the first of the new ideas for Club activities was broached by D.B.L. Hopkins in the January 1920 issue of *Camping*, when he suggested that an Annual Supper in a hotel was inappropriate for campers.

"Does it not strike anyone that, for a body calling itself a camping

Single-pole tents, mostly Itisas, in use in the late 1920s.

club to sit solemnly in a London hotel dining-room, everyone on their best behaviour, for a solid three hours and a half – even though the speeches and the accompanying entertainment be of the highest quality – is nothing but a negation of all those principles that members are morally pledged to support and promote?

"I propose to bring forward a motion for consideration at the Annual General Meeting to the effect that the time has come for the Club to consider whether it would not be better, next year and in future years, for us to have our annual feast in camp – in the open air.

"An *al fresco* stage might be managed, for a camp concert, and we could have a real camp fire in the evening. Other attractions would suggest themselves to the imaginative – and imagination is just what is wanted.

"Which will you have, my fellow campers; a formal stuffy town banquet, or an open-air reunion, full of fun and good fellowship?"

The first of these open-air suppers was held at Betchworth,

The first-ever special event pennon, designed and made by the Walton Site Committee for the 21st Birthday Camp in 1922.

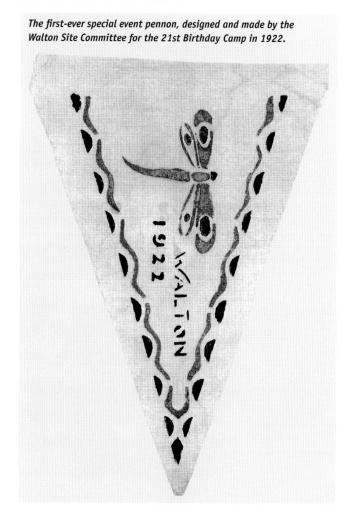

Aerial photo of Walton Club Site, 1934. **(Club Archive)**

near Dorking, at the end of June 1921. Despite poor weather, more than 100 members attended.

Later that year, musical members were asked to bring their voices and instruments, and all were asked to bring lanterns to the "Camp Fire and Feast of Lanterns", to be held at Deepdene, near Dorking. It was a great success, made more so by the glorious weather.

"When the light failed here, there, and everywhere the coloured lanterns peeped out in front of the tents. The great camp fire was lit, the Master of the Revels took the chair (on a fallen log) and song and story and chorus followed one another."

In 1922, the Feast of Lanterns (F.O.L.) – later to become the National Feast of Lanterns (N.F.O.L.) – was combined with the Club's Coming of Age camp and was held at Walton Club Site, as Deepdene had been sold for housing development. Over 200 members, including the Club President, the Club Chairman and his wife and D.B.L. Hopkins were in camp.

Among several early members of the Association of Amateur Campers (A.C.C.) attending was T.W. Lowther, one of the original six who camped at Wantage in 1901. As dusk fell "lamps were lit outside the tents, and up the river came a fleet of boats and punts, decorated with wreaths and fairy lamps, the crews singing old songs to the rhythm of the paddles". Despite extra ground being made available the event was somewhat crowded but it was, nevertheless, a memorable occasion. Plans for the following year, again at Walton, included a band, dancing, an illuminated river craft parade, sports, stunts, a grand camp fire and sing-song. Every tent was expected to be decorated or illuminated and, for the first time, traders would be on site to take orders for bread, milk and groceries.

After two more years at Club sites, special sites were found so that members from further afield would find it easier to attend. The founder of the F.O.L.s, D.B.L. Hopkins died in April 1925 and he was much missed. The F.O.L.s continued to grow in popularity and, by 1929, the numbers camping for the weekend at Knole Park had risen to more than 500 – the Feast was here to stay.

In addition to the F.O.L. it became the custom to hold Summer reunion camps, often during the Whitsun holidays, so that members from further afield could get together. One of the most successful was in 1923, when more than 100 members camped at Huntsmoor Park Club Site.

Some cycled from Derbyshire and Nottinghamshire while others came by car and motor-cycle from Manchester. The northern contingent stayed a week, visiting London, Windsor and other interesting places under the leadership of Percy Lindsey. For many it was their first visit to the capital and it was a huge success.

Another departure was the re-introduction of the foreign tour. Following the successful Dutch tour before World War One it was again to Holland that the first post-war

The Camping Club of G. B. & I.
4, NEW UNION STREET, LONDON, E.C.2.

TOUR IN HOLLAND, 1921.
APPLICATION FORM.

To the Tours Secretary,
    I wish to join the Club Tour in Holland during July and, in accordance with the particulars published with the May issue of "CAMPING," enclose fees amounting to £ _____ made up as follow :—
(please strike out items which do not apply.)

		£	s.	d.
* 2nd class fares London to Rotterdam and return to Tilbury		3	10	0
* 2nd class fares London to Rotterdam and return to London		3	12	6
Pedestrian itinerary		0	0	6
Registration fee (if not already paid) ...		0	2	6
	£			

Please send me an application form for Dutch visa to my British passport.

Signature _____

Address _____

Date _____

* See published particulars re carriage of cycles.

A rare photograph of Baden-Powell, for once not wearing Scout uniform, taken at Walton Club Site at the Club's 21st Birthday Camp and Feast of Lanterns, 1922. (Club Archive)

continued on page 95

First in the field A Century of The Camping and Caravanning Club

Lord Baden-Powell of Gilwell, the most famous camper of all

Born on 22 February 1857, Robert Stephenson Smyth Baden-Powell was the sixth son of the Rev. Baden-Powell of Oxford and Langton Manor, Kent. While a pupil at Charterhouse School he would often go out in the surrounding countryside and make a camp for himself but always managed never to be found out. Everything was cleared away so meticulously, including any fire he built, that no one could tell where he had been. These skills were later to stand him in good stead when writing Aids to Scouting (for army scouts) in 1899.

He served in Afghanistan, India and South Africa where he was assistant military attaché and was in command of native levies with the Special Services in Ashanti. He was most famous for the Defence of Mafeking and was several times mentioned in despatches.

One of his cunning disguises was to appear as an eccentric naturalist sketching the countryside. His drawings cleverly concealed plans of local fortifications and enemy lines. He was a very good artist and exhibited a sculpture at the Royal Academy in 1907.

After the Boer War he organised the South African Constabulary and then returned to England in 1903 as Inspector General of Cavalry.

An early postcard of Lord Baden-Powell and his wife, Olave. (Club Archive)

In 1907 he arranged an experimental camp for 20 boys from all backgrounds on Brownsea Island in Poole Harbour, teaching them to be self-sufficient using outdoor skills such as woodcraft, fire-making and tracking. He believed these skills would encourage a sense of discipline, duty, unselfishness and good citizenship in British boys. His ideas were circularised to a number of prominent people and the camp was such a success that the Scouting Movement rapidly became established. Three years later it was followed by the creation of the Guide movement, when he realised that the girls were not prepared to be left out of things!

In 1912 he married Olave St Clair Soames, who shared the same birthday but was 32 years his junior. She became the first, and only, World Chief Guide.

He was very proud of Scouting and Guiding and lived to see them grow into world-wide organisations. But he was also proud to be the President of The Camping Club, supporting its functions whenever he could. He believed that Scouts and Guides could learn much from members of the Camping Club, and he was always happy to welcome members at his home in Hampshire. He finally retired to his beloved Africa in 1938 and died in Kenya in January 1941.

"My wigwam tent by the lakeside near Encamp, 6,000ft up in the Pyrenees", by Alice Hicks, on the Spanish/Andorran tour, 1928. (Alice Hicks, Club Archive)

continued from page 91

tourists were to travel by invitation of the Nederlandse Toeristen Kampeer Club (N.T.K.C.). This tour was a huge success, with more than 20 members travelling to Holland in July 1921.

Fifty members of the N.T.K.C. – including its Tour Secretary, Mr Schoorl, who was also a Club member – returned to England with them for a tour of the south of England. The contacts made with the Dutch club led to many tours being made by it in England, and later contacts with the Touring Club de France, Camping Club de Catalunya and the Touring Club de Belgique made many other tours possible. The Club also had overseas members living in Alsace, France and Switzerland, who offered help in organising tours to these places.

In 1922 a group of 36 members toured the Pyrenees joined by members of the Touring Club de France. A detailed report was later published in *Camping* with a double-page spread of photographs and a page of brilliant cartoons by Percy Lindsey.

In the years that followed, Easter tours to Paris were arranged, and a holiday camp was held annually in Brittany. A tour to Norway with N.T.K.C. members took place plus tours to the Dolomites and the French Alps.

Left: The Camping Club Tour of the Pyrenees, 1922. (Club Archive)

Members who had been overseas individually were asked to send

The camp in the Restonica Valley, Corsica, 1927. This was the first Club tour to Corsica and, despite the long journey involved, was highly successful with 93 members taking part, of whom 29 were ladies. The tour was repeated the following Easter. (Club Archive)

Percy Lindsey (left, wearing beret), led many overseas tours for the Club and is seen here with other Club members in Andorra, 1928. (Alice Hicks, Club Archive)

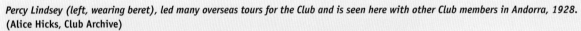

particulars to the Club to help them in planning future tours. No tours took place in 1925 but a base camp was arranged for three weeks at Chamonix, as well as the popular Brittany holiday site.

Percy Lindsey, already the Club's Art Advisor, became Tours Secretary in 1926. He was well qualified for the post having been on every Club foreign tour since 1921 and on many home tours.

His enthusiasm revived interest, and that year 78 Club members took part in two tours to the Vosges mountains and Alsace, twelve of them travelling independently. A tour to Corsica followed in 1927 to be repeated at Easter in 1928, when 30 members took part. Fifty-two members, half of whom were ladies, went on the Spanish/Andorran tour in May 1928.

On another successful tour to Spain in 1929, this time taking in the island of Majorca, Club members were joined by members of the Dutch and Danish clubs. J.A.C. Champion, the tour leader, remarked that it was truly an international camp. In the same year some 20 members went on a pioneering tour of Yugoslavia, and there were also tours to Paris, the Black Forest and – a new departure – a charabanc tour to Brittany.

Home tour itineraries were published in *Camping*, so that members could choose their own time to go. Very few organised home tours were arranged, an exception being the Scottish motoring tour in 1928 in which some 150 members took part.

Despite the huge success of the F.O.L.s, the Annual Supper was still held in a London hotel each year offering good speakers, entertainment and a bag of samples for every guest – a tradition since 1911.

At one of these events, the speaker was Lawrence Chubb. He was Secretary of the Commons and Footpaths Preservation Society and he stressed the need for co-operation between all outdoor clubs interested in the preservation of beauty spots: "It is only by such mutual co-operation that the heaths and moors and delightful resting places for the camper and

'Jay-Bee', a keen Club member and cycle camper from Lancashire, outside his tent at Copster Green after winning the Todmorden Cycling Club Memorial Cup 25-mile cycle race in 1925. (A.M. Payne, Club Archive)

rambler may be preserved from the inroads of the speculative builder."
He also suggested that, as a camping club, it should become the actual
owners of its camping sites. It is from this early incident that the Club
has maintained links with the various societies that preserve access
to the countryside.

When the Club was able to reduce subscriptions, partly due to a
large increase in membership – and, therefore, in income – a member
suggested that instead of a refund to members the balance should be
allocated to a fund for the purchase of sites, as suggested by Lawrence
Chubb at the Annual Supper. The Council, however, felt that the balance
should be returned to the members.

Much of the entertainment at
these events was provided by Club
members but in 1925 the final
items, and some of the best, were
provided by comediennes Elsie and
Doris Waters. Their turn was
"immensely liked". We have not
been able to establish whether or
not they were Club members but
this must have been one of their
earliest public performances. They

Cottage tents were very popular in the 1920s, especially for
car-campers.

appeared again at the Annual Supper the following year – many older Club
members today may still remember 'Gert and Daisy'. The Annual Supper
eventually became an Annual Dinner and Dance and continued to attract
large numbers of members.

The 1920s saw mixed fortunes for the District Associations. A small
number of them had been established before World War One but by the
beginning of the decade several were struggling and others had
disappeared. The most lively was Lancs, Cheshire and North Wales D.A.,
which had established active sections (Liverpool, Manchester and
Queensferry) for local districts within its overall area. In some areas
representatives were appointed to try and keep interested members
together and, where possible, to arrange an occasional weekend camp.

A big increase in Club subscription rates over two consecutive years
caused some country members to feel they were getting a raw deal, as most

*Left: Chertsey
Club Site stands
on the banks of
the River Thames
and was first used
in 1926. Once
part of the
grounds of a
large house, it
became the base
of the Canoe
Section after its
formation in
1933. It was
particularly
useful as it had a
small creek which
could be used for
bathing and by
canoes. In 1970
it was landscaped
and redeveloped
as the Club's
prestige site
near London.
(Club Archive)*

activities were still near London and the big cities. After a letter – from Topham-Steele (also known as Pajaro-Raro) of Lancs, Cheshire and North Wales D.A. pointing out that it was up to the members themselves to establish a D.A. in their own area – new D.A.s started to appear. Liverpool became a D.A. in its own right, to be followed by Kent D.A., Hants, Dorset and Wilts D.A. and Surrey D.A.

London D.A. (covering the London area postal districts) was revived, and would in future be responsible for camps in the area, except those at Walton Club Site. Bucks, Herts and Middlesex D.A. and Essex D.A. followed, but Kent D.A. soon disappeared.

Easter 1923 saw the first camp of the newly-approved Derbyshire D.A. at Hopping Farm, Youlgreave – a site which eventually became the Bakewell Club Site. Derbyshire D.A. was eventually absorbed into Leicester and Nottingham D.A.

Lancs, Cheshire and North Wales D.A. started to produce its own newsletter, called *Campers Pie*, the first of many D.A. newsletters. Others which were to follow before the decade was out include *The Essex Camper*, *The Camper's Companion* (from Surrey), *The London D.A.*

Nesting saucepans

Although campers often took pans from home, most preferred nesting pans as they took up less room, and some caravanners also liked them because they were easy to store. Originally available in six sizes, with fry-pan lids, two more sizes were later added to the range and separate flat lids became available.

Newsletter and the *Bucks Bulletin*.

A fixture list, published separately in 1925, makes it clear that some D.A.s were in abeyance, as only seven were listed. Glasgow and West of Scotland D.A. helped to arrange a tour for N.T.K.C. members, and both it and Northumberland and Durham D.A. arranged Summer holiday camps.

Notts D.A. had the unpleasant experience of stones and bricks being hurled at its tents during the night at a weekend camp. Apparently, neighbouring farmers bore a grudge against the site owner and attacked the campers, damaging their equipment. Fortunately no one was injured but one family of newcomers was, not unnaturally, put off camping.

The Club organised annual conferences of Council members and Representatives from D.A.s to consider matters of mutual interest. One of these matters was the question of the London and Home Counties D.A.s.

East Londoners were having problems getting to the London D.A. meets and some of them wanted their home area to become officially

Stephen Hilhouse (standing) and Alex Papps, both joined the Association of Cycle Campers in 1902 and became life-long friends and often camped together. Here they are seen at Mouldsworth, Cheshire, in 1928.
(Stephen Hilhouse's personal album, courtesy Miss S. Hilhouse)

part of Essex D.A. In those days, when not all areas were covered by a D.A., it was not possible to opt in to another D.A. and transport into Essex proper was much easier than transport to other parts of London. London D.A., however, objected and a referendum of members concerned was organised but this did not solve the problem. Further discussions were held between the Council and the Club members involved, and there was much correspondence in *Camping*. The dispute was finally resolved when the D.A.s were reorganised in 1929.

The D.A.s gradually began to organise their own special events. Surrey D.A. organised camps for Henley Regatta and the Aldershot Tattoo, and a cycle-campers' camp was held in Cheshire. The latter was much praised, as so many members were now using cars to get to camp. Lancs, Cheshire and North Wales D.A. also arranged its own tour to Chamonix, as well as a most successful two-day camp fire and exhibition in Manchester. By the end of the decade there were twelve D.A.s, a number of which had been revived.

Specialist Sections did not exist in these early days but in 1921 the Council was approached by a number of caravanners, asking for a special section to promote this branch of the sport of camping.

The subject of caravanning had been virtually ignored in the 1920 *Handbook* and caravanners felt left out. By March an official Caravan Group

A new, larger, magazine appeared in 1920. These three were cover competition winners.

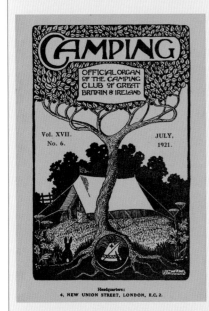

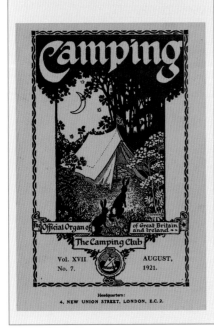

had been established, with F. Howard Mercer as Honorary Secretary but he was unable to continue and his successor also had to resign.

Despite several well-written articles on caravanning published in *Camping*, the Group failed so eventually the Council had to ask for the return of all the papers and records relating to the Group. Club sites, however, continued to thrive. Walton Club Site, which had been extremely profitable the previous year, was rented for six months in 1921.

The season ticket price was increased to £1 but despite this the site was very well used. Extra ground was rented for 1922 but even so there was a tendency to overcrowding. A site was found at Huntsmoor Park, near Iver, but this was available only on a short lease, which the Club was not able to renew.

A site at Savoy Farm, Denham, was found to replace Huntsmoor in 1924 and a reunion was held there later in the year. More than 50 campers from different parts of the country attended despite the bad weather. Owing to unforeseen circumstances the site became unavailable in September at very short notice. The Club was lucky to find an almost immediate replacement at Bury Farm, Rickmansworth. Bathing was available in the lake and the site proved to be popular. The Council was urged to try and buy a site near London to prevent any more unfortunate occurrences such as the loss of the Denham site earlier in the year.

The question of sites was thoroughly aired at the A.G.M. in January 1926 with suggestions that town clerks and railway companies might assist the Club in finding sites. It was stated that the town clerks and the railway companies had "an erroneous idea of camp sites, and that the sites already in the railway lists were not altogether suitable for Club members".

The Club acquired a new permanent riverside site

Fun and games at Walton Club Site, 1927, with Club Chairman R.T. Phillips "at the crease".

at Chertsey shortly after the A.G.M. in 1926. It was not then available for caravans and musical instruments were not allowed. However, folk dancing became a very popular activity at Chertsey almost immediately after the site was opened, and a gramophone had to be used for this.

The Club purchased the site in 1927 and the question of other sites around London was raised. "The cordon of houses penetrates further into the heart of the country, and the inevitable result will be that land will be scarce and, more important, costly." Members were now assured of the uninterrupted enjoyment of the Chertsey Club Site and the Council hoped to purchase other London sites for the future.

The Council was also concerned to find more suitable sites for motorists. A large number of motor-campers had now joined the Club, and some were disappointed to be turned away from sites they had chosen from the *Sites List* because access was unsuitable. This was a regrettable state of affairs that could only be partially remedied by other members finding suitable sites and letting the Club have details of them.

Restrictions had been imposed on the use of the Rickmansworth site by the ground landlords. It was clear that the site would no longer be available for Club camping. A new site in the area had been considered but negotiations fell through so the Site Committee set about to find another site in north London suitable for permanent site campers.

The situation was very difficult because both Walton and Chertsey were over-subscribed and had waiting lists for permanent pitches. Other members who wished to stay more than a few days on these sites had to notify the Chief Camp Steward by writing in advance.

The Club's international links were flourishing. A Council representative attended the tenth birthday celebrations of the N.T.K.C.

Camping Club of Great Britain and Ireland.

"Tudor House," 1, Princeton Street, Bedford Row, W.C.1.

A LECTURE, DEMONSTRATION OF LIGHTWEIGHT CAMPING AND "CAMP FIRE"

WILL BE HELD AT

The Royal Agricultural Hall, (Bertram's Rooms, Barford Street entrance), Liverpool Road, Islington, N.1.

ON

SATURDAY, MAY 1st,

1926. 3.—10.30 p.m.

The Programme will include a KIT DISPLAY, and DEMONSTRATIONS, SHORT TALKS ON CAMPING SUBJECTS, LANTERN LECTURE and MUSICAL ITEMS :: :: Teas and Refreshments will be on Sale ::

ADMISSION - - SIXPENCE,

Travel by Underground to "The Angel," Islington. Tram Services 5, 9, 13, 35, 37, 39, 51, 75, 79, 81. Bus Services 4a, 19, 30a, 38e, 43a, 73a, 138a, 173a, 174

Printed at THE GROVE PRESS, 28 South Grove, Rye Lane, Peckham, S.E.15

in Holland in 1922 and received a copy of its first *Handbook*. The Touring Club de France had helped in many ways, inviting Club members to some of its camps and helping with the arrangements for the tour to the Pyrenees; and the Camping Club of Catalunya, established on similar lines to the Club, reported a successful first season.

In 1928, the Touring Club de Belgique announced Rallye-Campeurs 1928 to be held over the Whitsun weekend. A Congress of Campers would also take place and campers from other countries were invited to take part. This was the first ever International Rally, as far as we are aware.

Throughout the decade the Club forged contacts with other organisations, both for mutual assistance with shared concerns such as countryside protection and for protection against anti-camping legislation.

At a Leisure of the People conference held in London early in 1920, the Club, as the premier organisation, was invited to take up the matter of National Camping Grounds. It convened a conference to discuss the matter, and suggestions were made as to where suitable sites could be obtained.

Even in 1920 it was "unfortunate that bands of gipsies had not favourably affected the attitude of the authorities towards campers in general". Conference delegates suggested the establishment of a federation of camping bodies, (Scouts, Guides, Boys Brigade, etc, and the Camping Club) thus making their own sites available to each other.

It was also suggested that the Club's own rules for the conduct of official camps should be modified to suit all organisations. The Club asked the National Trust to set aside land for camping on its properties but the Trust thought the idea undesirable and declined an invitation to attend the conference. At the conference, the Club was asked to help provide suitable leaders for Scouts and Guides, since "many Scoutmasters knew little about camping".

A Council for the Preservation of Rural Scenery was proposed in 1926 and the Club wished it every success. Within a few months it became established as the C.P.R.E. (Council for the Preservation of Rural England) and the Club became officially affiliated to the organisation.

The Moveable Dwellings Bill once more came before Parliament and the Council set up a Parliamentary Sub-Committee to watch for prejudicial anti-camping legislation, especially in connection with Bills promoted by local authorities. The Sub-Committee issued a strong warning to members not to risk polluting drinking water supplies and to behave responsibly. Other campers – non-members – were causing problems and the Club had to be able to state categorically that members would not cause nuisance, otherwise its camping rights would be gone for good.

Sports were a popular activity on the Club's permanent sites.

It was thought that a new Law of Property Act, passed in 1925, could also affect camping and an explanation as to its effects was published in the Club magazine. It made the question of camping on common land even more complicated.

In theory camping on common land was not allowed. This decision, though, had never been officially documented and so, in practice, it had been tolerated in some areas. With the new laws, only if a common in a rural district had been dedicated by application of the owner was it written down that camping was forbidden. Unfortunately, there was no way of telling which commons had been so dedicated, so the camper was none the wiser. The Club tried to establish whether or not a list of dedicated commons would be published. In the meantime members were asked not to camp or light fires on any common land.

Camping was becoming increasingly popular, in part due to adverse publicity that was being given to the Moveable Dwellings Bill in the national press. An appeal was made for members to help recruit new members to the Club. The greater the Club membership, the greater the chance the Club had of successfully opposing the Bill, which had appeared once again.

At the time, there were large numbers of caravan towns and colonies, which were causing problems. The Members of Parliament (M.P.s) introducing the Bill seemed to be completely unaware of the existence of pleasure campers, such as Club members, so almost every clause in the Bill threatened the whole sport of camping with complete extinction.

It was a very serious matter because local authorities would be given arbitrary powers to close camp sites on the flimsiest excuse. Allowances were made for travelling showmen but not for pleasure campers, who would be at the mercy of the Rural District Councils. No one would be allowed to camp without permission of the local councils and there was no provision for right of appeal. Furthermore, unless any land for camping was licensed by the local authority, owners allowing camping on their land would be guilty of an offence. This would have the effect of removing every private site in the country.

Clearly the Club had to act and act quickly. Members were asked to write to their M.P.s, asking them to support a motion for the rejection of the Bill by Lt. Cmdr. Kenworthy, M.P., who was acting in the interests of the Club. As a result of members' actions, the promoters withdrew the Bill.

How things have changed. The four-page leaflet above detailed the Club's foreign tours for 1923. It featured pedestrian tours in Norway and a holiday camp in Brittany in August. Today, the equivalent Carefree brochure runs to 128 pages and features holidays all over the world.

Both the London and provincial press strongly supported the Club's point of view and this must have helped the Club's cause. A very close watch would now be kept for any similar Bills, and every step would be taken to oppose the passage through Parliament of any measures likely to affect the rights of campers.

As a result of the Club's efforts, the Central Committee for Camping Legislation was established in June 1928, consisting of representatives from the Club, Scouts, Guides, and the Order of Woodcraft Chivalry, plus the Club's Parliamentary Agent, Hugh Shayler. It became obvious that to combat legislation effectively it would be better if all interested bodies were represented on one committee.

C. Dexter-Watts – known to all as Seedy – Chairman of the Club's Sub-Committee on Legislation, had done an enormous amount of work fighting the various Bills, but had to relinquish his position as Chairman for private reasons. The new Committee was chaired by D. Francis Morgan of the Boy Scouts Association. The Club's representative was J.A.C. Champion and the Honorary Secretary was L.M. Wulcko, also a member of the Club's Council.

C. DEXTER-WATTS (centre), was one of the members of Bucks, Herts and Middlesex District Association who founded the Rickmansworth site for the Club. Their representative on the National Council, he was also Honorary Press Secretary for the Club and organised the meeting of open-air bodies that formed the Central Committee for Camping Legislation.

The year 1929 started with eleven Private Bills before Parliament containing clauses affecting the interests of campers, proving the need for The Central Committee on Camping Legislation.

Regulations for camping in the New Forest were published by The Central Committee for Camping Legislation. It also submitted a Memorandum for the information of the National Parks Committee relative to the rights and privileges of campers in the event of the introduction of National Parks, as seemed likely.

Cloth cap camping – this is George Milne from Liverpool. (Club Archive)

The Club had survived internal disagreements and the threats of anti-camping legislation, and had greatly increased its membership over ten years. New ideas for Club activities had been extremely successful and once more the future began to look brighter.

There's nothing new by Hazel Constance

Tents based on a single hoop or a combination of hoops, forming a dome, are not new. Looking into some historical documents we find that a hoop tent existed even before the Club was formed.

Designed by Mr F.H. Gotsche of San Francisco towards the end of the 19th century, his V.X.L. tent was used for trading and hunting trips to Arctic regions and the tropics. To combat extremes of temperature he pitched two tents one over the other, thus providing the necessary insulation. Thomas Hiram Holding copied the idea and developed his Brigand, or Mushroom, tent.

Dome tents, re-introduced in the 1980s, are still popular in 2001.

Likewise the Beehive home-made dome tent, used by the Skinner brothers in 1903 and described as their favourite tent, measured 9ft in diameter. It was supported by eight lance-wood ribs, steamed and bent to shape, and pushed into the ground. The tops were bolted to an eight-armed iron star. The fabric was heavy cotton duck and weighed 28lbs. Its height was probably about 6ft and it was stated to have withstood a gale for over twelve hours without the use of any stays or guylines.

Another dome tent with shaped wooden ribs, mentioned in 1921 as "a useful tent for caravanners", looks remarkably like the pneumatic tents introduced more than ten years later.

In the 1980s lightweight single hoop tents appeared on the British market, with the Saunders Spacepacker and Spacepacker Plus becoming very popular.

Geodesic tents pitch inner first but are very stable.

Transverse ridge and tunnel designs by the same manufacturer offered the big advantage of two generous-sized porches giving access to either side of the tent.

Ultimate Equipment produced reasonably lightweight dome tents, a transverse ridge tent, and the Peapod, a sloping double-hooped tent.

In the early 1990s, Khyam introduced its quick-erecting tents, firstly in small sizes and later in family-sized models. Other manufacturers followed suit with family-sized dome tents, dome vis-a-vis (face-to-face) tents and large hoop tents. During this period the frame tent market collapsed. The last British manufacturer, J.J. Hawley, was bought out by the Andrew Mitchell Group (Vango) in 1998. Very few frame tents are now made as most people prefer light nylon touring tents that pack so much smaller.

Dome, frame and tunnel tents at an exhibition in the 1990s.

Although the U.K. was the primary instigator of the leisure tent market, very few tents are now made in Britain apart from a few quality lightweight tents from manufacturers such as Saunders, Omega and Terra Nova. Most tents are now made in the Far East or Eastern Europe and are imported by British companies.

A word about tent poles. Most early poles were made of bamboo, or, in the case of very heavy tents, turned hardwood with brass or iron sockets to join sections together. At the end of World War One Holding devised a nesting walking stick tent pole, made from different sizes of bamboo. Technology used for aeroplane wing struts was used to produce McGruer laminated tent poles, but these were very expensive and not a viable proposition.

The Saunders' Galaxy tent, developed from the single-hoop Spacepacker, is ideal for two persons backpacking or cycle-camping.

The advent of aluminium alloys led to lighter, stronger poles, including nesting poles from Camtors that were designed to fit on a cycle in place of the pump (but where did one carry the pump?). During World War Two nesting aluminium alloy masts had been supplied with pilots' survival dinghies. Many campers were able to make use of these after the war when they were sold as Government Surplus stock.

A vis-a-vis dome tent is ideal for families.

When glass fibre technology was discovered this, too, was used to manufacture tent poles, particularly for dome tents. Carbon fibre has also been used for flexible poles but it is extremely expensive and most poles on quality tents are now made from aluminium alloy. Although a few frame tents were supplied with alloy frames, most are now made of steel.

There's nothing new

1930–1939:
The end of an era
and a new beginning

The 1930s were to see great changes, both in society in general and within the Club. The Club's founder Thomas Hiram Holding died in 1930, and 1936 saw the death of King George V – the end of an era for both Club and country.

Threats of more anti-camping legislation, with over 100 Bills down for discussion in 1930, demanded greater efforts to increase the Club's influence of good camping standards. A fighting fund was established to help with the costs involved in opposing such bills. The Club was also concerned about the possible implications of the proposed Land Value Tax.

More Club-operated sites were obtained, more District Associations (D.A.s) sanctioned and new specialist Sections were inaugurated. The Club initiated the formation of the International Federation of Camping and Caravanning (F.I.C.C.) in 1932, and members benefited from special travel concessions offered by the shipping and railway companies and the new airlines. From a membership of 4,500 in 1929, the Club membership was to rise to 8,500 during 1939.

A new venture for the Club was a big indoor party, the first Club Reunion. It was held in 1932 at the Royal Horticultural Hall, Westminster. Almost a quarter of the Club membership attended and it was thereafter made an annual fixture.

During 1930 the Club's library, which had existed for some 20 years,

In the wider world

New fibre is stronger than silk: A new synthetic fibre material is discovered in America, stronger than natural silk. Called Nylon, one of its first uses was for ladies' stockings.

The monarchy in crisis: The death of George V in January 1936 was followed by the abdication of Edward VIII after less than a year, leaving his brother the task of restoring faith in the monarchy as King George VI. He and Queen Elizabeth were crowned in Westminster Abbey on 12 May 1937.

No peace in our time: Following Hitler's promises to Prime Minister Neville Chamberlain in 1938 that Germany had no more territorial aspirations, attacks on Poland, which Britain had pledged to defend, finally led to war being declared on 3 September 1939. Almost immediately, the Commonwealth and France joined Britain.

Left: Washing-up duty, Walton Club Site, around 1937. (Club Archive)

Folding caravans, which we now know as trailer tents, became popular in the 1930s. This one at the Charlton Kings Rally, near Cheltenham, was owned by Stephen Hilhouse, sitting in the caravan with his eldest daughter, Agnes. (Stephen Hilhouse's personal album, courtesy Miss S. Hilhouse)

was thoroughly overhauled and re-catalogued, and a new Honorary Librarian was appointed. Members could borrow books for up to two weeks and postage had to be paid unless the books were collected and returned in person. It was a popular service but difficult to control, especially when members failed to return the books!

At the end of the year T.H. Holding, the Club's founder, died. He was 86. He had last appeared at a Club function in 1925 when he was at the Annual Supper and had received a tumultuous ovation. It was a sad day for the Club but all realised just how great was his contribution to the enjoyment of the outdoors.

The decade was to see many changes at Club Headquarters, which were moved from Greville Street at the end of 1934. New premises were obtained at 38 Grosvenor Gardens, near Victoria Station, where a club room was again made available for members. H.W. Pegler was appointed Secretary in 1934 and Capt. S.J.C. Russell became Organising Secretary, a post originally held in an Honorary capacity by R.B. Searle.

Framed rucksacks

Introduced in the 1930s the Norwegian Bergans were considered to be the best in the world. Camtors also made rucksacks to the Norwegian pattern, but it was possible to buy the frame and make your own sack to fit. Camtors also introduced very light cane-framed rucksacks in this period. This particular sack was made by a Club member to fit a Camtors' steel frame.

Lectures on camping-related topics, held during the Winter months at Club Headquarters and other venues also proved very popular and helped in the recruitment of more members.

A Club publicity film, *With Tent and Rucksack*, was made during 1937. Although a silent film, it was an excellent method of showing the Club at work. It showed the Club's way of camping, the problems of casual campers trying to find a site and the solution – to join the Club. The two main characters, played by professional actors, were shown visiting Club Headquarters, selecting their equipment at Camp and Sports Co-operators and meeting members enjoying camping at Walton Club Site.

A scheme of temporary membership for up to three months for visitors from overseas was introduced. Members of recognised foreign camping clubs would automatically be given free temporary membership.

Percy Lindsey, the indefatigable Tours Secretary, broadcast on *In Town Tonight* in May 1938 describing his experiences when camping abroad. He told of camping in Algeria – where he unwittingly pitched over a dead dog – to camping on the slopes of Mount Olympus in Greece.

For years the Council had made many efforts to obtain incorporation.

Percy Lindsey often travelled to far-away places at his own expense, looking at possible venues for Club tours. Here he is on top of Mount Hermeticus, Greece, on one such occasion. (Club Archive)

Early attempts to obtain a Royal Charter did not materialise, so efforts were made to incorporate the Club under the Companies Act.

The Annual General Meeting (A.G.M.) finally approved the proposals and the Council and the Club's solicitor began work. Unfortunately, the legal wording could not be agreed to the Club's satisfaction and it was decided to make another attempt at a later date. World War Two, however, would result in even further delay.

In March 1933 Club members' discount on purchases, previously five per cent, given by Camp and Sports Co-operators was reduced to two-and-a-half per cent. The Club stipulated that the discount must not fall below this figure. The Society remained the Club's official suppliers, and members were urged to continue to support them in the mutual interests of both parties.

The Tucker family and friends camping together in the 1930s. Transport was by motor-cycle and side-car, a mode of transport used by many Club families. (Mrs B. Figg, née Tucker)

The shares that the Club owned in the Society were valued at £200 in 1930, but by 1934 their value had dropped to £105. Publication of the Annual Reports of the Society in *Camping* ceased after 1932, and apart from the occasional advertisement in *Camping*, Camp and Sports Co-operators ceased advertising in Club publications in 1936.

When the Club moved to Grosvenor Gardens, Camp and Sports Co-operators obtained new premises in Newgate Street, in the City.

The Club magazine, *Camping*, which had retained the same format since 1920, was improved and enlarged in April 1936. A cover price of sixpence was introduced, but the reason is unclear since it was not on sale to the public. The whole production of the magazine, apart from the printing, remained on a voluntary basis, with features written by members. Alex Papps remained as Honorary Editor and by the end of the 1939 had served a total of 22 years in the position.

Each magazine had a few pages devoted to the District Associations (D.A.s), Sections and permanent sites and included forthcoming fixtures, information, general activities and official notices. Proceedings of Council meetings, at one time fully reported, were now much abbreviated. Advertisements from a wide variety

Down sleeping bags

Considered to be warmer than quilts, the best quality down bags – some filled with eiderdown – were expensive but very light and packed very small. Most were square quilted with no internal walls, and often had cold spots where the down shifted away from the stitching lines.

First in the field A Century of The Camping and Caravanning Club

of suppliers were now accepted, helping to pay for the improved magazine and bringing in much-needed revenue, in addition to informing members about the range of equipment available.

At the beginning of 1930, the use of local bye-laws to restrict camping was on the increase, and the Club sought local representatives to watch for restrictive legislation. In particular, some authorities were using housing bye-laws to prevent the erection of any moveable dwelling, including tents and caravans.

Such bye-laws did not have to go before Parliament and it was very difficult to watch out for them. The big problem was that many people had erected small shacks on parcels of land for weekend use, which they often termed 'camping out'. These shacks were an eyesore, and had to be controlled, but not at the expense of true camping. The Club asked landowners and farmers who allowed camping on their land not to allow such shacks to be erected.

The new Central Committee on Camping Legislation also tried to maintain and extend existing facilities. Various public bodies were circularised to ascertain their attitude to camping, and a resumé of their replies was published in the *Yearbook* and *Sites List* for the information of Club members. While some, notably the

Cycle-camping was still very popular with all ages in the 1930s. This is Agnes Hilhouse, then a teenager, in the New Forest, Easter, 1933. (Stephen Hilhouse's personal album, courtesy Miss S. Hilhouse)

Metropolitan Water Board and the Office of Works (who were responsible for the Royal Parks) did not allow camping, most were happy to leave decisions to their tenants. The Corporation of London only allowed camping in Epping Forest, restricted to men and boys, not exceeding six in number. This rule had been in force since 1914.

Great costs were involved in fighting restrictive legislation and, despite the difficult financial situation in the country, Club members were urged to subscribe to the newly-established fighting fund. It was emphasised that the fund would not be used for the administration costs of the Committee. Sufficient funds were eventually raised but it took a long time to reach the figure required.

Surrey County Council introduced a restrictive Bill in Parliament and this was vigorously opposed. A clause was eventually inserted in the Bill to exempt national organisations that undertook responsibility for their members while in camp.

The Home Office and the Ministry of Health both criticised the Bill and eventually drastic alterations were made and the Club's opposition was withdrawn. Although the Club's own camping grounds were exempted, it was not possible to protect the rights of the unorganised, individual camper. Club members, however, provided they abided by Club rules, were exempted from the restrictions imposed by the Bill.

The Club realised it had to be able to show that it exercised control over its membership and, in December 1932, a Code for Campers was prepared. As a condition of membership of the Club all members were required to sign an undertaking to observe the Code. A new rule, that "The Council may refuse to accept renewal of any membership without assigning a reason for so doing" was introduced.

Parliament had to be satisfied that the Club had the necessary powers for enforcing discipline, and these needed to be in force *before* the framing of any Bill. At the time there were 24 Parliamentary Bills in the pipeline that could affect camping, and this new rule would afford the Club a large measure of protection.

There were also a number of town planning schemes that could affect camping. Since these were only advertised locally it was essential for every member to watch the local press for any which might cause problems.

Tylers' Causeway Club Site, near Cuffley, Hertfordshire, was leased by the Club in 1939. Used throughout World War Two, it had to be abandoned when the land was sold for gravel workings. **(Club Archive)**

Club member John Hayes and his wife at the International Federation of Camping and Caravanning Camp at Stresa, Italy, 1938. (John Hayes)

The 1936 Public Health Act, containing the first national measures for the control of camping, was passed. The restrictions laid down by some local authorities were horrendous: no tent to be pitched within 20ft of a hedge; no bread, milk or butter to be sold on site; only one moveable dwelling per acre; or *two* rubbish bins to be placed outside *each* tent!

Campers had to use a licensed site or apply to the local authority themselves for a license to camp. Some authorities tried to be even more restrictive but as new bye-laws had to be approved by the Ministry of Health they were unsuccessful.

Others opposed giving the Camping Club an Exemption Certificate, suggesting that these were only intended for certain youth organisations. The Club had support from the new Ramblers' Association that, while anxious to see adequate control of large camp sites and semi-permanent structures, was strongly opposed to any national or local legislation that would restrict the liberty of responsible organisations to camp for short periods.

Through strenuous efforts the Club did eventually get its Exemption Certificate, enabling it to run its own

FEDERAZIONE INTERNAZIONALE
DEI CAMPING CLUBS

•

CAMPO INTERNAZ. 1938-XVI
E VI CONGRESSO DELLA F.I.C.C.

MEINA-STRESA
30 LUGLIO - 16 AGOSTO
ITALIA

TESSERA D'ISCRIZIONE

N. 829

continued on page 120

KINDER S...
STORY OF HAND-TO-
HAND FIGHT.

INJURED KEEPER IN HOSPITAL
AFTER MASS TRESPASS.

CLASH WHEN CROWD
SURGED OVER HILLSIDE.
FROM OUR OWN CORRESPONDENT.
NEW MILLS, MONDAY.
SIX ramblers appeared at New Mills Police Court to-day
on charges arising out of the "mass trespass" on
Kinder Scout yesterday afternoon.
John Thomas Anderson (21),
Quadrant, Cemetery-road, Droylsden, cotton
special court on May 1st, ...

Kinder Scout and the battle for countryside access by Peter Frost

Ewan MacColl, who was to become the doyen of British folk song and known to later generations as the father of Kirsty MacColl, was a Club member and Press Officer for the Kinder Trespass. As well as many press releases and newspaper articles, he penned a song in support of the campaign. It's still being sung today.

The Manchester Rambler
I'm a rambler, I'm a rambler from Manchester way,
I get all my pleasure the hard, moorland way,
I may be a wage slave on Monday,
But I am a free man on Sunday.

Throughout its history the Club has always been a firm champion of the right to access to the countryside – even today it is consulted by government and civil servants on camping, footpath and other relevant legislation. The Club is recognised as a responsible voice in recreational use of the countryside.

Club members played their part in what was undoubtedly the biggest battle, and indeed biggest victory, for such access.

The year was 1932. In Britain unemployment was at record levels. What better cheap recreation for unemployed lads and lasses than walking and camping in the countryside? Yet vast acres of that very countryside were closed to them.

The fine mountain country between Manchester and Sheffield was one such area. It could provide country walking away from the smoke and grime of the cities, but it was closed to most people, open only to a small number of grouse-shooters protected by gamekeepers with their sticks and guns.

The Club's members and many others in the British Workers Sports Federation met together and proposed a mass trespass across Kinder Scout – even today one of the most spectacular and best walks in the area.

After a meeting in a quarry they set off only to be confronted by the keepers and the police. Many were taken to Hayfield lock-up and the next day they appeared at New Mills Police Court to be remanded for trial at Derby Assizes.

The jury brought in a mixed verdict – guilty on some charges, not guilty on others. The court decision was of no real consequence. The conscience of the nation had been stirred, and it is no coincidence that the first national park in Britain was the Peak District National Park.

The history of the struggle for access, the battles with gamekeepers and the mass trespass on Kinder Scout were not in vain – the public still enjoys its inheritance today.

UT RAMBLERS IN COURT.
ity Unemployed Demonstration.

ARMED MADMAN SCARES WOMAN.
FACING PISTOL ALONE IN TRAIN.
REFLECTION IN WINDOW.

TWO CHILDR BURNED TO DEAT
TRAPPED IN HOUSE F WHILE ASLEEP.
REFUSAL TO LEF FROM WINDOW.

This photograph of a camp at Lovat Bridge, Beauly, near Inverness, 1934, was entered for a cover competition for the Club magazine by Mr M.O. Sheffield of Sevenoaks, Kent. **(Club Archive)**

continued from
page 117

sites without a license from a local authority, and its members could

camp freely on any site where camping was a sideline, rather than a

business. Club rules had to be modified to ensure that members agreed

not to avail themselves of their exemption privileges when camping on

a commercial site.

Thus the Club became officially recognised as *the* national organisation

for campers and caravanners. At the time it was the only such organisation

to be granted exemption; other bodies had to change their rules to include

a member's undertaking before being granted an exemption certificate.

Anti-camping legislation had also come into force in Europe. Any

Dutch national who wished to camp had to buy a camping passport from

the authorities, no matter what their experience in camping. Nederlandse

Toeristen Kampeer Club (N.T.K.C.) members were not exempt from the rule.

They feared that the legislation could have a bad effect on the club,

stifling its growth. This kind of restriction was the reason that the

Central Committee was established. Swiss motoring

organisations also threatened to blacklist certain

Canton authorities if they did not withdraw their

opposition to camping.

Another attack on camping came with the Water

Undertakings Bill in 1939, when certain clauses gave

powers to the companies to make bye-laws controlling

the use of land within their catchment areas. They

would have the power to define the area over which

From the Club magazine

April 1931 *Clothing advice for ladies for Swiss tour: "I strongly advise a pullover and short skirt, or knickers. It is necessary to be as free as possible. No linen articles should be worn; they are a source of danger and extremely uncomfortable when damp through exertion."*

March 1939 *A slight encounter with the law: "We stood with an open map across the saddles, deciding on our route. Suddenly a car came roaring up the road, stopped abruptly, and two policemen got out. They eyed our loaded tandem and the open map, and suggested we might have an 'L' plate on the back."*

they wished to exercise control, and could also prohibit any activity they chose to specify in the bye-laws. Thus a water company drawing supplies from lakes or streams in a rural area could arbitrarily define an area of land surrounding their source of supply as a catchment area and could forbid any camping, or even rambling, in that area.

Another clause gave water authorities the right to refuse to supply water to tents, caravans, etc, thus attempting to evade the provisions of the Public Health Act where certain camp sites were excluded from local authority licensing requirements.

Lady Baden-Powell with Captain Russell, centre, and Stephen Hilhouse at Aldenham, 1937. **(Club Archive)**

The Central Committee on Camping Legislation had already successfully opposed four similar Water Bills in 1939, and to find such clauses in a government Bill applying to the whole country was disappointing. Members were once again urged to write to their M.P.s asking them to oppose the Bill. As a direct result of the Club's opposition, substantial amendments were made to make the Bill acceptable to the camping movement in general.

The general public has no real idea of the amount of work that the Club did in those days – and indeed still does – to protect the rights and freedom of the individual camper. Because of the wide publicity given to the restrictions in the national press, the Club gained a considerable number

Colonel and Mrs Lambert Williams with their caravan 'Hunter's Moon', preparing for a two-year caravan tour of Europe in 1937. **(British Caravanners' Club Archive)**

of new members. "My brother read that we had to get a licence to go camping, but that if we were Camping Club members we did not need one, so we joined the Camping Club," reminisced long-standing Club member Hilda Sykes in 1999.

At the same time as legislation was causing problems, the Club had to seriously consider its *Sites List*. All "undesirable" sites had to be taken off the list in order to keep its freedom to camp. Proper sanitary arrangements, not necessarily water flushed, had to be made on all sites. Farmers were advised of the proper means of providing sanitation, either by having a suitably screened earth closet or ensuring that the camper dug his own.

Voluntary Sites Inspectors were enrolled from among D.A. members to help eliminate unsuitable sites, and approved sites were issued with weatherproof and recognisable Camping Club Approved signs. Members prepared to assist in areas in which there was no D.A. were offered a contribution to their petrol costs. Later in the decade, the Club employed a full-time Sites Inspector to check the listed sites. Site owners were given every assistance in ensuring that their sites met required standards.

Club sites were still being sought and a new site became available at Rickmansworth in 1930. The Horsley site was also acquired and

At the official opening of the Holding Memorial Site at Clent Hills, 1937. (Gordon Salt)

First in the field A Century of The Camping and Caravanning Club

Two Coronation Camps were held in 1937: Alexandra Palace, north London (pictured here); and at Bagden Farm, Polesden Lacey, Surrey. (D.A. Newell, Club Archive)

purchased in December of that year. The poor state of the ground and the lake led to much voluntary work being done before it was finally opened in August 1931. Kelvedon Hatch site was acquired in 1936 and purchased the following year. A site at Box Hill, where there had been great problems for campers, was leased in 1939, as were Tyler's Causeway and Hurley sites.

After the death of the founder in 1930, it was decided to look for a new site in his memory. A fund was established but the money was slow to come in, partly due to the effect of the depression so it was a while before one could be found. Eventually, after much hard work by Mr Palmer-Cook and other members of Birmingham D.A., a beautiful site in the Clent Hills was found – it was finally opened in 1937. Other sites came and went, and in 1938 Middlesex County Council asked the Club to manage three sites – Denham, Grims Dyke and Theobalds Park – on its behalf in connection with the National Fitness Scheme.

The first of the Scottish sites, Balmaha, was opened in 1934. Ardgartan, owned by the Forestry Commission, opened in 1937. Another site, Dalavan Bay, was secured by Glasgow and West of Scotland D.A.

The fitness of the country in general was causing some concern. Dr Saleeby, a well-known exponent of the sunlight for health policy and a Vice-President of the Club, said that members should do all they could to further the great open-air movement in which the Club had led the way for so long: open-air exercise was the thing.

Speaking at the Annual Dinner in 1936, he said: "In many places abroad they are taking great care of their youth, bringing them up in the open air, but they are doing good that evil might come". A prophecy which unfortunately was to be proven before the end of the decade.

The Club urged the Government to proceed with the establishment of National Parks and strongly supported the views of Sir Lawrence Chubb with regard to the Rights of Way Bill and the need for an Access to Mountains Bill. They also set out their views on the rights and requirements of campers in these National Parks, should they be established. The Club also gave publicity to the new Pennine Way route, pioneered by Tom Stephenson, and fully supported the fight for access to the open moorlands, at that time forbidden to walkers. The Club became affiliated to the National Association of Rambling Clubs – later to become The Ramblers' Association – and The National Trust.

Overseas Club tours continued to be very popular. A special International Touring Pennon for members was suggested by Percy Lindsey. Three parties visited Oberammergau in 1930 for the famous Passion Play and had a wonderful time. When the play was staged again in 1934 (normally it is staged every ten years, but that year was the 300th anniversary of the first play) those who went found conditions difficult and very trying. In 1936, some members visited the Olympic games in Berlin, and indeed one member, John Dudderidge, a member of the Canoe Section, was in the British Olympic team.

JOHN DUDDERIDGE, O.B.E., with other members of the British Canoe Association (the Club's Canoe-Camping section) was in the 1936 British Olympic team. The section was re-named The Canoe-Camping Club when the British Canoe Union (B.C.U.) was founded as the sport's governing body. John is President of the Canoe-Camping Club and President of Honour of the B.C.U.

Spanish visitors inspecting Percy Lindsey's tent at San Pedro, near Cangas, Vigo, Spain, in June 1936. "The prelude to the battleground of Spanish discontent," said Percy. (Club Archive)

The opening of the International Camp at Weisbaden, 1937. (Club Archive)

Club tours headed further and further afield, and in this decade would include Algeria, Andorra, Corsica, Czechoslovakia, Denmark, France, Germany, Greece, Holland, Hungary, Italy, Majorca, Norway, Poland, Spain, Sweden, Switzerland and Tunisia. Base camps for Club members were established in some of these countries, enabling them to travel independently and stay for a few weeks in the area.

In 1932, due to the world financial crisis, overseas tours were cancelled. The base camps in Brittany, Denmark and Spain, which could be reached by British steamers, were still maintained. It was hoped to arrange a tour to Russia but after much work this proved to be quite impossible. In 1938, a tour to Canada and the United States of America was planned, sailing out on the *Empress of Britain* to Quebec, returning on the *Queen Mary* from New York at a cost of £40. More than a dozen members were due to take part but, owing to circumstances outside the control of the Club, only the Tours Secretary and one other member were able to go.

The Belgian Rallye Campeurs was again held in 1930 and 1931, and in 1932 a similar Rally was held at Saxenheim in Holland. Despite the cancellation of foreign tours that year, a British delegation attended. It was at this Rally that an international federation of campers was suggested, setting the wheels in motion for the founding of the F.I.C.C.

The Camping Club, being the first and largest club of its kind, and the only one to have its own office premises, was asked to act as Secretary to the Federation, prior to the next International Rally which would be held in 1933 in England, when a definite constitution would be formulated.

By gracious permission of King George V, Hampton Court Park was the setting for the first F.I.C.C. rally in 1933, when 390 campers from eight

JOHN A.C. 'Champ' CHAMPION, O.B.E., took part in the Club Pyrenees Tour in 1922, and in 1929 led the tour to Majorca, that he described as "truly international". He could be described as the father of the international camping movement. He was Club Chairman from 1931–1941 and the first President of the International Federation. He succeeded Stephen Hilhouse as Club President in 1960.

different countries took part. J.A.C. Champion, Club Chairman and the prime mover behind the idea of the federation, was elected Chairman of the F.I.C.C. with L.M. Wulcko as Secretary.

The International Congress would be held each year at an international camp, the next being France in 1934. Brussels was the venue in 1935 and Barcelona in 1936. Not long after the Barcelona meeting the Spanish Civil War broke out causing much anxiety among Club members for their friends in Catalunya. Germany was the choice for 1937. Members were asked by their hosts to "accept Germany as they found it, and not as portrayed in the newspapers". Those who went found most people very friendly. Italy was the venue for the Rally in 1938 and Switzerland in 1939.

Some Dutch friends recalled travelling through the night in complete blackout conditions through France and Belgium in order to get home, since travel through Germany was impossible. Some Club members who had extended their stay in Switzerland also had to hurry to get home safely.

Club members were also invited to join members of the N.T.K.C. in celebrating its Silver Jubilee at Soesterberg in 1937. Despite rather grey skies all had a very enjoyable time.

More members were helped to go on Club tours when the railway and shipping companies offered substantial discounts to Club members travelling overseas. Party tickets could be obtained for groups of 25 or more, giving substantial discounts on train and boat fares. Members on the Swedish motoring tour had their cars carried at special rates, plus an extra 15 per cent reduction as there was a minimum of ten cars.

LAURANCE M. WULCKO joined the Club in 1920 and was a founder member of Essex District Association, becoming Chairman in 1930. Elected to the National Council in 1926, he was Vice-Chairman from 1930–1935. In 1928 he was appointed Honorary Secretary of the Central Committee for Camping Legislation and was the first Honorary Secretary of the International Federation of Camping Clubs.

Crossing the Channel, 1930s-style. (John Hayes)

In 1937 a boat was chartered to carry the 60 or so cars belonging to members going to the International Rally in Germany across the Channel to Belgium. It was quite an adventure for a motorist to travel abroad especially as there were no roll-on, roll-off ferries. The cars had to be put in special cradles and hoisted on and off by crane.

Members staying at home were also able to purchase reduced price tickets from the railway companies, provided they had a special voucher from the Club. They could travel to and from different stations if they wished, making round trips possible. In 1933 the Club chartered a Heracles aircraft from Imperial Airways to take Club members from Hendon to Croydon, from where they were taken by the airline's luxury coach to a privately-arranged site at Nork Park, near Burgh Heath. The plane then returned to Hendon with a second party of campers, who camped at a

The Caravan Section's Easter Rally at Wookey Hole, Somerset, 1937. Note, no 20ft rule! (British Caravanners' Club Archive)

listed site at Mill Hill. Members flew over London at a height of 3,000ft, at 110mph.

"Members", said Percy Lindsey, "were greatly amused by the notice, in three languages: 'Please be sick in the bag'. But nobody needed a bag!" Unfortunately the airline had to discontinue its discount offer to members when it became a member of the International Air Transport Association, which did not allow its members to offer discounts.

National Feasts of Lanterns (N.F.O.L.s) continued to attract large numbers of members. An

The last appearance of Lord Baden-Powell, seen here with Percy Lindsey (right) at the National Feast of Lanterns, Aldenham, 1937. (Club Archive)

accident with a lantern at Shardloes Park in 1930 led to the complete loss of a member's car and camping kit. Thereafter, members were warned not to hang the lanterns too near the cars; at the time there was no 20ft rule.

In 1936 the Club introduced a successful Spring Festival to open the season. This too became an annual event. Lord Baden-Powell visited the N.F.O.L. at Aldenham Park, which was the last time members were to see him at a major Club event.

The Camping Club contingent march past King George VI and his family at the Festival of Youth, Wembley Stadium, 1937. (Stephen Hilhouse's personal album, courtesy Miss S. Hilhouse)

A successful overseas cycle tour through the Black Forest, Germany, took place in 1937. Club member Ernest Balint is seen here reading the map. (Ernest Balint, Club Archive)

A Silver Jubilee Camp was held in 1935 at Gatton Park, Merstham, and a Coronation Camp was held in the grounds of Alexandra Palace from 7–17 May, 1937. Another was held at Bagden Farm, Polesden Lacey, over the same period, and most D.A.s held special celebration camps. A Festival of Youth was held at Wembley, with Club members taking part in the march-past before King George VI and his family.

Camp Fires continued but were now arranged for venues in the provinces and organised by the local D.A.s.

In 1932 both the Club and Camp and Sports Co-operators exhibited at the Ideal Holidays Exhibition at the Royal Agricultural Hall where members were invited to help with demonstrations in the evenings.

In 1933 a National Exhibition of Camping, Hiking and Allied Sports, organised by the Club, was held at the Imperial Institute. For the first time the Club gave other manufacturers the chance to show their latest developments to both members and the public. This was so successful that the event was repeated in 1934, 1935, 1938 and 1939.

In 1934 the Club introduced Awards of Merit and Certificates of Fitness for specific items of equipment. Over the years these awards – highly coveted by the manufacturers – were given to various makers of quality tents, sleeping bags, cycle panniers and carriers, camp beds, etc. None of these went to Camp and Sports Co-operators, as they failed to exhibit after 1933, despite the increased competition.

Lean-to tents

Designed for use with either car or caravan, the car lean-to – the forerunner of today's awnings – had a window and doors, and was open on the side adjoining the car. A canvas panel over the car roof could be closed to allow the tent to remain free-standing when the car was driven away.

CAMPING

JUNE—JULY
1941

THE OFFICIAL ORGAN OF THE CAMPING CLUB OF G. B. & I.

TREES.

In 1936 a larger magazine was produced with photographs on the cover.

The Horsley Club Site was given over to the exhibition organiser for four weeks to enable various tents to be erected and tested over a period by Club members. Any Club member or member of the public could camp there and would be given a free ticket to the Exhibition in London. The camp itself formed an outdoor exhibition where the public could watch demonstrations of good camping and see tents being pitched.

The Club also held a competition, open only to members, for The Improvement of Tents in 1937. Submissions of new designs or improvements to existing designs were required. A prize of five guineas was given to T.E. Hicks for his improvement to the Itisa tent. Partial side walls were incorporated to give more headroom but added only 4ozs to the overall weight. The design also greatly increased the useable floor space. Another design for a much larger tent, built on a rubber-covered wire framework, was also submitted. The idea behind the design was that the wires would prevent sagging and would obviate the need for a ridge pole. The Club wanted to test the tent before giving it an award but we have found no further reference to that Club test. We do, however, have the tent, which carries a label saying it was an award-winner!

District Associations continued to grow, with new D.A.s being formed for Berkshire and Oxfordshire, Bristol, East Kent, East Yorkshire, Gloucester and Somerset, North Lancs, Sheffield, Sussex, Teesside and Wessex before the end of 1939.

October 1932 saw the beginning of the specialist Sections, with the founding of the Folk Dance Group. It met during the Winter months at a London venue, mostly on a weekday evening. In the Summer months members camped at various Club events, but mainly at Chertsey Club Site.

Many Folk Dance Group events and camps were organised in conjunction with the English Folk Dance Society. The Mountaineering Section had its inaugural meeting on Boxing Day at the Nag's Head, Edale. Many Club members were interested in this sport, having participated in a number of overseas tours that had taken them to high places.

The inaugural meeting of the Canoe Section took place at Club Headquarters in March 1933, when the British Canoe Association became incorporated with the Camping Club. T.H. Holding was at one time a champion canoeist and would have been pleased to see this sport encompassed within the Club. The Chertsey Club Site was the base for the Canoe Section for many years.

Thomas Black & Sons' **Good Companions** *catalogue from the 1930s.*

The Club's Caravan Section had its first official meet at the N.F.O.L. at Shardloes Park, Amersham, in September 1933. The Caravan Section became known as The British Caravanners' Club (B.C.C.) in 1937.

In December 1938 some B.C.C. members were "amazed to discover a well-advanced plan to bring about a fusion of the B.C.C. with The Caravan Club". Apparently The Caravan Club Chairman had put such a proposal to the B.C.C.'s Annual General Meeting without notice of such a motion being given. Opponents suggested that joining the two together would create an unhealthy monopoly. There was plenty of room for two clubs in caravanning as it was of growing interest and large numbers of members would be available to both clubs. That such plans were "well advanced" was denied by the B.C.C. Chairman. He did admit that four members of a

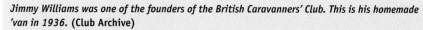

Jimmy Williams was one of the founders of the British Caravanners' Club. This is his homemade 'van in 1936. **(Club Archive)**

The first meet of the Club's Caravan Section at Benson, 1933. (The Caravan)

B.C.C. Committee and four from The Caravan Club had met to consider if it were possible to find common views to put before both Clubs.

The Honorary Secretary stated that the suggestion was nothing new, and had been considered on and off since before The Caravan Club had passed from Mr Stone, its founder, to the caravan press. There was no reason why the suggestion of The Caravan Club's Chairman should not be *considered* by B.C.C. members. No proposition had yet been put to members of the B.C.C, and members could be assured that nothing would be done without the approval of B.C.C. members. The matter was now being considered by the relevant committees of the Council that caravanning had always been, and must remain, an essential activity of The Camping Club. At the end of the year the Chairman said that the matter should be put behind them and best forgotten.

The Photo Group was introduced in 1935, with Percy Lindsey, one of whose many talents was photography, taking on yet another job, that of Honorary Secretary (*pro. tem.*) to the Group. Later Oscar Balint, a young Hungarian living in England, would become the Secretary. Many Club members were good photographers and were encouraged to submit their work for publication in the magazine and for the Club's album. Unfortunately these albums have long since disappeared.

The Club also increased its efforts to get motorists interested in camping. Various members organised runs during the Winter weekends, and endeavoured to find more sites suitable for motor-campers. An Honorary Motoring Officer was appointed but the Club did not feel a Special Section was needed.

On a more controversial note, when the cycle-campers asked if they, like the caravanners, could have their own Special Section this was refused. It was felt the D.A.s were the best way of catering for them. Some D.A.s (notably the Coventry section of Birmingham D.A. and the Sheffield section of Yorkshire D.A.) made special provision for cyclists.

Despite pleas from the cyclists, and also later from pedestrian-campers, the Council refused to sanction a Special Section. In 1936, however, a Cycling Officer, Wilf Groves, was appointed. A Pedestrian Officer was to follow. In May 1939 an Artists' Group was suggested. Once again the prime mover was Percy Lindsey, an artist and cartoonist who did many illustrations and tour maps for the Club.

It was obvious to members that storm clouds were gathering and the country was coming closer to war. A request from London County Council was published in *Camping* in May 1939. Volunteers were required to assist with the planned evacuation scheme for London, should such become necessary.

Members who had child care skills, catering and camping experience were especially needed. They would be required to escort evacuees to their Reception Areas or work in London escorting the parties between

Toilets

Suitable for motor-campers and caravanners, they appeared in 1937. Elsan's collapsible model closed to a height of just 12ins and was very compact for transport. The standard model had a ventilation collar in place of a vent pipe. Folding latrine seats were also available for use with earth closets.

Water-based activities were always a popular feature at Walton Club Site. This picture, from 1936, shows members having fun in a long canoe.

Manning the pump at Walton Club Site. (Club Archive)

assembly points and railway stations. They could either stay with them in the Reception Areas to help in any capacity required or could return to London – transport would be free.

A lengthy report of the first pedestrian tour to Poland from the end of June to mid-July was published in the September 1939 *Camping*, ending: "We look forward to the day when parties of Polish campers will be able to visit this country." In the next issue Percy Lindsey, who was on the tour, remarked: "By a margin of only six weeks we escaped the terrible ordeals to which that unhappy land has been subjected. It seems hardly credible that so awful a change could have taken place. I fear to think of what may have happened to our many good friends, whose hospitality, friendliness and gaiety and obvious delight at meeting a stranger, made us all welcome."

Members were asked to do all they could to keep the Club going by renewing their memberships. Those who wanted to maintain contact could perhaps renew as an Associate member at slightly lower cost. The Club reduced the staff at Headquarters to a minimum, leaving just a skeleton staff. Expenses would be cut to a minimum, Club sites would still have to be maintained and rates and taxes paid. Club Headquarters and some permanent sites were on period leases that had to be continued.

Members could continue to camp as long as their tents were properly camouflaged and they observed the blackout regulations. Campers on permanent sites had just 24 hours in which to camouflage their tents or pack them away.

Most of the large events had to be cancelled but smaller groups were urged to meet in each others' homes away from city centres to have get-togethers and assist Scout and Guide groups and Boys' and Girls' clubs. The Club intended to continue its recreational and social service as far as possible provided it did not interfere with National Service. Many younger members were quick to join up, leaving the various Club Committees and D.A.s to be run by those too young or too old for service. Members were encouraged to arrange small camp meets – provided camouflage regulations were complied with – outside restricted areas, or organise cycle runs and rambles during daylight hours.

Camping continued to be published at suitable intervals. Above all, the enthusiasm of members would enable the Club to weather the storm.

An original Itisa tent in use, Easter 1937. **(Club Archive)**

Camping accessories by Hazel Constance

In the early days of the Club the National Council insisted that members should be able to obtain special lightweight equipment in the best qualities of materials and workmanship at the lowest possible prices.

Thomas Hiram Holding supplied kit from his premises in Maddox Street, and in 1909 he produced a catalogue – *Refined Camping* – which included Primus stoves, pan sets, kettles etc, as well as rooksacs [sic], cycle clothing and carrying bags, quilts and canvas buckets and bowls, in addition to his tents. The Club's Supplies Department later issued its own catalogues, with a wide variety of equipment being for sale.

The earliest type of cooking appliance used by members was a Mersey Cuisine (left), a methylated spirit stove and pan set. Primus-type pressure stoves of all sizes were used by virtually all campers right up to the introduction of the Camping Gaz range of cooking appliances in the 1950s.

With the introduction of Camping Gaz, and later Calor Gas in cylinders, kitchen appliances were developed by several manufacturers to cater for families. Most were double-burner stoves, sometimes incorporating a grill, with or without a fold-out windshield (left). Various kitchen units were designed to take the stoves, such as the Beanstalk made from wire mesh on a frame.

Most campers used aluminium saucepans with detachable handles that packed one inside the other and were very light in weight, but some were rather thin and easily bent or dented. Steamers could be purchased to fit several sizes. The design of the pans did not change for over 40 years.

Trangia methylated spirit stoves were introduced to the U.K. from Sweden in the 1970s. Burning liquid methylated spirit and complete with pans, they were a popular choice for backpackers although controlling the flame for cooking was not so easy. Later Trangia

supplied an optional gas burner for fitting in place of
the spirit burner. These cookers were not a new
idea, however, as a remarkably similar spirit stove
was stocked by the Supplies Department in 1914.
The introduction of dehydrated and freeze-dried
food for campers in the 1970s was a direct result of
military developments during World War Two. Many early
examples were not very palatable, but later brands were better.

Sleeping in comfort in the early days of the Club meant getting straw
or hay from the farmer and laying it under the groundsheet. Sleeping bags
consisted of a long woollen garment like a sack with sleeves and a hood.
Down quilts, with a valance to tuck under the sleeper, were introduced
by 1908. Down sleeping bags followed in the early 1920s. These were
developed from simple sacks with through-stitching to
more complicated mummy models with internal walls
to eliminate cold spots.

The advent of polyester fillings led to further
developments, with inexpensive bags suitable for family
campers becoming widely used. The rapid development in
the use of synthetic fibres helped manufacturers provide
buyers with a choice of product. Air beds were popular in
the 1930s and lightweight versions for backpackers appeared after
World War Two, but their insulating properties were poor. The advent of
Karrimat offered campers better insulation, and later self-inflating
mattresses brought more comfort.

Rucksacks, initially simple canvas bags with slings for back-packing,
have developed into extremely complicated carrying systems with
adjustable back lengths to fit the body. The first framed sacks
introduced in the 1930s were D-shaped with an external D-shaped
steel frame. Camtors developed a cane frame, later copied by others,
which gave support to the load but was much lighter.

A revolution in rucksack design came after World War Two
when it was realised that a load carried high on the back was more
comfortable and produced less strain on the shoulders. Hip belts were
designed to take the weight off the shoulders. Later, internal-framed
sacks were devised.

Camping accessories

1940–1949: World War Two — and national recognition

W ith the beginning of World War Two in September 1939 the Club's policy was to try and continue camping as far as possible. Members were encouraged to do all they could to keep the Club going with those in the armed forces paying a reduced Full Membership subscription.

The year 1940 began with a warning: "We must expect a war of several years' duration. We should reflect, during the dark days and blackout nights, on the far-off happy days, the rows of tents and children's laughter. We must cherish the hard-won privileges embodied in Club membership and retain at all costs the organisation that is responsible for its administration. We must keep the pennon flying and keep for members on Active Service all the facilities for the resumption of their beloved pastime of camping on their return."

This was the period of what was called "the phoney war". The British Expeditionary Force (B.E.F.) was in France waiting for something to happen and at home every citizen was issued with a gas mask but it was not yet mandatory to carry it everywhere. Children who had been hastily evacuated began to drift back home, where they were probably just as safe.

Members of the B.E.F. were given home leave. Among them was a member of the Canoe Section, who arrived home in time for the Easter

Left: Just as in World War One, many men learned to live under canvas and would later use camping as a way to enjoy their leisure. In World War Two, though, it wasn't just men. These Land Army girls were in Barwick to help with the flax harvest – they seem to be enjoying life in a village of bell tents. No doubt many of those bell tents would turn up after the war as ex-army camping equipment – perfect for holiday accommodation. (Imperial War Museum Q30880)

In the wider world

Allied forces evacuated: German attacks on Belgium and Holland in May 1940 were followed by the evacuation of the British Expeditionary Force from the beaches around Dunkirk on the French coast. More men were being conscripted and the civilian population began to experience increasing air attacks on towns and cities.

Pearl Harbour is bombed: 7 December 1941 saw a surprise air attack on the American naval base of Pearl Harbour, severely damaging the U.S. fleet. This event led to America joining Britain and her allies in the war against what was now the German-Italian-Japanese axis.

Britain resounds to victory celebrations: Suddenly it was all over in Europe, though it took another four months and two atomic bombs before Japan surrendered. The return of thousands of men from the forces, food and fuel shortages and the massive rebuilding programme all affected the return to a way of life much different from that of pre-war times.

Frozen Britain works by candlelight: February 1947 brought heavy snowstorms and sub-zero temperatures, not helped by serious fuel shortages. Shop lighting with electricity was banned, including the use by one clever shop owner of a wind generator. By the following month the big freeze had turned to extensive flooding.

meet on the Teme at Ludlow. At the end of the trip he packed his canoe and camping kit ready for his next leave. While waiting on Bray Dunes, Dunkirk, in May, he began to wish he had taken his canoe back to France!

Club members were exhorted to undertake voluntary social work. At the height of the blitz small teams of three or four members went into the London Underground shelters at night to provide hot drinks for those seeking refuge. These teams were able to supplement the work of the Salvation Army and others, who were of course busy providing for the needs of the fire and rescue services above ground, and the work continued until it was no longer possible to obtain supplies of paraffin for the Primus stoves.

This picture reflects the typical attitude of the British public in the early days of World War Two. Everyone was determined, where possible, to carry on as normal. More than one vehicle was photographed carrying this telling notice. (Club Archive)

The Ministry of Home Security, realising the value of camping, was anxious to avoid imposing unnecessary restrictions, although some were bound to come. The main consideration was to ensure that blackout conditions were maintained after dark and that camouflage, where essential, was properly undertaken.

Caravans did not have to be camouflaged, although later in the war most owners painted the roofs a dirty-earth colour to make them less visible from above. Members owning quality tents were advised to make or buy a cheap flysheet and use it as camouflage rather than ruin them. There were restrictions on the use of radios and no caravan was allowed to have one installed.

Most camps that did take place appear to have been held on the Club's permanent sites. Members were encouraged to use these sites, getting there by bus, train or cycle. National Fitness Sites were at first closed to members, although Denham was later made available. After Dunkirk, Leysdown Club Site was closed as new restrictions forbade camping within ten miles of the east and south coasts of Great Britain. Camping at Kelvedon Hatch was also restricted for a while because of its proximity to North Weald airfield.

General Montgomery's purpose-built caravan was used for his living quarters throughout the war. Winston Churchill is seen leaving the caravan during the North African Campaign in February 1943. Monty is on the left, General Alan Brooke on the right.

Later in the war, Balmaha Club Site in Scotland was requisitioned for military use. Glasgow District Association (D.A.) managed to secure an alternative site at Carbeth, just eleven miles from Glasgow. Balmaha was returned to the Club in 1946, and Carbeth continued to be used until 1951.

Campers at Tylers' Causeway obtained the use of a blacked-out room in the local tea rooms in the evenings, and Kelvedon Hatch and Horsley blacked out their huts. Kelvedon allowed members to cook in the hut after dark, since flames from outside cooking stoves broke blackout regulations. The numbers of members camping at Chertsey, particularly popular with Londoners, was limited. Members helped there with breast-work protection – repairing the river banks adjacent to the site. Many bombed-out families later ended up here in a semi-permanent camp until accommodation could be sorted out.

An Air-raid Warden roster was established at the permanent Club sites, some of which remained open throughout the whole year. Others, including Rickmansworth and Horsley, established allotment gardens on site in support of the 'Dig for Victory campaign'. There was much rivalry to see who could produce the best crops. The severe Winter of 1940 greatly restricted all site activities, including vital maintenance.

In 1944 Hubert Visick presented the Club with 20 acres of land at

Graffham, Sussex, for the use of members who wanted a quiet and peaceful place to camp. This birch woodland venue remains one of the Club's most attractive sites, it is still possible to pitch out of sight of other campers. Unlike other Club sites, this one was never allowed to

have permanent campers and it was particularly popular with cycle-campers.

The freehold of Walton Club Site, which had been established in 1913, was purchased in 1946. Theobalds Park (a National Fitness Site) was also once again made available by Middlesex County Council. Two more sites were leased to the Club by the National Trust – at Polesden Lacey and Oldbury Hill. These, like Graffham, would not be allowed to have permanent campers on site but huts were erected for the storage of kit.

D.A. fortunes were mixed. East Kent had to suspend all camping activities and West Kent, Sussex and Essex were severely limited in where they could go. Camping was virtually impossible in all the southern D.A. areas but most arranged weekend rambles while others organised meets in their own homes. Members had to bring their sleeping bags and their rations. Teesside D.A. had little success with weekend camps but later devised a 'help-the-farmer' campaign, thus bringing out more members with a useful purpose to their weekend camping.

A Northern Section of London D.A. was started in 1940 and from the start it averaged between 20 and 25 campers at its meets. The Section became the North London and East Herts D.A. and was the only new D.A. to be established during the war. Wessex D.A. managed to do a fair bit of camping but Lancs, Cheshire and North Wales D.A. had problems due to ploughing. The fertile

Left: Graffham Club Site – this lovely wooded site in Sussex is perfect for those seeking quiet and secluded countryside. Given to the Club by Hubert Visick in 1944, a memorial shelter overlooks the South Downs. A huge fire on Lavington Common in 1956 jumped the road and spread to the site boundary, but campers and local residents beat out the flames and stopped it reaching the site itself. (P.H. Constance)

Motor-cycles were a very popular means of transport for campers after the war. This one belonged to Bill Sykes, although it does appear to be somewhat overloaded. (Mrs Hilda Sykes, Club Archive)

The President's last Greetings to the Club

TRANSMITTED FROM KENYA, JANUARY, 1941.

THIS is to offer you our hearty wishes for as Happy a Christmas as War will allow and a New Year bright with Promise. Out of evil good will come. We owe a statue to Hitler He has done more than any man ever to consolidate our nation, at Home and Overseas and has given us friends in America and in ALL the countries he has ravaged. Such wide friendship will help to world Peace so soon as he and his war clouds are swept away.

My wife and I, as evacuees, have settled here in Kenya, in the Africa we love, and in the same continent with Peter and Betty and their respective contingents of grand children where we hope that Heather and her husband may join us after their war Service. : As to you Scouts and Guides we are, geographically, more in the centre of things than before, nearer to N. Zealand, Australia, India and the East and not much further from Canada and West Indies than from England . So, from close up, we can watch you all at your various War Services. What you have done you have done well   Stick it out! Play up to the Scouts' slogan "SLEEVES UP! and with TAILS UP   GO TO IT TO WIN THE WAR" And after that to bring about Peace   with goodwill, and happiness for all.

Nyeri . Kenya   Baden Powell   Olave Baden-Powell   Xmas . 1940

The Club President, Lord Baden-Powell of Gilwell, died in Kenya, January 1941, just after the Club had received this message of greeting. Despite his age and failing health he was still able to draw the humorous sketches which were a trademark of his correspondence. (Club Archive)

Cheshire land was needed for more important things.

After the devastation of Coventry in November 1940, the Secretary of the Coventry section of Birmingham D.A., L.H. Sargeant, wrote: "There is still a Coventry and a Coventry Section. I am still able to live at the same address, at least up to the time of going to press. Many thanks for the offers of help from Birmingham friends – fortunately not needed, but very much appreciated.

"In these days of sudden destruction it is essential that each one of us has shelter to go to immediately should our houses be rendered uninhabitable, so please remember the above address. Although – due to the blitz – our family has increased, there is room for more. Further, I should like to formulate a scheme of mutual assistance. Therefore, members who are willing to help others in distress, please let me know, or members requiring a roof – apply to the Honorary Secretary."

Such is the camaraderie of campers that when one is in real trouble, no matter what the reason, another will come to his aid.

D.A.s in areas away from enemy action were, of course, more able to continue camping. Some managed to persuade site owners to allow them use of a site as a semi-permanent or holiday site for two or three months – this helped members to get the most from their camping. Base camps were arranged in several areas well away from the cities targeted by the German Luftwaffe and there was also one in Surrey so that Londoners could get away for a short break. Birmingham D.A., despite being in a target area, managed to organise a Summer camp for factory youth that was continued after the war.

Added to the fact that the blitz on London and other large cities was making travelling extremely difficult, a later Government ban on travelling by private motor transport compounded these problems.

The sections seemed to manage quite well. Canoeing in particular was very popular, with membership of the Canoe-Camping Club actually increasing. The Mountaineering Section managed to have a Christmas meet at Capel Curig in 1941 with 20 members attending despite the transport difficulties. The Folk Group, however, was finding it very difficult to carry on and had to suspend activities for a while. It emerged again in 1943, basing itself at Denham during the Summer.

Regional Groups were later suggested to overcome travelling problems and the lack of a Secretary, but the records show that a London and Home

From the Club magazine

Aug–Sep 1942 *Congratulations: "The Council has congratulated Mr and Mrs P.G. Rivett, popular in Folk Dance circles and as members of the Council, on the arrival of a son and heir, whose enrolment as a Club member at the age of six hours appears to constitute a record for the youngest Club member."*

June 1945 *From the* Victory *edition: "The Council have a most ambitious programme which should result in the Camping Club becoming even more powerful and giving even better service to the hundreds of thousands who will want, once more, to savour the delights of a life under peaceful skies." (Harry Pegler)*

Members of the West Kent District Association on a working weekend at Oldbury Hill, 1946, not long after the site had been made available by the National Trust. (Club Archive)

Counties Group was the only one to survive the war. The Artists' Group, sanctioned by the Council in 1939, was in hibernation having no Secretary. It began in June 1943 and kept going throughout the war. The Photo Group also continued to function, but it was difficult to get films and in some areas photography was forbidden. Nevertheless, both groups survived. The B.C.C. probably had the most difficulties as it was impossible to hold regular meets because of travel restrictions. It was possible to get a caravan towed to a fixed destination but many caravans were offered for war work and were also used to house bombed-out families. Probably the greatest setback came when caravan tyres were requisitioned. With no tyres caravans had to remain static. Members kept in touch and had wartime-style meets, consisting of cycle rides and rambles.

Gas for cooking

A new, small portable cooker using butane gas was launched in 1947. The Weedex cooker had a refillable cylinder and slid out from a metal box size 5ins x 4ins x 14ins and weighed 6lbs 6oz – not exactly lightweight, but portable.

In March 1944 Percy Lindsey expressed concern that the Club was not providing for the cycle-campers who, he felt sure, would increase greatly in number after the war. He and Stephen Hilhouse suggested that an Association of Cycle Campers (A.C.C.) be formed, as a section of the Club, taking the name of the pioneers of lightweight camping. Thus the A.C.C. came back into being in July 1944. By early 1945 it had over 800 registered members.

Tour itineraries were available for those who wanted to tour on their own. Home Tours for groups of members, although planned, did not take off, possibly because members couldn't get enough time off from war work.

Despite the war Club Reunions continued to be held and attracted relatively large numbers. All the Sections put on displays so that members could see what they were able to do, even in wartime. Everyone had to take their gas mask to the Reunions and a venue was always used that had an adequate air raid shelter nearby.

Arrangements were made for Club business to continue "in case of eventualities", and the Club's lease at Grosvenor Gardens was severed, with the co-operation of the landlords, as soon as it could be arranged. Smaller, less costly, offices on the third floor – more suited to the only two staff remaining – were obtained. A big problem for the Club was a large increase in postal charges. Members were asked to enclose return postage if a reply to an enquiry was wanted from Headquarters or any

FREDERICK A. 'Pa' COUSINS joined the Club in 1927 and practised both lightweight and permanent tent camping. He was on the Chertsey Club Site Committee and Camp Steward during the war years. Elected a National Councillor in 1936, he took an active part in the revival of the Association of Cycle Campers. He was Club Chairman from 1960–1962.

Watched by Stephen Hilhouse, Don Langridge demonstrates a flaring Primus stove at a Campcraft Course for prospective Youth Leaders in 1949. (John Corke)

official of the Club. *Camping* magazine reduced its number of pages to keep it within the minimum postage rate. Members were asked not to notify any change of address unless it was likely to be permanent because of the time and cost involved in cutting new stencils and altering records.

Camp and Sports Co-operators was bombed out of its showroom in Newgate Street in 1940 and opened a new one in the same premises as Club Headquarters. Its main offices and factory were moved to Hardwick Street, Finsbury. This was to be its last major move. The showroom was moved to Buckingham Palace Road in 1949.

Annual Reports for the war years highlight the comparatively large donations that D.A.s and permanent sites committees gave to help keep the Club running. Many relinquished all or part of their capitation grants, thus materially assisting Club finances. Any money surplus to the needs of the Club's immediate running costs was invested in 3% Defence Bonds to help the war effort.

At the end of 1940 the Club Chairman, J.A.C. Champion, was sent to Canada by his employers for the duration of the war. His wife, also a member of the Council, went with him. In his absence, Percy Lindsey was unanimously elected Club Chairman, a post he was to hold for nine years.

It was to be expected that membership would decrease during the war and by the end of 1941 almost 50 per cent of the pre-war membership of 8,770 had disappeared. Membership began to increase again in 1943 and it

This ridge tent is typical of the type used by family campers in the 1940s. This is the Gale family at Polesden Lacey. (Photo supplied by G. Montague for the Club Archive)

was noted that more members serving in the armed forces were renewing at the full rate. From the figures given in the Statements of Accounts in subsequent years it is clear that the membership continued to rise. By the end of 1946 it had reached 10,000 and was growing rapidly.

In January 1941 the Club's President, Lord Baden-Powell of Gilwell, died in Kenya aged 83. At the Annual General Meeting (A.G.M.), held just two weeks later, Fred Guppy suggested that a Memorial Fund be established and a camp site be dedicated to Lord Baden-Powell's memory. A later proposal was for a chain of sites to be established, starting with Balmaha – for which a Scottish 'Feu Charter' had been granted giving the Club use of the site in perpetuity. Lady Baden-Powell was very touched by the idea, but requested the site or sites be called B-P Sites rather than Memorial Sites.

By the end of 1941 a total of £500 had been donated to the Fund – a lot of money in view of the war conditions – which was invested in

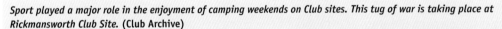

Sport played a major role in the enjoyment of camping weekends on Club sites. This tug of war is taking place at Rickmansworth Club Site. (Club Archive)

government securities until suitable sites could be purchased. Lady Baden-Powell, on hearing of these efforts, wrote: "The chances are I shall land in England sometime, and I shall then be able to supply you with some 'memento' to eventually be put on the proposed memorial site."

When she returned in the Autumn of 1942 she presented the Club with the three-acre paddock at her former home at Pax Hill, Hampshire, to be used as a Club site. This meant the Club would now have three B-P Sites: Balmaha, Pax Hill and Leysdown, which had also been designated as such, half the money for its purchase in 1943 coming from the B-P fund.

Leysdown was out of use owing to war restrictions and had been put under cultivation. It only became available for limited camping in 1946 and was fully open in the Summer of 1947. Unfortunately, the site was very exposed. Numerous bungalows and shacks had been erected all around and it was very difficult to reach without personal transport. Problems of adequate supervision led to the final closure of the site early in 1949. Fortunately, the Club was able to recoup the purchase price plus a small profit.

It was true to say the Club needed camping grounds but they needed to be good ones that would be a credit to camping. Pax Hill, too, was to have its problems but it was in use for eight years from 1945 before, due to unforeseen circumstances, it had to be closed.

In 1941 Percy Lindsey expressed his concern that the Club should be doing more for the youth of the country. Youth organisations took their members to camp at Denham National Fitness Site, where provision was made for youth campers. It was felt that there should be a proper organisation for young campers, under the auspices of the Club, offering training in campcraft. The Club's permanent sites would be used as base camps for groups of Youth members and special Youth committees and Youth Leaders would be appointed. The Youth Camping Association (Y.C.A.) was thus established in 1942.

Young people over the age of 14 were obliged to join a recognised

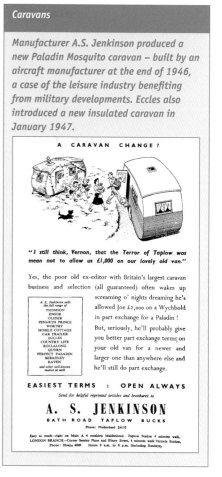

youth organisation or youth club during the war, and the Y.C.A. was available for those who were particularly interested in camping. Provision for the youth was included in the Club's plans for post-war camping. Local authorities were urged to provide camping grounds for young people throughout the country, in addition to the facilities being offered by the Club at its permanent sites. Club members were urged to let their own local authority know of the existence of the Y.C.A, and D.A.s were asked to try and form local mobile youth groups.

In 1943 a Memorandum on Post-War Camping was prepared by the Club. This envisaged permanent camping sites of no larger than twelve acres in size that had essential facilities. They would be located near large urban and industrial areas and at the seaside, perfect for weekend and holiday use. Small 'mobile' sites on farms, in National Parks, on Forestry Commission and National Trust land near places of scenic and historic interest for lightweight and mobile-camping, family-camping, canoeing, caravanning and mountaineering, were also needed.

This Memorandum was placed before the Government's Post-War Reconstruction Committee by the Club Chairman and, despite being "sympathetically and warmly received", it appears to have been completely ignored. "Our open-air friends cannot understand the omission of the Club's name from the Report or the main substance of our advice not having been accepted."

The Club had been asked, as a national body on camping matters, to act as a clearing house on all enquiries regarding camping during wartime. To have its advice ignored was very disappointing. "It becomes clear that a great deal more drive by all lightweight campers will be necessary if we are to obtain the freedom of action and recognition we desire after the war."

In 1944 the Club held a conference on Post-War Camping at which the suggestions in the Memorandum were discussed. Representatives from D.A.s were

Repairing a puncture on the Club Tour of Holland in 1947 on the way to the International Rally at Heemsteede.
(Photo Bill Sykes, supplied by Mrs H. Sykes, Club Archive)

present as well as invited speakers and suggestions were received from
those unable to attend.

Members were asked whether the Club should remain a small,
select Club or cater for all who spent their leisure time away from urban
surroundings, whether in tents or in shacks. Opinions were divided, but all
felt the Club should have nothing to do with camping in shacks. Sheffield
D.A. thought that the Club should cater only for the needs of the mobile
camper and they were not in favour of the provision of more permanent
sites to the detriment of the casual type of site. They thought the two
types of sites were complementary and others supported this view.

It later transpired that landowners were issuing new leases to tenants
that specifically banned camping on their land. Many individual campers
were finding it increasingly difficult to find a suitable pitch when touring.
The Club became concerned over the difficulties pedestrians and cyclists
were experiencing in finding places to camp.

Some suggested the setting up of a Camping Association to provide
for permanent-style camping in all its forms. Club permanent sites were
not intended as long-stay sites and it was undesirable that people "should
be allowed to squat throughout the year". The Club wanted to provide sites

Tea-time at Walton Club Site, 1945. (Club Archive)

for anyone to use, allowing them to benefit from members' experiences
and learn to camp properly.

It was often the non-member of any organisation, be it cyclist or
camper, that gave the activity a bad name, but no-one could be forced
to join a club. Most members agreed there was room in the Club for all
"real campers". If the activity was classed as camping, then it ought to
be brought within the Club, which should develop all forms of camping.
The Club, however, was still a private Club, and as such would not be
allowed to purchase land for use by other than its own members.

At the Club's A.G.M. in 1944 members decided to approve "any post-
war development which will add to the status of the Club as a national
organisation for camping". Proposals were made to establish a non-
commercial association that would operate side by side with the Club to
encourage camping in all its forms and to care for and protect the interests
of all campers, whether members of the Club or not. This would maintain
the traditions of the Club, secure high standards of camping everywhere,
and gain recognition by government departments and local authorities.

A trust company, limited by guarantee, was also proposed. It would
act not only for the Club but also for the proposed national association
and the Y.C.A., and would give the Club charitable status.

First in the field A Century of The Camping and Caravanning Club

To help counteract opposition to camping it was decided to make *Camping* a national magazine to be sold on bookstalls. It would offer advice on how to camp and local councils and farmers could be kept advised of Club policy.

A Special General Meeting (S.G.M.) in January 1945, formulating Post-War Policy, decided "that 'camping' within the scope of the Club shall be defined to include all campers and caravanners who provide for themselves, but to exclude users of fixed structures of any kind".

This was to have a big effect on Club camping in the coming years. The questions of a camping association and trust company were also agreed subject to further advice from the Club's solicitor being obtained. After long investigation the advice was that, as a constituent club of a national camping association, the Club would have to sink its identity, become one of a crowd, and sacrifice once and for all its position as the leading organisation. The Council decided that would be a betrayal of those who established the Club and brought it to its present "high estate". Advice on the trust company was that it would serve no useful purpose.

In 1947 another S.G.M. rescinded the decision to set up a national camping association and a Trust Company, and passed a resolution amending the Constitution to allow the Club to acquire and hold land and incorporate it as a Company Limited by Guarantee. The Company was formed on 10 November 1947.

"Insurance is available against damage..." This picture was taken at the Mobberley permanent site, near Manchester, in August 1943. (Percy Lindsey)

This was immediately followed by a decision to raise subscriptions and site fees, and tighten up on the management of Club sites. For the previous two years the Club had been running at a loss and, although the Club's financial position was sound, in a world of rapidly increasing costs members were simply not paying their way. The Council had been advised to increase the subscription to £1 the previous year but decided that 15 shillings would be adequate. Unfortunately, despite many economies, it was not enough.

Stationery and printing costs were soaring and extra staff were required at Headquarters to cater for the huge increase in membership. Permanent sites appeared well off because no proper maintenance had been possible during the war. They had to pay their way so that maintenance would not be done at the expense of the reserves.

The change of rules on permanent sites caused some dismay, but were deemed essential if the sites were not to deteriorate any more. Because of the war a blind eye had been turned to some practices, especially when bombed-out members had to live on a site in their tents, but it was now essential to show local authorities and Health Inspectors that there were high standards on Club sites.

Legislation again caught up with camping in 1947, when the Town and Country Planning Act became law, with extensive powers given to local authorities to control camping. This Act brought in the 28-day rule, allowing camping for 28 days in each year on unlicensed land without permission from the relevant local authority.

The National Feast of Lanterns in the lovely Surrey countryside at Bagden Farm, Polesden Lacey, 1949 was a big success. (Stephen Hilhouse, Club Archive)

First in the field A Century of The Camping and Caravanning Club

Campers at the International Federation of Camping and Caravanning Rally at Foots Cray Place, Kent, 1948. Foots Cray had been leased to the Club by Kent County Council and remained a Club site until 1963.

The Club was exempted from the provisions of the Act provided it continued to hold a Certificate of Exemption from the Public Health Act 1936. The Member's Undertaking once more had to be revised. Before this Act came into being a number of local authorities were discussing means of providing camp sites on seemingly amicable terms with the Club. Unfortunately, initial hopes for desperately needed sites in many areas faded despite much hard work by the Council and other Club members.

Part of the problem was that the Club was expected to provide the necessary weekend Wardens, and these would have to come from D.A. members, some of whom resented being told to help at these sites. The Club also had to consider the provision of Wardens on its own permanent sites. Walton had reported a number of thefts and permanent supervision was needed. The Council agreed to pay part of the cost, the remainder being raised by a levy on season ticket holders.

After the war, the Council started to hold its June meetings on a Club site. In 1947 the meeting was held at Milarrochy Bay, a great achievement for the newly-established Scottish Council whose hospitality was much appreciated.

The Club decided in 1948 to institute a Regional structure, based on the organisation of the Scottish Council. It was designed to decentralise much of the Club's work and place responsibility for local affairs more in the hands of Club members on the spot.

Up until that time every D.A. was entitled to send a Representative, with full voting rights, to the National Council. Since there were 22 D.A.s, the Council was clearly becoming far too cumbersome. The new Regional structure would allow more efficient operation with each of the seven Regions being entitled to send a Representative to the Council with full voting rights. Club sites had in the past also sent a Representative to the Council, but now the Regional Councils assumed responsibility for those in their respective areas.

It took a year for all the Regions to become properly established and, because the North East Region was very large and unwieldy, the Yorkshire Region was added to the network later in 1949. The Club's honorary officers – cycling, technical, motoring, etc – were entitled to attend meetings but in future would have no vote.

Also in 1948 H.M. King George VI was graciously pleased to become

Here is what was originally known as Balmaha Club Site. Requisitioned for military use during the war, it was returned to the Club in 1946 and is now known as Milarrochy Bay.

Patron of the Club. However, the Presidency left vacant since the death of Lord Baden-Powell, had proved difficult to fill.

Throughout the war, Alex Papps remained Honorary Editor of *Camping*, producing six issues per year. Apart from editorials and reminiscences, most of the content consisted of D.A. and sites notes, although there were some interesting articles about camping in war conditions.

Camping printed detailed instructions on camouflaging tents and how to get the maximum permitted light from car headlamps, which of course had to be shielded so as not to be visible from above. Many articles were printed recalling the pre-war days of camps in Europe, of the Swiss Rally, etc. As in World War One, some old-timers reflected on the camps of much earlier days.

Many of the photographs used for the covers of *Camping* were reprints of those previously used to illustrate earlier articles. All the D.A.s and Sections managed to write encouraging notes in each issue urging members to keep in contact even if conditions did not allow for camping. In June 1945 a special Victory edition of *Camping* was produced, with a full colour cover – the first in the history of the magazine.

In that issue were reminiscences from Alex Papps, Stephen Hilhouse and R.B. Searle, who was still after 25 years the Managing Director of Camp and Sports Co-operators. All three had been heavily involved in the running of the Club during World War One. Technical developments in caravanning by Ralph Lee, canoeing and news of the Photo Group and Artists' Group were included, plus an appreciation of the Club Chairman, Percy Lindsey, by H.W. Pegler, the Club's hard-working Secretary.

HARRY 'Peg' PEGLER was General Secretary from 1934–1958, and helped the Club through difficult years. A South African and a quiet man, he was proud that the Club had grown and prospered under his guidance, and made many friends. He appeared in the first ever television programme about camping and caravanning.

At the end of 1945, at the age of 72, Alex Papps stood down. He had been actively associated with the Club's magazine, either as Editor or on the Editorial Committee, for more than 40 years. His devotion to the Club was rewarded – a Testimonial Fund was established in order to make a presentation to him.

Camping magazine became a commercial operation in 1946, and changed its title to *Camping and Outdoor Life*. Camping and Open Air Press was set up as a limited company to publish the magazine, with the Club holding a controlling interest.

Permanent campers at Walton Club Site enjoying a communal tea-party, 1945. **(Club Archive)**

With the change of title came a radical change of content to make it appeal to the general public. Articles of general interest were included, but information on Club matters was published in a separate leaflet called *Camping Club News*. It was edited by Alex Papps and sent separately to members, who still received their magazine free of charge. Unfortunately, few copies of these newsletters have been kept so there is a gap in recording of the Club history for the late 1940s.

The change-over to a consumer magazine could not have come at a worse time. Shortly after being appointed, the new Editor became ill and died the following year. Paper was very expensive, in very short supply and the quality was extremely poor. Although 12,000 copies were sold in the first year of the new venture this cannot have helped sales. The magazine had a new Editor in 1948, the format became smaller and there was an

Mapledurham – site of the first national meet of the British Caravanners' Club after World War Two.
(British Caravanners' Club Archive)

improvement in the quality of the paper and typography. A greatly improved content, with more emphasis on the Club style of camping became evident.

September 1946 saw the first post-war National Feast of Lanterns (N.F.O.L.) at Aldenham Park. At the N.F.O.L. at Lullingstone Castle the following year a presentation was made to Alex Papps, by then aged 74 and still camping, in front of over 1,000 members. This was the largest-ever attendance at such an event at the time and no one realised just how big the N.F.O.L. would grow. In the following years N.F.O.L.s were held at Theobalds Park and Polesden Lacey, respectively.

The year 1947 was a dreadful year, with one of the worst Winters on record. There was a terrible fuel crisis, power cuts and – when the thaw finally came – floods, rain and burst pipes. Yet despite all this, the Club's membership figures soared to 11,000, with applications pouring into Headquarters at double the 1946 rate. It should be remembered that new applicants had to be recommended by an existing member. The Club announced a Fund for Farmers to help those who had suffered through the bad weather earlier in the year. It was one way of returning their hospitality to members who were able to camp on their land during the war.

Exhibitions had been a regular feature of Club activities before the war so in 1947 a small exhibition was held at the Tea Centre in Piccadilly, London. It was reasonably successful. The Club sponsored and took a stand at a Health and Holidays exhibition in London the following year. At this exhibition the Club arranged a public meeting to call on the Government to implement legislation in regard to National Parks, Footpaths, and Access to the Countryside. The Act was finally passed in 1949.

Touring abroad was quite impossible during the war but news of overseas clubs and personalities trickled through. Sweden and Switzerland both sent greetings to members who had been on tours to their countries, although letters took months to reach London. The Spanish clubs had begun camping again after the terrible Civil War and a Portuguese club was established in 1944.

Despite being occupied by the Germans, news from Holland reached the Club to assure members that some Dutch camping friends were well. The Club later heard that the Nederlandse Toeristen Kampeer Club (N.T.K.C.) President, Professor Dresden, who was Jewish, had been taken to a concentration camp in Germany. He survived the war and everyone was delighted when he made the opening speech of welcome at the first post-war International Rally at Heemstede, Holland, in 1947. This event was originally planned for 1940 and because much work was done before Holland was invaded the N.T.K.C. had lost quite a lot of money. Despite these problems, plus rationing being in force, they organised a good Rally.

In 1948, the International Rally was held in England to coincide with the Olympic Games. The Club had organised a site in Bushy Park but,

Family Camping at Llangollen, North Wales at the end of the 1940s. **(Club Archive)**

First in the field A Century of The Camping and Caravanning Club

as late as the end of June, plans had to be abandoned. The Rally was finally held at Foots Cray Place, Kent, with a subsidiary camp at Henley. The 1949 rally was held at Fontainebleau, near Paris, and over 400 Club members went to France to enjoy the scorching hot weather.

The year 1949 was the best ever for the Club. It now had 12,000 members and the number of renewals was greater than ever before. Renfrew D.A. was established in Scotland and Teesside D.A. was revived.

It was also the end of an era for the Club. Percy Lindsey stood down as Chairman after nine consecutive years. He had piloted the Club through the difficult days of the war, through all the plans and pitfalls of legislation and reorganisation and had continued with many other duties as well, not least as Honorary Tours Officer. He had already organised tours abroad after hostilities – to Holland and Switzerland in 1946 – as soon as it was possible to go. Plans were well in hand for many more interesting tours that he would in many cases personally supervise. All was set for the next half-century.

George and Florence Montague in fancy dress at Polesden Lacey Club Site National Feast of Lanterns in 1948. **(Photo supplied by the late G. Montague, Club Archive)**

Motor caravans – from austerity to boom by Chris Burlace

A custom-built 1957 Landliner, with a body by Lasts of Chelmsford based on a 30cwt Commer.

This do-it-yourself model was first completed in the early 1950s, it was later cut in half and lengthened. It uses Austin mechanicals.

Unwittingly, the British motor industry, with the introduction of 10-15cwt vans with pressed-steel bodies such as the Morris J-Series and Bedford's CA, was sowing the seed for the development of more affordable motor caravans. Volkswagen (V.W.) began selling its Transporter in 1950 and just a year later caravan makers Westfalia unveiled its Camping-Box conversion.

In Britain, a car was liable to the old Purchase Tax. A van – not liable – became a car if side-windows were fitted. Caravans, however, escaped the tax. Customs and Excise drew up regulations – cooking facilities, a 6ft bed, prescribed wardrobe space, etc – by which a vehicle qualified as a caravan and was tax exempt.

Peter Pitt was first to launch a V.W. conversion in 1956. Maurice Calthorpe showed his Bedford Home Cruiser at the 1957 Ideal Home Exhibition, and Martin Walter Ltd., which already had its Dormobile with seats converting to beds, added the extra features to meet the Customs and Excise requirements. Home Cruiser and Dormobile both had raising roofs to provide headroom.

The Purchase Tax hurdle was just one that had to be overcome to make the post-war motor caravan an attractive proposition. What about road traffic law? Light commercial vehicles (and cars with caravans) were limited to 30mph. Would that still apply after conversion? To instigate a test case, Peter Pitt drove his V.W. around Windsor Great Park where commercials were prohibited. Sure enough, he was stopped and prosecuted but he won his case. Motor caravans were now subject to the same speed limits as cars.

By the end of 1957 six firms were offering conversions on Austin, Morris and the newly-arrived Ford 400E vans as well as V.W. and

This display at Turners of London in the late 1960s includes, from left: Bedford Dormobile Romany; Bluebird Wanderer, Auto-Sleeper and Canterbury Commers; Dormobile Roma on a Bedford Beagle base in front of a Bluebird Highwayman; Transit CI Wayfarer; Car Campers Commer; and a Bedford CA Dormobile Debonair.

Bedford CA. By 1962, when 24 converters were listed, the Standard Atlas and the Commer had been added. Commer, incidentally, was the only motor manufacturer to produce an own brand motor caravan. From 1958 coachbuilt models joined van conversions in the fast-growing market.

Van conversions were dominant in the first 25 years after World War Two. Dormobile was the number one marque and the V.W. came to be the most successful base vehicle, with over half of the market by the early 1970s.

The Paralanian was the first series production post-war coachbuilt. A quality two-berth, it cost nearly £400 more than Bluebird's Highwayman four-berth. It was built initially on the Austin 152 but later mainly on Commer and was priced at £870 on its debut a year later in 1959.

Kingscote & Stephens Ltd produced the Cotswold motorhomes – another quality marque. The Series C made its debut in 1962 on an Austin 152 and with bodywork particularly well styled to that of its base vehicle. It won high praise in a report in *Autocar* (that magazine together with *Motor* gave good space to motor caravan features in the 1960s). Cotswold built on the Ford Transit later in the decade and its flagship was the Series D on a BMC FG four-litre ambulance chassis. In 1968 it cost £2,950 for this 20-footer. Other large coachbuilts of the 1960s were the 21ft Adventurer on a 30cwt three-litre Commer chassis built for Wilson's Motor Caravan Centre, Brixton.

At the other extreme, of course, were the coachbuilt Wildgoose creations. These were built in Worthing based on the famous BMC mini-van. The Popular version had an elevating roof for headroom where needed, and the Brent an inner shell winding up with the rooftop to almost double internal space.

Bluebird added a new coachbuilt model following the arrival of the Ford Transit. Its side-entry Sprite was well specified and even boasted a shower in its toilet cubicle – fill the sink with warm water and an electric pump delivered it to the shower head!

However, history ends on a high note in the early 1970s. That was the boom time for motor caravan sales, reported to have reached around 15,000 units per year, although no official figures exist. Then came Value Added Tax and car tax – both imposed on motor caravans – an oil crisis and a recession. After that boom, motor caravans never had it so good again.

Pitt sold out to Canterbury and this model is on a 1967 V.W.

A 1966 Airborne. The four front seats converted to two single beds, the couch extended to make a double.

Just a one-off, the 1967 Jennings Roadranger on a Vanden Plas Princess.

What's in a name?
Motor caravan constructors were often as inventive with their names as with their designs. Bedmobile, Sleepa-Kar, Slumberwagen and Auto-Sleepers (the only survivor into modern times) implied a good night's sleep; Autohome, Autochalet and Carawagon were obvious combinations; and Car Campers direct, if short on imagination.

1950–1960:
A Golden Jubilee and
50,000 members

Rationing was still in force as the Fifties began. Sterling was in crisis and overseas travel was severely limited by currency restrictions. This decade was to see the death of the Club's Patron – a beloved King who had never expected to accede to the throne. Both celebrations and problems would affect the Club.

The Golden Jubilee would be celebrated in 1951, at the same time as the Festival of Britain. High costs due to devaluation would lead to financial difficulties, several Club sites would close, and could not be replaced. The Baden-Powell Memorial Site at Balls Park, Hertford, would open and Headquarters would move to Old Kent Road. A phenomenal growth in Club membership would see the total rise from 13,000 in 1950 to 51,000 in 1960, and the Club would mourn the loss of Stephen Hilhouse, Percy Lindsey, Alex Papps, Harry Pegler and R.B. Searle. Even more controls on camping would be introduced.

The Presidency of the Club had remained vacant since 1941 and King George VI suggested that it might well be that one of the Club's own members was deserving of this honour. Clearly, Stephen Hilhouse was such a man and he was elected President at the 1950 Annual General Meeting (A.G.M.).

A record 500 members attended that meeting, many intent on getting the statement that "as a matter of policy the Council has decided that Club

In the wider world

A second Great Exhibition: One hundred years after the Victorian's Great Exhibition, the King and Queen opened the Festival of Britain on 27 acres of what was bomb-derelict land near Waterloo. Nothing remains of the Dome of Discovery or the Skylon, just the world-renowned Royal Festival Hall.

Petrol rationing ends: In 1950 the first Whitsun holiday since petrol rationing ended brought out traffic described as an all-time record. Queues stretched out of London for ten miles and hotel share prices rose. Petrol had been rationed for ten years.

East coast devastated by floods: In February 1953 hurricane force winds and high tides brought disaster to Britain's east coast, where collapsing sea defences along the coast from Lincolnshire to Kent flooded vast areas and killed over 500 people.

Vivat Regina: May 1953 saw the Coronation of Queen Elizabeth II, who went on holiday as Princess Elizabeth with her husband the Duke of Edinburgh, and returned as Queen following the death of her father, King George VI. Coronation Day was marked by the news of the conquest of Mount Everest by Hillary and Tensing.

Small, and smaller still: 1959 saw the birth of the Mini, the British car described as being bigger inside than outside. Even smaller were the latest radio receivers using transistors instead of valves. A handbag-size model weighed just 7lbs.

Left: Members of the 'mobile group' of the Youth Camping Association at Walton Club Site, 1950. (Club Archive)

sites to be acquired in the future shall be administered mainly in the interests of mobile camping" deleted from the Annual Report, but they were unsuccessful. Many permanent campers wanted more permanent sites, not less, because members with families and with no transport of their own often relied on this type of site so they could leave their tents erected for the whole camping season and occupy them for weekends and holidays. It must be said that there were also many families without transport who regularly camped lightweight and who felt they were treated as second class campers when using some of the permanent sites.

The Council's view was that the Club's growth was based on mobile camping and this declared policy had gained it exemption from the Town and Country Planning laws. It was the Club's strongest negotiating card and was the basis of all efforts to counter the disrepute brought upon the good name of camping and caravanning by colonies of immobile moveable dwellings. The Club dared not allow its own sites to be confused in the public mind with such colonies so it had to remain geared towards mobile camping. "The protection of our interests compels us to disassociate the Club from them and the problems they create."

The Scottish Burghs threatened to restrict camping and, despite great efforts by the Scottish Region, the Club was unable to obtain an amendment to give exemption from the new Act, which it had had in the past. Effectively it meant an end to the use of unlicensed sites in and around Edinburgh and much of the surrounding countryside. The Club's exemptions under English law did not, of course, apply in Scotland,

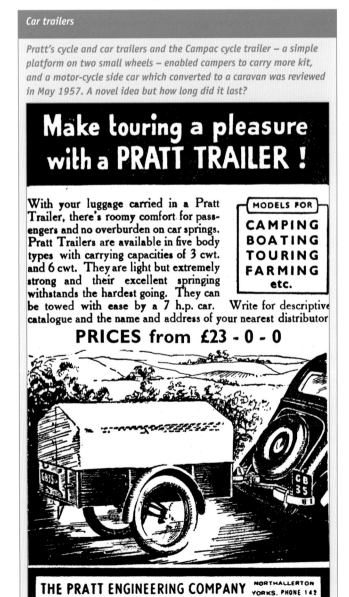

Car trailers

Pratt's cycle and car trailers and the Campac cycle trailer – a simple platform on two small wheels – enabled campers to carry more kit, and a motor-cycle side car which converted to a caravan was reviewed in May 1957. A novel idea but how long did it last?

Make touring a pleasure with a PRATT TRAILER !

With your luggage carried in a Pratt Trailer, there's roomy comfort for passengers and no overburden on car springs. Pratt Trailers are available in five body types with carrying capacities of 3 cwt. and 6 cwt. They are light but extremely strong and their excellent springing withstands the hardest going. They can be towed with ease by a 7 h.p. car.

MODELS FOR
CAMPING
BOATING
TOURING
FARMING
etc.

Write for descriptive catalogue and the name and address of your nearest distributor

PRICES from £23 - 0 - 0

THE PRATT ENGINEERING COMPANY NORTHALLERTON YORKS. PHONE 142

Typical 1950s set-up: large ridge tent with extended flysheet sheltering a large kitchen and living area – a typical permanent pitch. **(Club Archive)**

so this was a big blow to the Club and a huge drain on the fighting fund. It was imperative to boost the fund considerably in order that such bills could be challenged and to stress yet again the fact that the Club catered only for those who used tents or caravans "for recreational and instructional purposes".

Caravans were defined in 1951 to include "any horse-drawn caravan, motor caravan or motor trailer, especially built for use as a mobile caravan, conforming in all respects with the requirements of the Road Traffic Acts". For a number of years the Club had not admitted motor caravanners but those owning such vehicles were soon to be seen on Club sites, although as yet not in great numbers. Only converted vehicles in which it was possible to stand up were classed as motor caravans, any other vehicle designed for sleeping in being classed as a car and therefore ineligible for use on Club sites.

Local authorities and government departments still did not appear to understand the difference between the Club's style of camping and the collections of wheel-less caravans, shacks and bell tents that were used for residential purposes or let for holiday camping.

From the Club magazine

May 1954 *Club sites: "Regional Councils shall have power to authorise a capital expenditure of a maximum of £50 per annum to each site under their jurisdiction. Expenditure in excess of this amount must be referred to the National Council."*

December 1959 *Account of a winter camp on Yes Tor, Dartmoor: "During the night drinking water froze solid in the buckets and rime formed on the inside of the tents. The temperature was estimated at something like 20°C below freezing. Eggs had to be thawed as they too were frozen solid in their shells!"*

In 1953 the Report of the Central Committee on Camping Legislation stated: "It is clear that in every part of the country the interests of mobile and recreational campers and caravanners are being seriously prejudiced by the vast numbers of fixed caravans, shacks and other structures which masquerade under the name of moveable dwellings. Almost as much harm is done to mobile camping and caravanning by the large number of sites engaging in holiday letting, which tend to develop into holiday camps, and it is inevitable that local authorities, in the stress of coping with these various needs, tend to overlook the requirements of genuine mobile campers. There is the grave danger that true mobile camping may be smothered by planning, however well-meaning."

The Club was vigilant in watching for any restrictions that might appear as a result of the proposed Town and Country Planning Act. The danger was that where public sites were established local authorities might restrict occasional camping on unlicensed sites or impose extra conditions on existing sites. Every effort was made to explain the needs of "mobile, self-contained campers and caravanners, and emphasise our objection to regimentation". Regional Councils, it was hoped, would be able to assist in putting these views to their local authorities and keeping an eye out for local bye-law notices.

This lovely view of the lake at Horsley Club Site in 1950 shows some of the permanent caravans pitched where today (left) the reception and toilet buildings are situated. **(Club Archive)**

Taken at the inaugural meet of the Bedfordshire, Cambridgeshire and Hunts District Association at Little Paxton, in 1950. The photo shows the newly-elected officers and committee. Front, left to right: Peter Rowell (Honorary Secretary), Woodbine Haylock (Chairman), Bill Todd (Honorary Treasurer). Back, left to right: Committee members W.P. Kingdon, Enid Gill, Fred Day, and Mrs Haylock.
(Biggleswade Chronicle and Bedfordshire Gazette)

Concern was expressed in 1954 regarding lack of provision for mobile tent campers, particularly in seaside areas, where planning consent was often given for sites exclusively for the use of caravans. The Central Committee on Camping Legislation suggested that, as a condition of planning approval, at least 20 per cent of the land should be reserved for mobile tent campers.

Although the response was said to be "encouraging" there is little evidence that these suggestions were put into practice and since the Fifties it has been very difficult for the genuine touring tent-camper to find a pitch in many popular seaside areas. Throughout the land the lightweight cycle-camper or backpacker is even worse off, since he cannot travel as far as a motorist, and all tenant farmers of the National Trust, plus those of many other large estates, are prevented by their tenancy agreements from allowing casual campers to spend even one night on the property.

More local authority bills were introduced to try to control the use of moveable dwellings in their areas. These were closely monitored and where necessary counsel were briefed to appeal against them. Most authorities, but by no means all, accepted the Club's view that genuine mobile camping and caravanning should not be penalised and gave exemptions to those belonging to recognised organisations.

The Caravan Sites and Control of Development Act, brought before Parliament entirely as a consequence of the huge development of residential and holiday caravan sites and their attendant problems, was passed in 1960 despite strong representations by the Club and other organisations concerned with caravanning. A completely separate system of controls for caravans was introduced. The exemption of individual Club members under the previous Health and Planning Acts now disappeared in relation to caravans, the Club's exemptions now only applying to sites under its control. It became essential for the Club, as an exempted organisation, to provide many more sites under its control for the use of caravans. Consequently five-'van sites were introduced. The Club still had the right to manage its own sites without being licensed by local authorities, and unlimited numbers of caravans could use a piece of land for up to five nights for Club caravan rallies.

The Regional Councils took much longer than expected to become fully operational, only Scottish Region (which had a head start) and North London and Eastern Counties making any real progress. It wasn't until the end of 1953 that all were working successfully. A new Regional Constitution was approved in 1954, the aim being to spread the burden of administration and to give Regional Councils wider control over Club activities in their areas. They organised National Feasts of Lanterns (N.F.O.L.s), helped to find and run new sites for the Club and protested against restrictions. The Regions also began to arrange the Club's A.G.M.s, some of which for the first time were to be held outside London.

The number of District Associations (D.A.s) grew rapidly, with 15 new D.A.s and two revived ones getting off the ground in the 1950s. Birmingham D.A. celebrated its Golden Jubilee and Sheffield its 25th anniversary. In 1958 it was noted that some D.A.s were growing so large that it might be necessary to divide them into smaller units – Staffordshire D.A. was the first new D.A. to be formed after this proclamation.

The Club had to exercise the utmost economy in its business activities and relied heavily on enthusiastic volunteers. The future of the Club's development would

Tents

Benjamin Edgington introduced a simple frame tent in May 1955 and Pindisports advertised the continental Auto Tents in 1956. The latter were to prove extremely popular in the next few years, with British companies making similar models. Marechal frame tents were first advertised in Camping and Outdoor Life *in September 1957.*

BY APPOINTMENT
TO H.M. THE QUEEN, TENT AND FLAG MAKERS

BENJAMIN EDGINGTON
(Silver & Edgington Ltd.)

**69 GREAT QUEEN STREET,
KINGSWAY, LONDON, W.C.2**
Telephone: HOLborn 6070

"THE CONSORT"
THE **HEADLINE** TENT WITH **HEADROOM**   Wt. 28lbs. **£20.12.0**

For full details of this and the range of the WORLD'S BEST TENTS
and SLEEPING BAGS, etc., send for FREE fully illustrated catalogue.
5% DISCOUNT TO MEMBERS

| 18 ARWENACK STREET, FALMOUTH, CORNWALL Phone: Falmouth 1134 | 2a EASTCHEAP, LONDON, E.C.3 Phone: Man. House 0814 | 18 LLOYD STREET, ALBERT SQUARE, MANCHESTER, 2 Phone: Deansgate 4949 |

Despite the development of frame tents, lightweight camping was still very popular. The Association of Cycle Campers' Easter Rally was held at Calverton in 1956. (Club Archive)

"depend on an increase in the number of these helpers". Total membership was 13,783 in 1950, of whom 8,569 were full members, and it was hoped to increase this number to 10,000 within the Jubilee year. Unfortunately, the full membership only increased by 80, so the dream was not realised. The increased rate of renewals was encouraging, especially in view of the financial constraints placed on many citizens.

Stephen Hilhouse, Club President, speaking at the opening of the Balls Park (Hertford) Club Site in 1953. Olave, Lady Baden-Powell can be seen just behind him. (Club Archive)

On joining the Club new members were asked for a member's reference and had to state the length of their camping experience, if any. By the beginning of the 1950s many were allowed to join without a reference and with no camping experience because of the need to have a large body of membership to back up the fight against punitive legislation.

Unfortunately, the standards of camping practiced by those who were not Club members were poor. Indeed reports of bad camping by members reached Headquarters in 1952. This could have had a very detrimental effect on the Club's ability to sustain its exemptions so the Council decided to issue a leaflet – *Good Camping* – to all new members. Articles on good camping practice were included in the magazine, which by then had ceased to be available on the bookstalls. Despite this, standards were beginning to fall and letters in *Camping and Outdoor Life* reflected this problem. Members were anxious to maintain quality rather than quantity but the Council felt an increase in membership was essential and that "standards would improve because new members would see for themselves the best way to camp". Unfortunately, this did not always happen.

New developments in camping equipment changed the scenes on camp sites. The first frame tent advertisement appeared in the Club magazine in May 1955 – a simple square tent with a conical roof from Benjamin Edgington, followed by a similar one from Blacks the following year. Two large French-style frame tents were seen on the Polesden Lacey Club Site in 1954.

One unforeseen problem was the arrival, with the frame tent, of

Left: Originally known as Balls Park Site and opened in 1953 as a memorial to Lord Baden-Powell of Gilwell, President of the Club from 1919–1941, it is the Club's largest site, with 32 acres of grassland. Now redeveloped, Hertford is a most attractive site within easy reach of London but it still has a good country feel about it.

sewn-in groundsheets. These also started to be used in lightweight tents. The groundsheets could not be taken up to air the ground, resulting in large dead or dying patches of grass where a tent had stood for a week or more. A simple change of rules to ensure such tents were moved after one week would have gone a long way to controlling this problem but campers were now using so much equipment that re-siting would have been a major operation and such a rule would have been very unpopular. Permanent tents on some Club sites already had to be moved every four weeks. Most of these had removable groundsheets or duck-boards allowing the ground to be aired to a certain extent.

Large frame tents and Camping Gaz cookers began to arrive in force in 1958. The arrival of these products was reflected in the huge growth of camping – but camping of a different style to that which many members recognised. Some of the old hands did not approve, although others were converted. More and more people wanted to camp and more and more joined the Club. Stark warnings about camping controls were regularly appearing in the press, making it even more likely that people would opt to join a club.

By 1952, membership had reached 15,000, with a total of over 400 youth members joining the Camping Club Youth (C.C.Y.) in its first year. Increased renewals kept the membership above 15,000 the following year, although new membership was down, a matter for great disappointment.

The Club was unable to renew the tenancy of Box Hill site in 1950, and in 1952 the Redhall site at Edinburgh – a council-owned site administered by the Club – and the Carbeth site were both closed. The Club also lost the use of the site at Lower Burleigh but acquired a piece of land on the Isle of Man for lightweight camping.

In 1952 a new 30-acre site was found at Balls Park, Hertford. This was to be the Baden-Powell Site and was opened by Lady Baden-Powell in June 1953. The site at Pax Hill, her former home, had been returned to the Girl Guides Association the same month. Unforeseen

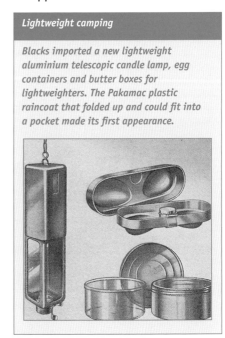

circumstances had forced them to put the house and surrounding land on the market, and it could not be sold without the inclusion of the three acres that the Club had been given. An intensive search was made for replacements for all the sites lost since 1950 but these efforts met with no success.

In 1957 Matt Smith, a member of the Glasgow and the West of Scotland D.A., and a group of volunteers began to develop Ardgartan site. Up to that time it had been under-used and access was difficult because of poor forestry roads surfaced by logs laid by the Forestry Commission. Matt organised the work of building new roads and a new toilet block, as well as completely re-building

Published in 1951 this leaflet outlined the benefits of Club membership emphasising the exemption from restrictive legislation. At the time it cost just £1 to become a full member, but family members paid extra. (Club Archive)

the derelict boat house as a wet-weather shelter. His volunteers also cleared the site of brambles and scrub to make more pitches, and improved the site drainage.

This work, mostly done by six permanent caravan owners meant that a greater number of permanent campers were able to use the site, thus bringing in more finance as well as more volunteer workers. To obtain a permanent pitch on Ardgartan members had to take part in the working party weekends but Matt insisted that the site was for all members – not just the 'perms'. Improving the site enabled more mobile campers, especially those coming to Scotland for their holidays, to use the site.

Voluntary work was the way in which all the early Club sites were developed. Dedicated teams of volunteers often permanently camped on the sites. Sites such as Graffham, Oldbury Hill and Polesden Lacey, which did not allow 'perms', were maintained by volunteer teams from D.A.s, which formed Site Committees to oversee the work.

In the case of Graffham, the first Site Committee was established by the Association of Cycle Campers (A.C.C.), whose members were very fond of the site. Buildings on Club sites were erected by volunteers, although some professional help was given. A memorial shelter at Graffham was dedicated to Hubert Visick, who gave the land to the Club.

Dogs – or perhaps it was their owners – were beginning to cause problems on some sites, and the rule that dogs must be kept under control was changed to read that they must be kept on a lead and under control at all times.

The Club magazine improved once more, with many articles showing the best ways to camp and a woman's page was introduced.

In 1951 there was a detailed article by the Editor concerning *Freedom to Camp*, which included a report of a conference of regional officials who were briefed concerning possible legislation and what to look out for. Many non-members read the article and wrote in to say how impressed they were with the Club's work as they had not realised that independent campers could benefit from Club membership. It was emphasised that more than two thirds of Club members preferred camping on their own and did not take part in local activities.

A coach was organised to take members to the International Federation of Camping and Caravanning Rally in Belgium, 1958, after which a tour was made to Germany and Denmark where this photograph was taken. (Pauline Rook, Club Archive)

CAMPING – ODENSE 1958

A view of the National Feast of Lanterns, Trent Park, Cockfosters, London, 1951. **(Club Archive)**

The article and subsequent letters resulted in another boost for Club membership. A special Jubilee issue, in June 1951, was full of nostalgic articles by, among others, Stephen Hilhouse, H.P. Mitchell (who joined in 1901) and Alex Papps. There were also earlier reminiscences by the late W.F. Skinner in which he mentioned the incident when he was almost arrested as a spy while camping at Land's End in 1914. Ralph Lee described caravanning, past and present, and Archie Handford wrote an interesting article on T.H. Holding.

In 1952 *Camping and Outdoor Life* once more became a members-only magazine. All Region and D.A. information, Headquarters notices, tours information, etc was published in the main body of the magazine, with no more loose copies of *Camping Club News* to mislay. Three volunteer Editors followed in quick succession until 1958 when Alan Ryalls took over the reins as Honorary Editor.

By this time concern was growing about permanent sites. A member complained that Ardgartan was "fast becoming a caravan park even though caravans dominate two other sites in the vicinity". Another complained of loud radio noise and talking after 11pm – which he had never encountered on a Club site before – and asked that the Code for Campers be printed once again in the magazine.

Another asked why the Club could not provide more sites for tents only, and yet another complained of the large number of caravans using the Holding Memorial Site at Clent Hills. It appeared that the interests of the mobile camper were being swallowed up in favour of the permanent camper. The Club was seen as providing benefits for those only interested in a cheap holiday and not for the more enterprising camper.

Not all Club members wished to camp on Club sites or with the District Associations. Here, two members are camping in windy conditions on Swinhope Moor using Tinker and Arctic Guinea tents from Thomas Black & Sons. (Bryan Miller, Club Archive)

"When the Club's attention appears to be fixed on the more unenterprising forms of camping its reputation suffers, and already one meets many keen campers who fail to appreciate that the Club is, in fact, interested in what they term 'real' camping. Nor is it easy to convince them otherwise from the written record."

After all this correspondence, the Editor asked members for their views: "Should we be more selective or restrictive in our membership? Can we continue to cater for all types of camper and yet give real service to each? Does the Club really succeed in educating the novice camper to a reasonable standard?" A two-guinea prize was offered for the best essay on the subject. The winner, *A lightweight camper looks over the fence*, was a thought-provoking essay written by a member of the Surrey D.A., who was also a prominent member of the

A.C.C.: "My immediate reaction was that a marvellous opportunity had been offered for a frank, logical and ruthless 'clean-up' of our organisation – the chance to cast away the 'perms', cut loose the caravans and return to the mobile lightweighters their rightful inheritance. As I pondered on the method of attack, gradually the realisation dawned that to take the

Wash day at Balls Park in the early 1950s – Hilda Sykes and her daughter, plus nappies. (Club Archive)

offensive would really be a revolt against the Club itself, not just a section of the so-called 'over-privileged' members.

"The Constitution of the Club is not specific as to the meaning of the word 'camping' and by this very fact it is impossible to say whether mobility, for example, is the main object of our organisation. The Club's aim is to help all to enjoy the open-air life by means of camping and kindred activities, and to stimulate the invention and adoption of appliances for camping. It must surely be admitted that these clauses can embrace every possible aspect of camping by virtue of the words 'to help all', 'kindred activities' and 'appliances for camping'.

"The word 'camping' springs from *campus*, the Latin word for a field. Military camps, explorers' base camps, and even Roman soldiers' camps were all just that, and some were very permanent. It cannot be said that only a nomadic existence in tents constitutes 'camping'.

"Times have changed since the Club was founded, and it has had to keep pace with modern trends. It would be of no great advantage to anyone in the long term to split into smaller specialist Clubs, even if it could be done. Personal viewpoint is the crux of the problem, and every member should learn to 'live and let live'. Everyone has a reason for their particular style of camping, and we should not be critical.

"There is surely plenty of room in this country for all members of the Club – whether 40,000 or 50,000 souls – to enjoy camping in their own particular way without clashing with those of different tastes. Provided everyone observes the Code for Campers, what does it

The Club's Golden Jubilee in 1951 coincided with the Festival of Britain. The design of the commemorative pennon reflects this, with the Festival emblem prominently displayed in the centre.

When Club Headquarters moved to Old Kent Road in 1955, temporary membership cards were issued showing the new address. The subscription was still £1 for a full member.

matter if many only join to spend a mere two weeks camping holiday once a year, or if many others prefer permanent sites or comfortable caravans? They pay their subscriptions and appropriate fees for the facilities they enjoy and, remember, they leave the rest of the year and the rest of the country free to the light-weighter."

The question of equipment was another topic of correspondence. In 1953 members asked why there were no British tents like the continental ones seen at the International Rallies, and how could a newcomer discriminate between good equipment and poor quality stuff?

John Jackson, of Jackson and Warr, a quality camping retailer, remarked that continental tents were designed for the continent, and British tents for our own islands. He had had to replace many broken and bent poles of continental tents damaged during rough weather at the Sidcup International Rally!

John Jackson offered a prize of five guineas for a new tent design that was not merely a modified version of current well-tried designs. He pointed out that the quality of British tents was the best in the world although the manufacturers seemed content to stick to the old designs. One suggestion was that the Club should re-introduce its Awards of Merit and Certificates of Fitness so that every potential purchaser would know what was good and what was not. Unfortunately, this suggestion was not followed up. Archie Handford wrote to say he still had, and used, his original home-made tent

Spriggs Alley – a special permission site, 1953. (Club Archive)

Friends lightweight camping at Triberry, Germany. (Club Archive)

designed by Holding and made with his help. One wonders what R.B. Searle would have said, but by then he was very frail and died in December 1955.

With the hope that international camping would become a normal activity again, the Council proposed that the German Camping Club be invited to send a party to England in 1950. Members spoke both for and against the motion at the A.G.M. that year. One man turned the majority in favour – a pre-war refugee from the Nazis, now naturalised, most of whose relatives had died in concentration camps. "It is the only way," he said, "to show them how democracy works."

With the end of petrol rationing in the same year, members were soon able to extend their horizons. Some 300 British campers went to the International Rally at Spa in Belgium, which coincided with some of the worst internal clashes ever known in that country. Some Club members had to make long detours to avoid trouble spots, while others managed to get into Luxembourg and hitch a lift on some of the Italian coaches going

Sports Day at Rickmansworth in the 1950s. (Club Archive)

Stephen Hilhouse at the National Feast of Lanterns, Stratford, 1955. (The Birmingham Gazette and Despatch Ltd)

to Spa. For once, the British contingent was not the largest overseas one. In 1950 the number of Dutch members exceeded those of the British. All who went had a good time.

The first overseas Club tour by charter plane took place in 1951 when a group of members flew to Helsinki to tour Finland and Finnish Lappland. Unfortunately, the plane that should have brought the party home was not as large as the one that took them out and a few members were "unavoidably delayed in Finland"! It seems the company had allowed for the number of passengers, but not for the volume of their camping kit.

A total of six foreign tours took place that year and it looked as though the pre-war enthusiasm for such events would soon revive. Fourteen tours were arranged for 1952 and 15 for 1953. By then prices for travel were rising steeply but the number of tours planned – still around twelve each year – seemed to attract sufficient numbers. Even more motorists were going independently, particularly to International Rallies but the coach and train trips still remained popular. Another charter was arranged by Silver City from Lydd to the Rally at Saarlouis in 1955.

The whole Club, and in particular the international tour parties,

First in the field A Century of The Camping and Caravanning Club

suffered a devastating blow early in 1956 with the sudden death of Percy Lindsey. He had already arranged seven tours for the year. Miss Marion Dennis, an accomplished linguist and a regular member of the Club's foreign tours, took over the job of Honorary Tours Secretary in 1957. This was the year in which the Club introduced a combined Holiday Travel Insurance, giving cover to members should they become ill when overseas. The large number of individual campers going abroad prompted the Club to publish its first overseas sites list, *International Camping*, in 1960.

The International Rally was once more held in England, in 1959, when the Club organised the Rally at Oaks Park, Carshalton, with 4,500 campers attending.

Many successful camping exhibitions were held before World War Two and in the 1950s the Club was again to become involved. For the Club's Golden Jubilee in 1951, which coincided with the Festival of Britain, the Club arranged demonstrations in the Sporting Arena on the South Bank site. Several members erected their own tents and displayed their kit. Club members answered questions from the public and, although the display took place during the opening weekend, it was quite successful.

In June 1952 the Club had a stand at the Food Fair at Olympia. It was

Ethel and Leon Starkey, outside their own home-made tent, Windsor, 1954. **(Club Archive)**

honoured by a visit from the Queen, who was shown round by Stephen Hilhouse. This was one of her first official engagements after the death of King George VI, who was succeeded as the Club's Patron by Prince Philip. In January 1959 the Club again sponsored an exhibition – the Camping and Outdoor Life Exhibition at Alexandra Palace. Despite appalling weather, with snow, fog and ice, some 50 members camped in the grounds in 20 tents during the middle weekend. The show was a resounding success for both the Club and the camping trade, which was there in force, and it set the scene for more exhibitions in the years to come.

The Club played a large part in the training of teachers in lightweight camping at courses arranged by the Ministry of Education and other bodies. A leading light in this venture was Don Langridge, the Club's Vice-Chairman, who had greatly inspired members of the Youth Camping Association (Y.C.A.) at Denham, where he started his Club camping during the war. Sadly, he died very suddenly in November 1959, aged only 57.

At the end of 1950 the National Council invited the Y.C.A. to come fully under the Club's umbrella and officially become the Youth Section of the Club. It was pointed out that the Y.C.A. was established as a separate organisation in 1942 in the expectation that grants would be forthcoming and that in post-war years it would make rapid strides to become a truly national organisation for young campers. In fact, this had not happened,

Decorated tents were a feature of the National Feasts of Lanterns. This is at Debden Green, 1952. **(Club Archive)**

First in the field A Century of The Camping and Caravanning Club

Stephen Hilhouse's last camp at the National Feast of Lanterns, Manton Forest, Nottinghamshire, 1958.

the only grant being one for foreign travel that only benefited a few members. The Association had not grown into a national organisation, most of its activities were based on Club permanent sites around London.

Efforts to form local groups outside the London area had not succeeded and only about ten per cent of the membership bothered to take the Test of Good Camping. As it stood, the Y.C.A. was never going to be financially independent of the Club. Headquarters staff already did much work for it free of charge. Very few Y.C.A. members joined in D.A. activities or became full Camping Club members, most preferred to go off on their own. The Club felt that a separate Youth Section within the Camping Club could offer more opportunities for development than the present Y.C.A. In this way it could extend training and activities into the D.A.s and it was felt that D.A., Club Site and Section committees would feel a closer bond with, and responsibility towards, young Club members than they did towards Y.C.A. members.

Percy Lindsey, founder of the Y.C.A. and still its Chairman, was very unhappy about the idea. He felt that the Y.C.A. had always worked with the parent body, and as such, being tied to a private Club, had not attracted grants from philanthropic societies. Membership had been badly affected after the war by National Service and the lack of adult leaders. He did not accept that young people wanted to be "tied to the apron strings of an adult order", and he did not think that a Youth Section of the Club would fulfil the same purpose as the Y.C.A.

For their part, the Y.C.A., after discussions with a delegation from

National Feast of Lanterns, Debden Green, 1952.

the National Council, decided that it could not accede to the Club's proposals. Its decision was accepted with regret. All services hitherto rendered to the Y.C.A. by the parent club were withdrawn in September 1951 and the National Council began work with the formation of a Club Youth Section. The rules for membership were published in March 1952.

N.F.O.L.s continued to grow in both popularity and size. In 1951 the venue was Trent Park, Cockfosters, and in Coronation year, 1953, it was at Mapledurham, Oxfordshire. In 1954 the new Baden-Powell Site at Balls Park was the N.F.O.L. choice, and in 1955 it was Stratford-on-Avon Racecourse, the furthest north it had ever been held. It was to go even further north in 1958, when Sheffield D.A. organised the N.F.O.L. at Manton Farm, Worksop. Nearly 5,000 members attended the event. In 1960 the N.F.O.L. was held in the west country at Rood Ashton, Wiltshire. Numbers were down because of poor weather on the days leading up to the event, but over 3,700 campers were present, mostly in tents.

In June 1955 Club Headquarters moved to Old Kent Road, near the Elephant and Castle. The new premises were obviously cheaper as they away

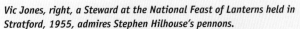
Vic Jones, right, a Steward at the National Feast of Lanterns held in Stratford, 1955, admires Stephen Hilhouse's pennons.

from the more expensive Victoria area, but they were not convenient for the members who needed to visit Headquarters. Harry Pegler, the General Secretary of the Club, continued in office until December 1958, when he retired at the age of 68. His successor, W.T. Rainford, previously the Deputy Secretary, had already been appointed in the previous August.

The two men worked together until the end of the year. Sadly, Harry Pegler did not have much time to enjoy his retirement, he died in October 1959.

The year 1959 also saw the death of Stephen Hilhouse, the Club President, who had worked so tirelessly throughout his life for the Club. He was succeeded as President by J.A.C. Champion, the Club's International Officer and a President d'Honneur of the International Federation of Camping and Caravanning (F.I.C.C.).

This year was another landmark for the Club – the first holiday and touring site opened at Norman's Bay, near Pevensey. This was the first site to be geared specifically to holidays. It had a resident Warden on the site. It was a tent-only site and members could not stay longer than 28 days in a season. No permanent tents were allowed and there was plenty of space for touring campers. The venture was so successful that it was followed in 1960 by a site at Slapton which would also accept a few caravans. These sites were, of course, strictly for members only.

The year 1960 began with another very successful Camping and Outdoor Life Exhibition, this time at Olympia, and another good programme of foreign tours was planned. Alex Papps, perhaps the most tireless worker ever for the Club from the time he joined in 1902 until July 1960 died in September. He continued to hold office as Honorary Club Librarian right up to two months before his death at the age of 88.

It was the end of an era, no original Club members were still alive, the last of them having passed away during this decade. In the last ten years membership had risen from 15,000 to 51,000 – one wonders what these pioneers of the Club would have thought

Hampshire District Association's Christmas Party in the village hall at Bentley, Alton, 1952.

Tourers from the 1960s
by Andrew Jenkinson

Swift, Ace, Mardon, Elddis, Fleetwood, Royale, Silverline, Viking and Lunar were just some of the names that became established in the decade that saw caravan production increase on a yearly basis. Ci had been formed with its takeover of Eccles in 1960 and merger with Bluebird in 1963. Founder Sam Alper also took over Fairholme, a respected Cardiff manufacturer, in 1965 to add to his caravan empire.

"Hey lady, your outfit clashes with the interior somewhat" – inside the Eccles Topaz from 1968. Modern and clean design interiors made the Eccles a big favourite amongst club members.

Alper also bought out foreign manufacturers such as Wilk (still known today as Ci) in Germany as well as opening new tourer manufacturing plants in the rest of the world. Thomson too was breaking production records with 2,000 being made at its Scottish plant in 1966.

Smaller concerns were setting up to compete with the bigger tourer makers, such as father and son team Siddle and Ray Cook with their mid-priced Elddis clubman tourers in 1965. Ken Smith, with his wife Joan, began the famous Swift brand back in 1964 producing the Swift Flying Clubman series.

As Hull, East Yorkshire, was becoming "caravan city" the north west saw Lancastrian manufacturers Knowsley produce mid-priced popular clubman tourers.

The Ace Airstream from 1969 with glass-reinforced plastic (G.R.P.) front and rear panels which caused quality problems with leakages. G.R.P. – being used on a medium-priced tourer – panels were ahead of their time .

The 1960s saw some early "swinging tourers" with some ultra modern interiors. Reg Dean, who served his early days working for Sam Alper, took the 1963 Eccles tourers by the scruff of the neck and redesigned the interiors using white plastic wall coverings and teak-veneered furniture. Dean moved over to the makers Lynton in Manchester and gave the range a classic new exterior and also an Eccles interior to boot.

Over at Astral and Bluebird a slight American influence was in progress, with both companies marketing Luton top rear end door tourers in the early 1960s. Both flopped in the market so the idea wasn't tried again. Trendsetting continued with the Siddall Delta caravan, which boasted continuous roof lockers and a rectangular profile – designed by Conran it was too radical and didn't sell.

The Bluebird Europe 1 from 1966, designed for small car towing.

Mid-priced caravans in the 1960s still boasted fitted carpets, water pumps (hand or foot operated) 12V interior light, awning channel, and "stable towing" as selling points. By the end of the decade another feature was added to this list – pre-finished acrylic exterior panels. Up to this time most caravan manufacturers had their own spray booths – a time-consuming and expensive operation, plus the paint usually peeled off in later years. So this advance in technology was a major breakthrough although some of the smaller makers carried on into the early 1970s with spray-painting.

Construction was very traditional, with wood framework and glass fibre matting wedged in with hardboard fixed to the interior and the outer aluminium skin screwed into place. Insulation was also a major advance, with at least the walls and roof being insulated. Thomson used mineral wool produced exclusively for them, while tin foil and polystyrene were also favourites. Interior woodwork was, in many cases, real wood that was topped with melamine for work surfaces. In those days caravans were used until around early October and put away till Spring, with only the hardened caravanners using them in Winter.

The 1968 Eccles Moonstone – a 13ft family tourer, whose shape was distinctive and modern.

Sites were basic in many ways with just a toilet and wash basin being the only luxuries and those that did have these facilities charged around five shillings a night. Many caravanners then, my parents included, would stop in a quiet lay-by for a weekend, getting provisions from a nearby farm – very back to basics!

The British Caravan Road Rally was in full swing in this era, with cars towing caravans round a race track and then going on a rally route. Many caravans came back in a sad state – but it was all good fun. The 1960s saw caravans develop slowly but the industry was nearing its strongest position with many U.K. tourers ending up in Belgium, France, Germany, Holland, Italy and Scandinavia – those were the days.

1961–1970:
Sixty glorious years –
and lots of milestones

The culmination of 60 years existence was celebrated in a rather muted manner. Special Regional events and the National Feasts of Lanterns (N.F.O.L.s) were prefixed by the wording Diamond Jubilee and a Club pennon was designed to celebrate the occasion. There was also a Club Reunion at Alexandra Palace, but unfortunately we have found no reports of what actually went on. This was, in fact, the last Reunion to be held by the Club. In June 1961, Capt. D. Frazer-Allen, who had done much research about T.H. Holding and the beginnings of the Club, suggested a plaque be affixed to the bridge at Wantage close to the site where the first camp was held in 1901 and it was placed in position in July the following year.

In 1961 an avenue of lime trees was planted at Balls Park (now re-named Hertford) site in memory of some of the Club's outstanding pioneer members. Unfortunately, only two trees survive and only the lower stake of one of the plaques remains embedded in the base of one tree. The magic '60' was reached in Diamond Jubilee Year with a membership of over 61,000. Although there was a drop in membership at the end of 1962, the growth recovered until in 1970 membership reached 110,000.

One sad note was that in August 1961 W.T. Rainford, the Club's General Secretary, suffered a stroke. Although he returned to work on a part-time basis for a short while in 1962 it was clear he would not be able

In the wider world

First man in space: For 108 minutes the Russian astronaut, Yuri Gagarin, circled the Earth before returning safely. During his flight he reported on instrument readings and what he could see, but did not control the spacecraft during orbit.

Mersey beat: Although an undoubted success on Liverpool's music scene, the Decca record company's experts believed the Beatles would never make it to the music charts. Manager Brian Epstein and the Fab Four considered producing their first album themselves.

State funeral for a commoner: Led by the Queen, representatives from almost every country and from the royal families of Europe mourned the passing, at the age of 90, of Sir Winston Churchill in January 1965. The state funeral service in St Paul's followed three days of lying in state in Westminster Hall. Tributes to Churchill's leadership through two world wars and many times of crisis came from all sides.

There really is a man in the moon: 21 July 1969 was the day on which the world watched on television as American astronaut Neil Armstrong set foot on the surface of the moon, soon followed by colleague Edwin "Buzz" Aldrin.

Left: Washing up on the Lindsey Field, Chertsey, 1965. (Photo Mrs Langton, Club Archive)

to continue working and he took early retirement. He died in May 1969.

The Club's priority was to seek out new sites for members, especially in popular holiday areas, and a record number of 22 new sites was acquired between 1961 and 1970 including several provided by local authorities.

The 1960s proved to be a trying time as far as legislation was concerned. The Club set up a Joint Standing Committee with The Caravan Club to deal with common problems including those caused by legislation. Proposals were made for joint action by the two clubs in establishing a federation of camping interests to promote united and concerted action on policy matters by all user bodies. Thus the British Federation of Camping and Caravanning was founded in 1963. The Joint Standing Committee remained, but it would only meet to discuss co-ordination and agreement on specific policy matters as they arose.

Go-Placer trailer tent

A streamlined trailer which, when closed, could hold equipment for up to five persons and capable of carrying a 12ft sailing dinghy on top, was shown at the Camping and Outdoor Life Exhibition in 1961.

Article Four directives were increasingly being invoked as a means of controlling camping and the Club was extremely concerned. Such directives could nullify the Club's exemptions, therefore reducing the capacity for camping in popular areas. Several attempts were made to enforce these directives in south west England, where it was already difficult to find sites close to the seashore. If enforced, members would have to find sites at least two-and-a-half miles from the beach. Fortunately, the Club was successful in opposing a large number of such applications. In 1965 the Ministry of Housing and Local Government Report stated that the Club should have the opportunity to comment on proposed Article Four directives. Members of Parliament (M.P.s) who were Club members offered to help oppose them where necessary.

The Club continued to oppose all attempts at restrictive legislation against camping, including the implementation of local byelaws. Some planning officials were also allowing extra caravans to be sited on many existing sites but were rarely providing for extra tents, thus causing real problems in certain areas.

A number of local authorities were approached in 1961 with the suggestion that if they could provide a site the Club could help with its management. Some local authorities also approached the Club to ask if they would develop a site themselves and make it available to all-comers. Clearly, the Club was not happy about using members' money to develop sites to be used by non-members. It did, however, welcome the opportunity of co-operating with those local authorities who were prepared to develop sites for the Club to manage. The Club was quite prepared to offer advice but felt that sites wanted by local authorities for public use should be paid for by the authorities themselves. The first council to provide a site for the Club to manage was Folkestone in 1965.

A Memorandum on Camping was submitted to the Minister of Housing and Local Government. A deputation from the Club to discuss the matter was "well received" by the Minister, who was said to be favourably disposed towards camping. The Club was later asked to submit recommendations for sanitation standards suitable for various types of site.

At the end of 1963, L.M. Wulcko retired from his appointments as Secretary to the Central Committee for Camping Legislation and as the Club's Parliamentary Officer, posts he had held for 35 years. The Club would miss his great expertise but he was prepared to remain as an ordinary committee member for the time being. George Cubitt, appointed General Secretary in September 1963, took over as Secretary to the Central Committee. A Parliamentary Agent was also appointed in place of an Honorary Parliamentary Officer. The Central Committee was finally wound up in October 1966 when the fighting fund of over £5,000 was transferred to The Camping Club. A special account was opened for

From the Club magazine

January 1961 *No frills please: "I decided to try one of the popular butane stoves... On the second day I was back to lighting a fire... I had bought a paraffin pressure stove. I am wondering if all the frills that camping has grown since I started are really any improvement."*

November 1961 *Are we losing the best people?: "Let us get away from the mentality which segregates perms from non-perms, and caravans from lightweights, and simply make it radios-and-dogs, and non-radio-and-dogs."*

January 1967 *The life of canvas: "How much modern equipment will be in use 60 years hence? My advice to these campers with old tents is look after them and keep them for happy camping."*

GEORGE CUBITT M.B.E. joined the Club's staff in 1958 primarily to help organise the 1959 International Rally but was soon absorbed in general administration. He was appointed General Secretary in 1964 and served the National Council and all committees of the Club as well as closely supervising all aspects of its administration. In the 1960s he saw the Club grow to the point where it was hard to believe the frustrations he and those before him suffered as growing pains.

In 1958, Headquarters was under-staffed and under-resourced, and all paid staff "had to do as they were told by the elected officers". This did not engender the kind of loyalty which might have been helpful in difficult times. It was due to his efforts that attitudes changed and the divisions became non-existent.

As Secretary General, he represented the Club on many outside bodies, including the Central Council of Physical Recreation of which he was Deputy Chairman, Chairman of the Outdoor Pursuits Division for many years and a member of the Executive Committee. He also played a vital role in the activities of the All-Party Parliamentary Group. He is an Honorary Member and a Vice-President of the Club.

With the advent of the Mini car, extra space was needed to carry the larger and heavier camping kit being used. This Turtle Top Campers' model roof rack appeared in 1969.

the fund, and a Camping and Caravanning Liaison Committee was later set up to carry on the work of the old Central Committee.

In 1966 the All-Party Parliamentary Camping and Caravanning Group tabled a motion in the House of Commons calling on the Government to sponsor a camping site in the heart of London. Later that year The Caravan Club asked The Camping Club for a grant of £12,000 towards the provision of a site at Woolwich. The Club offered to take a half-share in the project, equally sharing all capital expenditure, running expenses, profit, losses and general management but leaving the day-to-day management with The Caravan Club. The offer was not accepted and subsequent negotiations with other bodies enabled The Caravan Club to proceed without the help of The Camping Club.

At the same time The Camping Club was negotiating with London County Council (L.C.C.) – later to become Greater London Council (G.L.C.) – to open a site in Hainault Forest, which the L.C.C. was very keen to have. After many objections and petitions they finally lost the battle at the Committee stage in Parliament, without the views of the Club or the G.L.C. being heard. This was a great disappointment to both organisations after the end of two years' work, during which a considerable amount of time and money had been spent.

The Club's General Secretary wrote that the Club had learned an important lesson, that any weak points in the case would be fully exploited by Counsel for the opposers, so the Club would need to be especially careful in the future. It was clear that "a lot more public relations work was needed to make the general public understand the needs of campers, as it was evident during the whole history of this case that most people have little idea of camping except the fallacy that we are noisy, untidy, vandalistic and beauty-destroying people. Despite much verbal support from leading personalities of all political parties and other bodies connected with land use, the fact remains that nothing has been done, nor looks like being done in the immediate future to promote better mobile camping and caravanning facilities in Britain. We are sick and tired of making excuses, not only abroad but at home also, for the inadequate facilities in Britain."

A Caravan Club Working Party report published in 1967 implied that greater control should be exercised over tent camping. The Club's views on this matter were circulated to interested Ministries and other bodies. There were constant reports after this in the national press that tighter controls would be introduced and that tents would be brought under similar control to caravans.

A Development of Tourism Bill was introduced in 1969 and the Club's

Tents

Tentomatic tents were first advertised in 1967 but the advert did not show the tent!

When camping at Graffham one year, a member came to the Steward for help. "'We've got a new tent,' he said. 'We got it up, but we can't work out how to get it down.' It was a Tentomatic, and we never saw them get it packed before we had to leave, but it obviously was taken down eventually."

Known throughout the international camping movement as 'Uncle and Auntie Plum', Mr and Mrs Plumridge of Cranleigh, Surrey, were the Camping Club's oldest camping couple in 1966, and had just celebrated their Diamond wedding. They had camped at 21 of the 26 International Federation of Camping and Caravanning Rallies held up to then. (Club Archive)

"What a mess." Sorting out the gear for a week's camping holiday in Cornwall involved packing up a perm pitch for this camper. (Club Archive)

views were given to members of the All-Party Group. In the House of Commons several M.P.s stressed the importance of camping in the field of tourism. A network of transit sites for tourists, near main towns, was proposed but this came to nothing despite the obvious need for such sites.

The National Council agreed to oppose any amendments to the 1960 Caravan Sites and Control of Development Act that may affect tents in the same way as caravans, and to press for separate legislation to deal specifically with touring tents and caravan matters, thereby keeping the legislation apart from that dealing with static or residential 'vans.

In 1970 the Ministry of Housing's Working Party report was published. It stated that tents should be subjected to the same type of control as exercised over touring 'vans, on the grounds that there was no difference between modern tents and caravans. The problem was that they had only thought of exempting from the proposals "Expeditions", as an activity of youth organisations. No consideration had been given to the needs of adult or family cycle-campers or backpackers. It was suggested that a maximum of five units (tents and/or caravans) could use an unlicensed site, but a licence would be required for more than this number.

The needs of backpackers and cycle-campers, both individuals and families, were brought to the notice of the National Council by the Association of Cycle and Lightweight Campers with the suggestion that "small" tents should not be counted in the five units. The Club pointed out that there might well be a crisis and a great shortage of sites if these restrictions were brought in too quickly and notified the Ministry of these problems.

Canoeists were having difficulties in the north-west of England, particularly on the River Ribble, where they were being prevented by anglers from using a large part of the waterway. Canoeists had been using the rivers for years and the Council and Headquarters staff promised to use their endeavours to support their claims. Eventually, access agreements were sought through Lancashire County Council, which accepted "in principle" the need for access agreements to allow canoeing on the lower reaches of the Ribble.

Two Club Holiday and Touring Sites – West Runton and Culzean – were opened in 1961 but the Club was to lose its popular London site at Rickmansworth. London County Council gave Rickmansworth Urban District Council (U.D.C.) a grant of £9,000 towards redevelopment of the Aquadrome. It was stated that: "Rickmansworth U.D.C. will continue to develop outdoor activities that have previously been provided for public enjoyment."

The land occupied by the Club site was apparently to be used for fishing and games. No provision was made for camping and the Club had to vacate the site by 31 December 1961. The L.C.C. was informed of the

Chertsey Club Site always held an annual regatta, and some weird and wonderful outfits appeared on the Thames. Visitors on Chertsey Bridge in 1964 look down in amazement at the caravan afloat. (Mrs Langton, Club Archive)

The Motor Caravan Section, founded in 1963, has become one of the Club's largest Special Interest Sections. This early motor caravan belonged to National Councillor Jack Avery. The extension tent virtually doubled the accommodation and provided a useful pitch marker when the 'van was driven away. (Bob Reynolds, Club Archive)

termination of the Club's tenancy, and was asked for any assistance it could give, but it was unable to help. In any event, the L.C.C. was unable to persuade Rickmansworth U.D.C. to continue to provide a camping site. All efforts made by the Club to secure another site in the area came to nothing.

Another interesting development was the opening of Damage Barton Holiday and Touring Site in 1962. A private site, it would be operated as a lease and service site by the owners for Club members only.

A dispute over the ownership of a small piece of land on a Club site and the eventual sale of a piece of land on the same site, led to the necessity of registering all titles and land owned by the Club at the Land Registry Office. This would prevent any further disputes, which could continue at some length and cost the Club dearly in legal fees.

The Club was anxious to obtain sites in the Lake District, and were co-operating with the National Trust over the provision of a site in Borrowdale. However, local residents – already being plagued by overcrowding on illegal sites including common land by non-Club members – opposed the plan. The Club and National Trust views were that, although there was a problem with camping in this area, the provision of a properly wardened site would help to control the situation. After a meeting of the Lake District Planning Board, at which the General Secretary of the Club was present, an application was submitted for planning permission for the site. Unfortunately the decision was "deferred". It had been suggested that the proposed site was unsuitable and trespass on commons and other land

Left: This lovely site at Blackmore, Worcestershire was officially opened in 1969, one of a complex of three sites made available by Worcestershire County Council, the other two being operated by The Caravan Club and Worcestershire Girl Guides. Originally an army camp and with views of the lovely Malvern Hills, it has been landscaped into a number of informal camping areas, broken by trees and hedges.

The Association of Cycle Campers held its Diamond Jubilee Rally at Charlton, near Wantage, in 1961, not far from the site of the first A.C.C. camp in 1901. (Fred Frost, Association of Lightweight Campers Archive)

had been caused by the practice of closing down sites which were "too visible". The Borrowdale site was later abandoned in favour of a new Holiday and Touring Site at Grizedale in 1963.

On a lighter note, negotiations for a site at Dunstan Hill were in progress during 1963 but doubt was expressed as to whether the site could possibly be a paying proposition. Fortunately, this view was not unanimous and the site was opened in 1964. Foots Cray closed in 1963, as Kent Education Committee needed to use it for schools camping, and again no replacement site was available.

In 1965 the Club stated that it was "the proper function of the Club to manage and administer sites on behalf of national organisations, local authorities and other approved bodies". It also reiterated the urgent need for Club holiday sites. In the same year, Vic Jones suggested that holiday meets should be organised by District Associations (D.A.s) and Sections for Club members, especially in the peak holiday season. Details of two Temporary Holiday Sites (T.H.S.s) were published in the Club magazine in May 1967. It had been planned to list all of them and an article about them in the June magazine but this never materialised.

The Club began to purchase more sites and land for sites and a Sub-committee was set up to consider

Car-top tents

First shown at the Camping and Outdoor Leisure Exhibition in 1967, these were amazing frame tents that attached to the roof rack of a car. A ladder was used to climb into the tent. Similar models were made by other manufacturers.

This is a car-top tent still in use by a Club member.

Club site fees which were "absurdly low". Many protests were received, but the costs of development were high. Official bodies envisaged sites of a high standard, in many cases higher than those found on the best Club sites, and modern campers demanded more facilities of a higher standard than were acceptable in the past. It was considered fair that site users should finance the sites rather than finance them by raising the Club subscription. It was felt that fees should be competitive with those charged at other sites in the localities of Club sites.

Some of the permanent site committees complained that it was unfair to charge for amenities that had been installed by voluntary labour at little or no cost to the Club. Before the end of the decade a paid Sites Manager was working at Headquarters. Chertsey Club Site was being redeveloped as an international site, which would be managed by the Club's Site Committee and not by the South East Region, as in the past. Season tickets would no longer be available on the site.

Extra land adjacent to Kelvedon Hatch Club Site was acquired in 1966 and land at

The Club Chairman Pa Cousins (left) and his family joined the Association of Cycle Campers for their Diamond Jubilee Rally near Wantage. (Association of Lightweight Campers Archive)

Hopping Farm, Youlgreave, was purchased the following year, when the Club also bought Slapton and Llanystumdwy sites. A new lease was being negotiated for Denham site but the G.L.C. wanted the Club to replace chemical toilets with W.C.s with provision for 150 units. The Club was concerned at the high cost involved, especially as only a 21-year lease was proposed. In view of the short term of the lease and the prohibition of caravans, the cost of complying with the terms of the lease was outside the Club's capabilities. However, the site remained open for the time being.

Sutton Hill Club Site was opened in 1968 and received a Civic Trust Award the following year for the design of its amenity buildings. Another Club site in Scotland – Barns Ness – was officially opened in June 1969, and was the first to receive a grant under the Scottish Countryside Act. Blackmore Club Site was opened on a site shared by Worcestershire Girl

Guides and The Caravan Club; this was later to receive a Duke of Edinburgh Countryside Award.

The Club got a shock in 1968 when it heard that a compulsory purchase order was likely to be raised for the Clent Hills site, as it was intended to build a reservoir there. Another enquiry into the proposed reservoir, which would affect the site, was held in the summer of 1970. Fortunately, the results of geological tests proved that the ground was too porous, and therefore unsuitable for a reservoir – the site was safe.

In January 1970 it was announced that no new season tickets would be issued for any site and that all seasonal pitches would cease at the end of the 1973 season, although this would be reviewed at that date. Until that time only those with season tickets in 1969 would be allowed to continue to hold one. The control of all Club sites was transferred to the Sites Management Committee in November 1970.

The 1960s were also times of great change within the Club's organisation. The offices in Old Kent Road were earmarked for demolition in conjunction with a road-widening scheme and the Club would once more have to find new premises. Unfortunately, costs in London were soaring so it was decided to look for premises in the suburbs where the rents would, theoretically, be cheaper.

Several premises were inspected, but nothing suitable was found and the matter became urgent. Eventually, a property was found in Lower

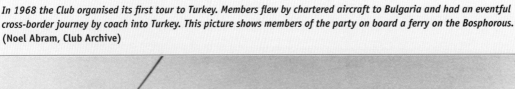

In 1968 the Club organised its first tour to Turkey. Members flew by chartered aircraft to Bulgaria and had an eventful cross-border journey by coach into Turkey. This picture shows members of the party on board a ferry on the Bosphorous. (Noel Abram, Club Archive)

Many new District Associations were founded in this decade. This picture shows the founder members of Lakeland D.A. at their inaugural meet in April 1969. (Ken Crawley, Club Archive)

Grosvenor Place, Victoria which seemed suitable and the offices moved there in June 1963. Unfortunately, the cost of the lease would affect Club expenditure on other matters. A maisonette above the offices was part of the deal and this was let as a residence.

At the end of 1970 planning permission was obtained to turn the top three floors of the building into office accommodation. Better offices were needed but the cost of office accommodation in central London was beyond the means of the Club and this was the best solution which could be found. The Club was able to obtain some compensation for the loss of its Old Kent Road premises, although the figure was lower than it had wished for.

It was decided that the Club should provide a publicity and information service to organisations interested in camping and to the press by producing regular information sheets and special press notices. Publicity improved by the mid-1960s and in 1966 the Club sponsored a radio programme about camping on *Radio 390*.

A lunch for 31 guests to promote National Camping Week was held at the Café Royal in May. The chief guest was the Minister for Land and

Early frame tents were very simple, often square in shape with no windows. This Bukta Kingfisher tent, made in 1960, was still in use in 1974 when this picture was taken. (John Birrell)

Natural Resources. National Camping Week itself was a great success, gaining much good publicity – and new members – for the Club and congratulations were offered by the All-Party Camping Group.

Exhibitions organised by the trade were supported by the Club. During 1968 the Club promoted Campers' Week, designed by the Public Relations Committee to put camping more firmly on the map of Britain and to bring local authorities, landowners and local dignitaries into direct contact with well-practised modern camping and so correct any misconceptions still held. These old-fashioned prejudices had held back the development of the camping sites so badly needed to cope with the

Folk Dance and Song Group at Blockley, Easter 1965. (Pete Mac)

expansion of the game. Over 100 meets were organised throughout the U.K., the aim being to have 100,000 Club members camping with the Club during that one week. The week was successful and was to be repeated in the following year. The appointment of a Press Officer was considered in 1969, but was not implemented.

In 1967 W.V. Jones advocated the Club change its name to make it clear that the Club was concerned with both camping and caravanning, as outside bodies assumed the Club was only interested in tent-camping. However, his suggested title of The Camping and Caravanning Club of Great Britain and Ireland was not available for registration.

At that time the Club staff were having difficulty processing membership applications and renewals, and it was suggested that volunteers should be recruited to help the Club in this work at busy times, particularly as some Sections were unable to obtain up-to-date details of their membership. That same year it was decided to keep computerised membership records and there would be a complete change in the Membership Subscription structure. Special subscriptions for members of the forces had been withdrawn in 1962 and the new subscription would cover the husband or wife of the full member together with children up to the age of eleven. Older children would have to pay for Youth membership. All those over 18 would need to become full members, with the exception of Youth members who had passed the Camping Test before their 18th birthday – they could continue with Youth membership until they

This commemorative pennon was produced to celebrate the Camping Club Diamond Jubilee in 1961.

were 21. These new rates were to be introduced in 1969. It was suggested that a twelve-month subscription from the date of joining should also be introduced but the National Council rejected the suggestion.

Proposals for the future development of the Club were discussed fully in 1969. It was stated that the Club must take a more business-like approach towards administration and become more efficient. For this it was necessary to employ adequately qualified, experienced and competent staff. It was decided that the staff and salary structure should reflect this to offer it as an attractive career. It was also necessary to maintain the Club as the premier camping organisation of Great Britain, improve services to members and intensify public relations activities.

There would be new committees, including Sites Management and Sites Development committees, an International Committee, a Public Relations Committee and a Disciplinary Committee. The Finance and General Purposes Committee would become the Management Committee. Twelve new Regions were suggested. Smaller D.A.s were required and a Boundary Commission was set up to examine Region and D.A. boundaries. Representatives of Regions and of Sections with more than 3,000 full members would have a vote on National Council, and other Sections could

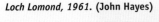

Loch Lomond, 1961. (John Hayes)

Cuppa at Kielder, 1961. **(Photo John Hayes)**

send a representative in an advisory capacity. The major policy of the Club
would be to acquire sites – preferably freehold – to safeguard the future of
the Club and provide a vital service to members. Club units would also be
encouraged to provide T.H.S.s but the arrangements would first have to
be approved by the National Council's appropriate Sites Committee.

At the same time as these proposals were made it was agreed to
produce a Club publicity film. However, a suggestion that the Club
should acquire its own computer instead of using an outside company
was considered to be "impracticable".

Just after these proposals were approved in 1969, the Club President
J.A.C. Champion died. He had a long association with the Club during
which he had made vital contributions to its development. Special mention
must be made of his work abroad where he was held in very high esteem.

In June of the same year the Council accepted an offer from Black
and Edgington, a leading supplier of camping equipment, to present a
Chairman's Jewel to the Club.

Concern was expressed in 1961 at the small number of members
participating in Club tours. It was suggested that two types of tours should
be planned – one for those interested in party tours and one for those
interested in independent foreign touring, with separate planning meetings
for each category. The new Tours Secretary proposed that the Club should
look at broadening the basis of tours programmes. Consideration of the

Youth members at Chertsey, 1965. (Mrs Langton, Club Archive)

International Committee's idea that a foreign touring department be set up at Headquarters was deferred until the policy for the future of the Club was discussed. An air tour to Canada was arranged for July 1967, with over 300 members filling two chartered planes. It was fully booked well in advance and had a waiting list of 150 people.

To satisfy the charter regulations, the Social and Cultural Section was formed and at the same time the Tours Committee was disbanded. In 1968 a Club tour to Turkey was arranged and, although there were some hiccups with the transport, everyone seemed to have a good time. Sterling devaluation did, however, affect air charter prices with possible cost increases of at least 14 per cent. A tour to Canada and the United States for that year had to be cancelled because of lack of support.

Members continued to attend the International Federation of Camping and Caravanning (F.I.C.C.) rallies, with a large number going to Lake Balaton, Hungary in 1966. British campers received a trophy for the largest total number of miles travelled by individual campers to the Rally. The International Youth Rally was held in England in 1967, and in 1968 over 800 British campers went to Norrköping, Sweden, for the F.I.C.C. Rally. Of these, 166 had booked through the Club, which had organised a coach party.

In 1969 more than 13,000 campers attended the rally held at Woburn Abbey, organised by the Club in co-operation with other members of the British Federation. In 1969 the proposals for a foreign touring service were adopted and the Club's Carefree travel service was brought into operation the following year. This was operated by means of commission-earning activities, such as booking ferry crossings, insurance, etc, and was another landmark for the Club.

In 1966 the F.I.C.C. Caravan Commission tried to bring about some international standardisation of laws and regulations concerning mobile caravanning. Britain in particular was asked to give details of experiences with static caravan sites as they affected the availability of touring pitches. In 1969, a common International Carnet (F.I.C.C., A.I.T. and F.I.A.)

D. 'Del' FRAZER-ALLEN, T.D., F.R.G.S., joined the Club in 1948, and researched much of the Club's early history. He traced the exact location of the first camp at Wantage and the commemorative plaque on the nearby bridge was his idea. A lightweight camper and expert on tent fabrics, he was for many years the Club's representative on the International Federation of Camping and Caravanning Tent Commission.

was introduced and Capt. D. Frazer-Allen, who was by then the Advisory Officer to National Council of the Association of Cycle and Lightweight Campers and an expert on fabrics used for tents, was appointed Chairman of the F.I.C.C. Tent Commission.

On the home front, the Club lost more of its hard-working members. Bill Ferris, Chairman of Scottish Region, died as he was getting ready for a special dinner at which – unbeknown to him – he was to be given a presentation. Bill Austin,

a dedicated cycle-camper and Youth supporter, also died. The Austin Trophy, competed for by Camping Club Youth (C.C.Y.) groups every year, is a permanent memorial to his memory. E.K. Blyth, who had been the Club's Honorary Solicitor for many years, also died during the decade.

W.L. "Bill' AUSTIN, was a keen cyclist who helped to revive the Association of Cycle Campers in 1945. He was a Club delegate to the General Assembly of the International Federation in 1949 and took the lead in establishing the Camping Club Youth in 1952. He was Club Chairman from 1953–1956. After his death the Austin Trophy (below) was given in his memory, and it is still competed for annually by Camping Club Youth.

On a brighter note in 1970 Bill Whiteman, a member for 37 years, over 25 of them as a Vice-President of the British Caravanners' Club (B.C.C.), was given Honorary Club Membership. He was also President of the F.I.C.C. Caravan Commission, a specialist on caravan law and a leading campaigner and journalist in the caravan field. At the same time, Ralph Lee, at that time already a Club member for 50 years and the current President of the B.C.C., was also given Honorary Club

membership. It was proposed to nominate both men as Vice-Presidents of the Club at the next Annual General Meeting (A.G.M.).

The number of D.A.s was growing rapidly. South Yorkshire and East Essex D.A.s were founded in 1961, and Gloucester in 1963 with the consequent re-naming of Bristol D.A. West Wales D.A. was founded in 1964 and in April 1965, Central Lancs D.A. and Northern Ireland D.A. were approved, followed by South Lincs in 1966.

Leinster D.A. (the only D.A. ever to be founded in the Republic of Ireland) was started in 1967, as was Hereford and Worcester D.A. In March 1968 Huddersfield D.A. and Durham D.A. were formed. Solent D.A., Lakeland D.A. and a new Oxfordshire D.A. began operating in 1969 and Leeds D.A. was founded in 1970. Unfortunately, all outdoor Club activities had to be cancelled at the end of 1967 when there was a bad outbreak of Foot and Mouth disease preventing access to much farmland in the countryside. Fortunately, this was cleared in time for most of the camping season.

In 1962 the Folk Song and Dance Group was revived at the suggestion of Bob Whitlock and it has never looked back. At the same time, Ron Harding suggested that a Motor Caravan Section be formed. After presenting his views to the National Council, he was given permission to set up an *ad hoc* committee to start things off. A special area for motor caravans was made available at the forthcoming N.F.O.L., and the Section was finally given approval in 1963.

RON HARDING, journalist and newspaper editor by profession, founded the Motor Caravan Section and was Club Chairman from 1978–1980. He wrote the Crosspatch *comments in* Camping and Caravanning, *and such was his dedication that in 1991, although he knew he was dying, he wrote about his repatriation from France by Carefree to emphasise the value of the service to members.*

The Association of Cycle Campers was having difficulties as the number of cycle-campers seemed to be declining. A successful Diamond Jubilee Easter Rally was held at Wantage in 1961. More members were needed, so in 1965 the name was changed to the Association of Cycle and Lightweight Campers to encourage other like-minded campers who used lightweight equipment but who travelled by means other than a cycle to join them.

With the increasing interest in and growth of trailer tents, a Trailer Tent Section was proposed and officially formed in June 1967. The Club then announced that no more Sections would be allowed, although there had been strong pressure for a Tent Camping Section. Tent camping groups had to be attached to the Regions, in the same way as the D.A.s were.

N.F.O.L.s continued to grow in size, with all records being broken at the Diamond Jubilee N.F.O.L. in 1961 at Colchester. Over 5,000 people attended, occupying some 80 acres of land including three overflow fields. Around 7,000 members attended the N.F.O.L. organised by Central Counties Region at Teddesley Park in Staffordshire 1963 and in 1964 some

BOB WHITLOCK was a keen folk dancer and singer and in 1962 suggested that the pre-war Folk Group should be restarted as a Folk Dance and Song Group. He was its first Chairman and led the group from strength to strength. He became President of the Group in 1969 and was actively involved until his death in 1996, by which time it was the fourth largest Section of the Club.

10,500 members – one in eight of the Club membership in the British Isles – put "a strain on the administration" at Bourley Camp, Aldershot. About 1,500 others camped in the area, often directed by the police to any open ground. These of course were not officially registered.

At Blackpool the following year, over 11,500 members attended the N.F.O.L., and at a wet Longleat in 1966 and Newby Hall in 1967 over 8,000 attended each event. In 1968 the National Council was asked to consider the future organisation of N.F.O.L.s as they were becoming so large. North London and Eastern Counties Region, which organised the event for that year at Woburn, had 3,500 pitch bookings and had to refuse 1,000 applications. The next year 1,700 units with over 6,000 people went to Wynyard Park in the north-east, while over 9,000 attended Mallory Park, Leicestershire in 1970.

Miss World, Lesley Langley, and Dougal Haston, mountaineer, at the Charing Cross Underground Station Exhibition, National Camping Week, 1966.

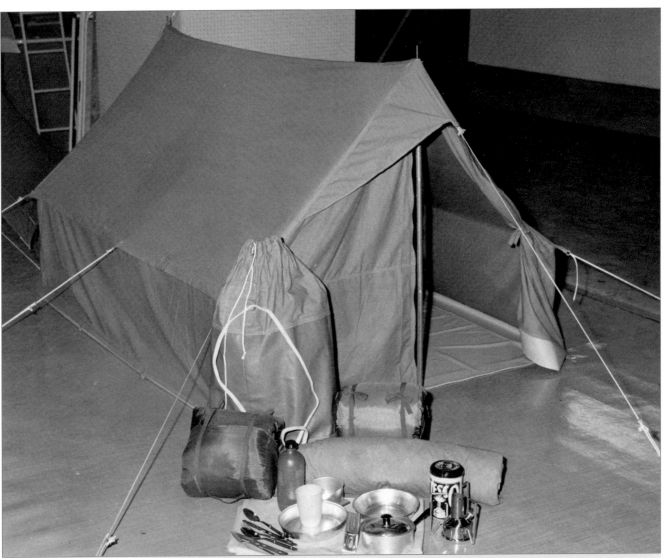

Yours for just £9 19s 6d – the complete camping outfit for two that goes into a duffel bag. Headquarters and General Supplies Ltd showed this kit off at the Camping and Outdoor Leisure Exhibition, 1964.

In 1962 the National Council decided that frame tents would not be permitted on season ticket pitches because of the inability to air the ground properly. In 1970 members were encouraged to provide their own chemical sanitation at Club Meets but South East Region stated that it was the duty of all Club units to provide for those who did not have their own. This was confirmed by the National Council. Sleeping in cars – long forbidden by the Club – was to be allowed provided that the car had specially designed seats converting to beds and that such cars were used in conjunction with a properly designed tent attachment.

Perhaps one of the greatest leaps forward in the 1960s was in the development of camping equipment. With the frame tent now firmly established, all kinds of ancillary equipment was being produced for use inside. Restrictions on the use of fabrics and metals were no longer in force and a lot of new gear was being imported from the continent.

First in the field A Century of The Camping and Caravanning Club

Camping and Outdoor Life magazine was full of advertisements for all kinds of kit. Indeed there were nearly as many pages of advertisements at the beginning of the 1960s as there were editorial pages and space-saving measures had to be devised. (Secretaries' names and addresses were no longer listed every month in *Regional Roundabout*, the forerunner of *Out & About*.) The cover design was changed in July 1964 when different coloured headings were introduced. In September of that year the first full-colour photograph was used on the cover.

The Club sponsored the popular Camping and Outdoor Life exhibitions throughout the decade. On the whole they were very successful, although there was growing concern at the number of exhibits unconnected with camping. The Club's stand in 1965 was excellent although members asked if there could be a Club lounge. This was later agreed to. Other regional exhibitions were manned by volunteers from D.A.s and North-West Region received a gold award certificate for the design of its stand at the Liverpool show.

National Camping Week enabled members of the public to visit units on site and see how the Club worked.

Trailer tents and folding campers by Geoff Timberlake

Traditional trailer tents and the evolved variant, the folding camper, are popular camping units which provide most of the comforts of modern caravans but avoid their pitfalls. The difference between a trailer tent and the folding camper is that the former opens up from the trailer and has canvas walls which are pegged out at ground level in a similar manner to a frame tent, while the folding camper opens up to form a self-supporting unit without the need for pegging.

Trailer tents and folding campers came to the fore after World War Two, but similar camping units capable of being towed behind a motor car appeared before World War One. At that time all towed units were known as caravans but those of the folding variety used much canvas in their construction and thus by our modern definitions would be classed as a trailer tent or folding camper.

Typical of those early units were the Cocks Collapsible Trailer Caravan introduced in 1921, a Folding Trailer Caravan by H.B. Fenwick in 1923, and a home-made trailer caravan reported in *Camping* in 1925. A French model, the Chalet-Remorque Stella was advertised in May 1930 in the *Revue de l'Auto Camping Club de France*.

In the 1960s, when camping as an alternative means of holiday and leisure activity became the accepted norm, trailer tents (or tent trailers as they were first known) were produced by manufacturers large and small both in the U.K. and on the Continent. In 1968, no less than 26 different makes of trailer tent, many from British manufacturers, were used by campers attending the First Birthday Meet of the Trailer Tent Group.

Barry Bucknall, the designer of the Mirror Dinghy, had also designed a trailer tent intended for the D.I.Y. enthusiast. He challenged Peggy Ryalls, the wife of the then Editor of the Club magazine,

to build one of his kits – this she did in 70 hours. She and her husband Alan used it at the Birmingham D.A. Jubilee Meet on 9 June 1967. At that meet an inaugural meeting, chaired by Hickey Liversedge, the Club Vice-Chairman, took place between other trailer tent owners to explore the possibility of forming a new Section within the Club, and the Trailer Tent Group was formed. The first Birthday Meet was held at Billing Aquadrome, where 501 adults and 269 children camped in 244 units. Initially the Group was sub-divided into five U.K. Regions and later, as demand grew, five other regions were added. The Group has issued its own newsletter since the Group's conception in 1967, the newsletter is now named *The Silhouette*.

American folding campers were introduced to the U.K. in the mid-1970s, initially from makers such as Starcraft, Coleman and Jayco. These non-pegging models wooed campers who wanted a trailer tent but not the associated pegging. The Canadian Bonair also made a popular appearance for a time.

An early British version came from Dawman, but as its roof had to be raised by means of an overlarge broomstick, it failed to oust the transatlantic

opposition. Conway, which initially solely made trailer tents, marketed Jayco models and from them eventually developed its own designs more suitable to the U.K. conditions. Pennine, a Lancashire-based company produced its own range of folding campers, becoming arguably the founder of this sector in the U.K. Continental manufacturers, especially Trigano, have dabbled in folding campers, but not to the same numbers as Conway and Pennine.

Nowadays, the number of manufacturers has stabilised, the models are much more sophisticated, with mains electrics, water heaters, washrooms, kitchen units and storage lockers to suit the demands of the modern camper who no longer has the urge to improve his unit. Indeed the level of comfort in a modern trailer tent/folding camper is on a par with most touring caravans.

1971–1979:
A new structure and a Royal Jubilee

To celebrate the Club's 70th birthday in 1971, a grand Anniversary Ball and Dinner was held in London. The Club was presented with a large quartz crystal by the International Federation of Camping and Caravanning (F.I.C.C.) and the Federation of French Clubs presented their Gold Medal to the Club. George Cubitt, the Club's General Secretary, received the M.B.E. in the Birthday Honours List in 1974. He was the first person ever to receive such an award for services to camping.

The decade also saw the celebration of three-quarters of a century of the Club, and the Queen's Silver Jubilee. In celebration of this latter event, two of the Club's Honorary Officers, Jack Avery and Vic Jones, received the Queen's Silver Jubilee Medal for services to camping. Another well-known Club member, Frank Grant, also received the medal for his service in the police force. Celebrations for the Club's 75th anniversary included a reception at the Mansion House attended by the Club's Patron, H.R.H. Prince Philip, at which he was presented with six tents for his Award Scheme by Camping Club Youth (C.C.Y.) members.

A special "Nite Out" was arranged for members at Cesars Palace, near Luton, in place of a celebration dinner and dance which, because of inflation, would have been beyond the means of many members. The nightclub was exclusively booked by the Club for this occasion. This was followed in

Left: Although black and white photographs were the order of the day for front covers in 1976 a Royal event produced a colour picture for the front of the April magazine. Sadly, sharpness and quality weren't as good as they are now. The picture marked the attendance of the Club's Patron, Prince Philip, at the 75th anniversary reception at London's Mansion House. (Club Archive)

In the wider world

LSD to PP: 15 February 1971 saw the demise of the traditional, but rather illogical, British pounds, shillings and pence (£-s-d), and the introduction of decimalised currency in the form of the pound divided into 100 new pence. Old coins such as the half-crown, the florin, and the even older guinea ceased to be legal tender.

Yes to E.E.C.: In June 1975 nearly 70 percent of voters in a national referendum voted in favour of Britain joining the European Common Market. In spite of early fears of apathy, the voting turn-out was nearly up to general election standards.

Record drought: 1976 saw the worst drought in Britain for 250 years. Temperatures in London reached 95°F (35°C), reservoirs dried up, forest fires became a threat and water rationing was imposed. The Government appointed the Sports Minister, Denis Howell, as Minister for Drought. On 31 August the rains came and Britons once again complained about their awful climate.

Country-wide bonfire chain: 7 June 1977 began a week of Jubilee celebrations marking the Queen's 25 years on the throne. The events started with the lighting of a chain of bonfires on prominent sites stretching from Land's End to the Shetlands, and ended with the Queen and Prince Philip attending a service in St Paul's Cathedral followed by a banquet at the Guildhall.

DON DEWEY joined the Club in 1929 and camped with Surrey District Association and at Horsley. He then bought a caravan and was a founder member of the British Caravanners' Club. On moving to Birmingham he became its representative to the National Council, and helped start Central Counties Region in 1948. He became Club Chairman in 1958, the first from outside London, and was Club President from 1971–1980.

March 1977 by a Club Reunion at the Royal Albert Hall.

In 1971 the Club had a new President, Don Dewey but its senior Vice-President, Lady Baden-Powell died in 1977. She had been formally associated with the Club since 1919 and had been one of its staunchest supporters. Don Dewey stood down as President at the end of the decade due to ill-health. He died at the end of December 1980. His place was taken by Sir John Cripps, a former Chairman of the Countryside Commission and a great supporter of the Club and its ideals.

The Club continued to grow apace, with membership increasing from just over 110,000 to over 190,000 in 1979. Unfortunately this figure dropped to 187,000 in 1980, mainly due to the economic recession. The number of Club sites for members increased from 43 in 1971 to 66 in 1980.

At the beginning of 1971 the National Council accepted a suggestion from the International Committee that an award for services to camping be instituted, and it was agreed to award Certificates of Honour to such persons. The first three were awarded to F.I.C.C. officers – members of overseas clubs – on the recommendation of the International Committee. The first Club member to receive a Certificate of Honour was Don Dewey in 1976. Club Regions and the voting Sections were then asked to nominate one Club member whom they considered to be eligible. The Club Chairman could also nominate persons for the Award but it would be well into the 1980s before the non-voting Sections were able to nominate anyone.

Ten private Bills related to camping were introduced in Parliament in 1971. Because of the postal strike at the beginning of the year the costs in time and money in opposing these Bills were quite substantial because the Club Chairman had to sign papers and petitions, sometimes on a daily basis. Since these could not be posted, a messenger had to travel by train to the Chairman's home to obtain the necessary signatures in time to submit the petitions. The postal strike also played havoc with voting papers for the 1971 A.G.M. and with magazine distribution.

Cornwall County Council asked for Part 1 of the Caravan Sites and Control of Development Act 1960 to be made applicable to tents within the county and the Club's Parliamentary Agent was instructed to object to this proposal. Many local authorities sought restrictions on the parking of caravans on estate roads. One Welsh council wanted to prohibit the parking of caravans "within the curtilage of a dwelling house" – in other words in private gardens.

Perhaps the most dangerous piece of anti-camping and caravanning legislation of all appeared in 1976, the Club's 75th anniversary year, when West Midlands County Council proposed banning the parking of caravans, trailers, boats and certain other vehicles anywhere on private premises. A meeting was arranged at the National Agricultural Centre, Stoneleigh. So many people attended it was necessary to find a much larger room at the last minute to accommodate them. Officials from District Associations (D.A.s) and Sections of The Camping Club, Centres of The Caravan Club, a large number of works caravan and camping clubs from the area, the Auto Camping Club and Motor Caravanners' Club as well as numerous sailing and boating associations were all represented, together with the Scouts and Guides, the Automobile Association and the Royal Automobile Club.

VIC JONES, M.B.E. joined the Club in 1943 and after war service was active in both the Birmingham District Association and the British Caravanners Club. He was Chairman of Central Counties Region for seven years and later Region President. He also became President of the British Caravanners Club. He joined the National Council in 1959, was Chairman from 1972–1974, Honorary Treasurer of the Club for 14 years and is now a Vice-President of the Club.

The Club's Immediate Past-Chairman, Vic Jones, explained the implications of the Bill, which would give the County Council unprecedented control over an individual's private property and which clearly was an infringement of basic rights. Although the County Council stated that it only intended to apply the restrictions in special circumstances there was no guarantee that once the bill was approved, such promises would be honoured by succeeding councils. The Council was offering no alternative parking and the proposed time of one hour to load and unload was ridiculous.

A lot of work was involved in successfully opposing the punitive clauses in these Bills and in some cases the Club had to continue the fight on its own, so there was great satisfaction at the successful outcome. It also made the point that the Club was concerned for all campers, not just those using tents.

Despite plans for the creation of extra pitches for touring caravans in the peak season, Torbay Corporation sought powers to "prevent the amenities of the Borough being prejudicially affected, and for preventing annoyance to the residents in, or visitors to, the Borough by the conduct of occupiers of the moveable dwellings on any camping ground". The Club strongly objected to "the implications that camping sites were unwholesome places and that campers are a section of the general public more inclined than others to be unruly or disorderly".

Cagoules

First introduced by the major camping stores in 1971, they were made from polyurethane coated nylon. Originally designed for hill-walkers, cagoules soon became very popular with campers. A smock-style garment, they were later made with full-length two-way zips, making them easier to put on in a hurry and much easier to ventilate.

The Corporation suggested that it would accept exemption for Club members camping on Club sites within its area but this was refused since the Club had no sites of its own in Torbay and the exemptions would therefore be worthless. A similar bill was proposed by Teesside Corporation. The Club's Parliamentary Agents were again instructed to oppose both Bills on the grounds that they wrongly implied that campers were unruly and required special control, and in any case the Corporations already had powers to deal with matters of amenity and nuisance. Once again it was necessary to publicise, and boost, the fighting fund.

A Night Assemblies Bill, designed to control open-air overnight assemblies of more than 1,000 people, and primarily aimed at pop festivals, could have seriously affected the organisation of Club meets, especially N.F.O.L.s. The Club took action to seek exemption from the provisions of the Bill which, in the end, did not pass through Parliament.

Hampshire County Council's Bill for the control of parking of commercial vehicles was carefully studied to ensure that motor caravanners were not caught by the provisions of a Bill designed to control commercial vehicle parking.

Unfortunately the N.F.O.L.s were to be affected by bureaucracy. They were becoming more and more popular, with over 10,000 members in more than 3,000 units attending the 1971 N.F.O.L. at Lingfield Park, Surrey. There were highly complimentary press reports about the organisation of the event and the behaviour of the campers. Despite this, Lancashire County Council insisted on a planning application being submitted for the event due to be held at Ribby Hall in 1972, even though the Club's legal advisers categorically stated that the event was exempt from such planning applications.

Planning permission was refused and the event had to be cancelled at the last minute, resulting in a large financial loss for the Region and disappointment for members and traders alike. Lancashire County Council had succeeded in doing what only Hitler had achieved before!

Folk Dance and Song Group founder Bob Whitlock playing his melodeon at the National Feast of Lanterns, Stoneleigh, 1976. (Pete Mac, Folk Dance and Song Group)

Fortunately other N.F.O.L.s were not affected, with all of them attracting more than 5,000 people. A record was set in 1976 when 16,000 people in more than 5,000 units attended the N.F.O.L. at Stoneleigh, with all but 90 being booked in advance. This was one of the most successful N.F.O.L.s ever held. The spirit of early N.F.O.L.s was rekindled in 1979 at Northington Down Farm, Hampshire, when over 11,000 people camped, some of them on stubble fields. The weather was hot and windy and dust blew everywhere.

Efforts were made to resolve the problems of canoeists on some of Britain's waterways when the Central Council for Physical Recreation arranged a meeting at which a measure of agreement was reached between anglers and canoeists for the separate use of rivers and other waterways.

In 1974 a Working Party was set up to consider how the Club could best establish and maintain lines of communication with local authorities throughout Britain. The growing awareness of the need for central and local government to become more deeply involved in the provision of facilities for sport and recreation meant that it was of the utmost importance for the Club to maintain contact at all levels.

The Club's right to operate Temporary Holiday Sites (T.H.S.s) under its Certificate of Exemption was questioned early in 1974. It was thought planning permission would be needed in future but the Department of the Environment informally supported the Club's view that the exemption that applied to the Club's permanent sites did in fact also apply to T.H.S.s. It was decided that in future, all T.H.S. applications would have to be submitted through Club Headquarters and a T.H.S. Sub-Committee was set up in 1976 to deal with these.

In April 1976 a Government Report on National Parks suggested limiting the number of camping and caravanning rallies each year within any national park that did not have specific planning permission. In July the Department of the Environment endorsed the Club's

Force ten tents

The well-known orange cotton canvas ridge tents, designed to stand up to a gale, first appeared in the early 1970s. They were very robust but also very heavy, as many Youth members soon found out. The advent of nylon flysheets for these and other lightweight tents began to make carrying the load a little easier.

views on voluntary control over meets in the national parks. District Associations and Sections had to submit details of proposed meets in a national park by pre-determined dates, well in advance of the event, otherwise permission would be refused. Although the scheme was already working well in some parks by the end of 1977, it was a challenge to the Club's traditional activities when other national parks authorities were proposing additional restraints and even withdrawal of exemptions. Regions, D.A.s and Sections had to recognise the seriousness of the situation and act responsibly.

The new Humber Bridge authorities were also proposing very high tolls, especially for cars with trailers and caravans, so the Club sent a letter of objection to the Secretary of State for Transport, stating that they would oppose these charges. Despite the Club's efforts the high charges were introduced and, of course, have increased considerably since the bridge was opened.

In September 1978 the Department of the Environment again circulated its Consultation Paper. It was obvious that the existing freedom from control of tent camping would be severely curtailed when and if legislation was introduced.

In 1980 the Dartmoor Commons Bill was amended to the Club's satisfaction, but an Article Four directive covering 73 square miles of the Gower Peninsular Area of Outstanding Natural Beauty was noted with "extreme concern". This meant that all camping, including that of exempted organisations, would be restricted to licensed sites in the area unless prior planning permission had been obtained. This caused great difficulties for the Cambrian and Wyvern Region, and especially West Wales D.A., who, in addition to getting planning permission for meets, also had to restrict the numbers attending in many cases.

Club sites were developing rapidly and in the 1970s great strides were made. Twenty-four new sites were added to the network. Chertsey Club Site was closed and completely redeveloped as a holiday and touring site for members only, although members of foreign clubs could also use it. The holiday and touring sites were distinct from the ordinary Club sites, which at the time were run by voluntary committees, in that they were primarily

Left: Bakewell Club Site situated near Youlgreave village, from which it took its original name. The site was first used by Derbyshire D.A. at Easter 1923. It became a Club site in 1970 and is a memorial to A.W. Snowden, an early Chairman of Sheffield D.A., who often camped here. It is set in beautiful countryside and is popular with many members.

From the Club magazine
June 1971 *Club Cross-Channel Charter?:* "*Perhaps the Club could charter one ferry crossing a week for Club members during the high season, and let members have the benefit of – we hope – a low-cost crossing more in keeping with the distance involved.*"

July 1971 *Comment: The* Financial Times *concludes that "30 years ago camping was the activity of the rich who could afford expensive equipment and the poor who could only afford a camping holiday".*

June 1976 *Toyota advertisement: "A holiday in a motor caravan should be spent under the sun, not under the bonnet."*

Sir Charles Fergusson(left), Lord Mansfield (centre) and Club Chairman Ray Cripps at the opening of Scone Club Site in 1975. (Club Archive)

intended for holiday base camps, near the sea or attractive countryside. They all had a Warden or Site Manager, had water-flushed sanitation and a few also had showers. They were usually only open for the main holiday season from Easter to September but Chertsey was an exception as it was the first to remain open all year. At the time it was equipped to the highest of any known standards in the U.K. A Warden was sought who could preferably speak both French and German, accommodation was provided and there was a shop available on the site. New flush toilets were installed at Oldbury Hill and Kelvedon Hatch was extended by the purchase of another field and the provision of extra toilet facilities.

Minehead Club Site, provided by Somerset County Council and managed by the Club, opened at Easter 1971 and Kirkby-on-Bain (now known as Woodhall Spa Club Site) opened as a minimum facility site at the same time. Development of a site at Kilkerran was approved and a Countryside Award was made in respect of Blackmore Club Site. On the down side, a lease and service agreement for Wood Farm, Charmouth, was terminated as there had been so many complaints about the site from members. It was also removed from the *Sites List*.

Studying the local map at Cranleigh, Surrey. (P.H. Constance)

First in the field A Century of The Camping and Caravanning Club

Current trends required better facilities on sites so it became necessary to introduce an extensive programme to improve Club sites, requiring considerably more finance for the work than the existing annual rate of expenditure on site maintenance and improvement.

Early in 1972 the Management Committee decided that no additional charges would in future be made for hot water to hand basins on Club sites, and that, where technically possible, charges for showers should also be withdrawn. A new site, developed on land leased by the local authority, opened at Bodmin in June. A minimum facility site at Slindon, owned by the National Trust, and one at Saltram, near Plymouth, also opened during the year. Chertsey Club Site was opened after being redeveloped and the Club agreed to purchase Dunstan Hill site when the lease terminated.

Bob and Jean Reynolds, the first Wardens of the redeveloped Chertsey Club Site, at their retirement party.
(Ron Harding, Club Archive)

The Club had decided that in future all of its sites would be managed by a Warden instead of by Site Committees. Laleham site, owned by Staines Urban District Council (U.D.C.), was one of the sites affected. In 1973 the U.D.C. asked for the decision to be rescinded, saying that it would not accept a Warden and that the Site Committee was to remain in place. The National Council could not agree to these demands so the Club withdrew from the site. By 1974 all sites had been re-designated as "Club sites", no distinction being made between them as by that time all were Wardened.

By the end of 1973 it became obvious that the costs of developing Scone Club Site were rising rapidly but because it was in an area where demand for camping sites was heavy it was decided to proceed as planned. A decision was made to increase the level of subsidy. A substantial grant toward the cost of development was later received and the site was finally opened in 1975.

In March 1974 Wolverley Club Site was opened. In the following year the Club acquired the site at Great Shelford, Cambridge. In 1976 sites at Freshwater East and Slingsby were purchased and the new site at Moffat was opened. The following year new Club sites were opened at Ebury Hill and Luss and the management of sites at Crowden, Jedburgh, Beadnell and Dingwall was undertaken on behalf of local authorities.

All season tickets for Club sites were terminated at the end of 1977. There were, of course, the inevitable objections but camping was changing and Club members had to accept the fact. In 1978 sites opened under the Club's auspices at Bangor-on-Dee and Ludlow racecourses, followed in 1979 by new Club sites at St Neots, Machrihanish and Lingfield Racecourse. Finally, in 1980 the Club Site at Sheriff Hutton was opened with minimal facilities and an undeveloped site at New Quay, Dyfed, was purchased and opened, again with minimal facilities. By the end of 1980, the Club either owned or managed over 60 sites.

It was suggested that reduced fees in early and late season might encourage D.A.s to use Club sites. This was considered to be impracticable at the time but the Sites Management Committee was looking into the possibility of lower fees for all in off-peak periods. In April 1975 it was agreed that reduced fees for pensioners receiving state retirement benefits would be offered at certain Club-operated sites during off-peak periods.

Ralph Lee suggested that the Club should take the initiative in calling meetings to agree a possible standard electricity outlet for use on camping sites to which both caravans and tents could be connected. Later on the International Electro-Technical Commission proposed a standard

Easter 1970 – lightweight campers at Ashover, Derbyshire. (P.H. Constance)

Presentation of the new Camp Steward's sign at Oldbury Hill Club Site in 1971. (Ian Henderson, Club Archive)

that it was expected would be accepted and Ralph hoped that the Site Committees would endeavour to supply electricity to caravans on Club-operated sites. On this occasion, however, he felt that it should not be supplied to tents. For safety reasons the 20ft rule, now very familiar to Club members, was introduced in 1977. Not only was it enforced on Club sites but also at all D.A, Section, Regional and National Meets. The first Club sites' map for use with the *Sites List* was produced in co-operation with the Ordnance Survey in January 1978. The Club also stressed the importance of obtaining more five-'van Certificated Sites, and of encouraging members to use them.

More staff had been taken on at Headquarters to cope with the increasing workload. Both senior and junior staff positions were unfilled at Headquarters, which was causing problems. There were plenty of jobs on offer so staff were moving to positions offering better salaries. A full-time Public Relations Officer (P.R.O.) was appointed but only stayed for three months. The P.R. Committee said that little could be achieved without appropriate staff and that candidates for the post of P.R.O. should be specialists in written communication. Much of the Club's P.R. work was done by Alan Ryalls, the Honorary Editor of the magazine. Before the decade was out, the Management Committee had decided that providing information about the Club was more important than concentrating on P.R. so a full-time Information Officer was appointed. The possibility of establishing a travel department at headquarters was suggested in 1972.

In 1973 the Club started looking again for new premises in London. The preference being for accommodation all on one floor. The problem was that rents for office properties were rocketing to astronomical figures and new premises simply could not be found. Headquarters was designated a Grade Two Listed building, meaning that any work anywhere on the

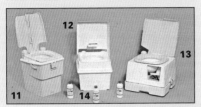

premises had to be specially approved. Financial forecasts for the next three years were drawn up in 1976 so that the Management Committee could establish the level of priority for the acquisition of new premises. Eventually, in 1977 additional office space was obtained in Grosvenor Gardens, round the corner from Lower Grosvenor Place;. This was the best which could be done to keep the offices in central London. Subscriptions, which had already risen several times since 1970, had to be increased again to provide the necessary working capital to keep the Club on a sound financial footing. No further projects could be considered unless more capital became available. Club subscriptions rose from £3 per full member in 1971 to £9 in 1980 – a reflection of the spiralling costs of the time.

In 1979 the handling of Club membership was contracted to an outside computer agency. There were difficulties with a small Headquarters-based Membership Department, which was over-stretched during the renewal season (all renewals were due at the same time each year) and which also had wildly fluctuating work flows at other times. This created problems that could not be handled satisfactorily, even with extra temporary staff and adjustments to the system in co-operation with the Club's computer agents. The clerical aspect of the work was the cause of major delays, even though members were asked to volunteer to help out at Headquarters – which they did – and temporary staff were also employed. As the Club Chairman remarked: "One volunteer is worth more than a temp." New membership cards attached to the renewal form were sent to members,

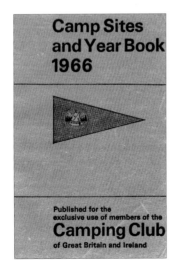

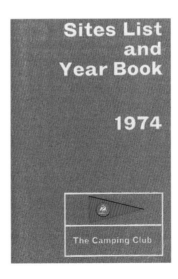

and subscriptions were acknowledged by the continued receipt of the magazine, saving the Club more than £5,000 in postage.

In 1972 a proposal was made by the British Caravanners' Club (B.C.C.) that the membership fee should include all youths up to the age of 17 years of age, because many aged twelve and over who were not members of the Youth Section regularly attended Club events and took advantage of Club membership while in the company of their parents.

The National Youth Committee was asked to consider the matter but it strongly opposed the idea. The Chairman of the Committee, Jack Pitfield, said the proposals would seriously undermine the Youth Section, leading to a reduction in its membership that would be bad both for the Club and for the Youth Section as a whole. Ray Hughes, the Regional Youth Liaison Officer for North West Region and the Vice-Chairman of the National Youth Committee, wrote an open letter to all parents which was published in the Club magazine in 1973, pointing out that membership of the Youth Section was not automatic. Unless they filled in a form for their children aged twelve and over and paid the very small subscription for them they could not take the Camping Test nor could they take part in Youth activities. He had even had youngsters attending for testing who were not C.C.Y. members.

Camping Club Youth members map-reading while on a backpacking trip in Surrey, 1974. (P.H. Constance)

He pointed out the advantages of membership – eligibility for National and International Youth Rallies once the Test was passed, plus continuing with Youth membership rates until the age of 21, again once the Test was passed. This was – and still is – a considerable benefit, saving the young member quite a sum of money in membership fees. "The C.C.Y. of today are the Club members of tomorrow. Let us all build our Club for its future."

Sadly, Ray Hughes died not long after he wrote that letter, in fact it was published posthumously. He was held in high esteem in his Region and a trophy for endeavour by Youth members was established in his memory.

Ralph Lee pointed out to the National Council that, for a family in the B.C.C., the requirement to pay for youth over the age of twelve meant that the subscriptions were uncompetitive with other caravan organisations. In practice, the rule requiring twelve-to-17 year-olds to become Youth members was widely abused. The B.C.C. proposal was not carried by a narrow majority in 1974 but eventually the Council agreed to include children of Youth age within the full membership subscription in 1979. Anyone wishing to take part in Youth activities or take the Camping Club Youth Test had to become a member of the Youth Section. Unfortunately Jack Pitfield's prediction came true and the Youth Section was drastically reduced.

Backpacking takes off! Watched by mum, two-year-old Paula strides out with her own rucksack at Polesden Lacey Club Site in 1979. (P.H. Constance)

In 1975 the Club's Solicitor advised that notice of motions for an A.G.M. should have the support of at least 20 per cent of the total voting membership but it was accepted there was a moral obligation to allow members a say in matters affecting the running of the Club. In future, the A.G.M. would be held in London and run on strictly formal lines in accordance with the Companies Act, but members could air their views at Members' Meetings to be held throughout the country.

In 1971 the Club magazine was radically changed. From a small pocket-sized monthly magazine it became an A4 publication with fewer, but larger, pages. The new format allowed the Club to display articles better and to use a larger typeface, thus making a more readable magazine. The methods used to produce the magazine were also changed and it became possible to introduce colour into the magazine itself, not just on the covers. Advertisers would also have better facilities for advertising.

The paper quality, however, was variable because of an acute paper shortage and the Club had to get whatever was obtainable. Some of the poorer quality paper was also unfortunately heavier. The number of pages had to be reduced to keep postage rates as low as possible. The change-over took place in April, and in November the magazine title was changed to *Camping and Caravanning*. The decision to change the title was not taken lightly. "It has, to some extent, been forced upon us by the

In April 1971 the Club magazine changed to A4 format and a new logo for the Club appeared on the front cover. In 1977 the logo changed and, with variations, the Club has been using that logo ever since. Early in the 1990s the wording 'The friendly Club' was added. A special logo was created for the Centenary of the Club.

Winter camping, popular since the Club was founded, continues today. Members of the Association of Cycle and Lightweight Campers at Croydon, Surrey, 1978. (P.H. Constance)

persistent misunderstanding on the part of planners, local authorities, advertisers and potential Club members who seem to think The Camping Club only caters for tent campers."

The Editor pointed out that there had already been several changes in the title of the magazine since the Club's inception. Just after World War Two camping struggled to get back on its feet, cars were few and caravans hard to come by. No-one had thought of the frame tent let alone the motor caravan and trailer tent as they existed in 1971. The tendency towards 'wheel camping' had become more marked, and around 35 per cent of Club members could be termed 'wheel campers'. Therefore, to more accurately reflect the trend and to make quite clear to everyone that the Club and its magazine catered for all, the new title was introduced. The Editor, Alan Ryalls, retired at the end of April 1975 after nearly 20 years work as Honorary Editor. His place was taken by Iain Morris, a full-time member of headquarters staff as paid full-time Editor. He was ably assisted in his job (in an honorary capacity) by Ron Harding, a professional journalist and Editor and a member of the National Council. Iain Morris had a rough start, as there was a dispute in the printing industry, resulting in a late June magazine, no July edition and a combined July/August issue.

The Club's *Technical Handbook of Camping and Caravanning* ceased to be issued after 1971 and the decade also saw the demise of the Club's

International Camping Sites Guide, the last of which was published in 1974. It was followed by four separate booklets devoted to recommended sites in four specific areas. *The Club Yearbook and Sites Guide* would in future be produced by Headquarters staff and continued to be published annually until 1977, when it became a biennial publication to try and save costs.

Other changes took place after the Boundary Commission reported in 1971. The new Regional structure was introduced in 1973 at an additional cost of between £500 and £600 per year. There was an urgent need to recruit new members to increase the surplus on the Annual Accounts to enable the Club to expand on solid foundations. Many members criticised this need to recruit all and sundry, as they considered that standards in camping were rapidly declining. This sort of argument had taken place decades before when proposals to limit numbers were first raised for the same reason. The Club pointed out that new people brought in new ideas and we should not be selfish and close the door on those who wanted to join. It was up to experienced Club members to pass on their expertise to those who had never before camped but who wanted to join in.

Five new regions were formed, namely North Central, West Central (which became Cambrian and Wyvern), Eastern, Southern, and South Central (which became Chiltern Region). North London and Eastern Counties Region was wound up. Members of Leinster D.A. had resigned from the Club *en bloc* in 1972 and formed the Irish Camping and

The opening of Wolverley Club Site, March 1974. (Club Archive)

First in the field A Century of The Camping and Caravanning Club

CAMPING
& OUTDOOR LIFE
MAGAZINE OF THE CAMPING CLUB OF GREAT BRITAIN & IRELAND LTD

VOL. 66   No. 3
MARCH, 1971

In April 1971 the Club changed its magazine printer and the method by which the magazine was printed. Previously the A5-sized magazine (left) was printed use the letterpress technique. It was set in metal type and each picture had to be made into a metal block before printing.

April 1971 saw the Club magazine being printed by Eden Fisher Ltd, in Southend. Eden Fisher was an early practitioner of the web offset technique recently arrived from the U.S. The new technique allowed second and third colours, and colour photos could be used on the cover as the April issue (below) shows.

The Club magazine is still printed by web offset although, today of course, the magazine carries colour pictures throughout.

camping
outdoor life
NE OF THE CAMPING CLUB OF GREAT BRITAIN AND IRELAND LIM

Vol. 66
APRI

In this iss

* Quiet Day
  on the
  Isle of Arr

* News on Lo

* Chairman's
  Corner

* Campavan
  Trailer Tent
  Test

The Camping Club

Caravanning Club. This was not entirely unexpected and all good wishes were sent to the new Club. Northern Ireland D.A. was not attached to any Region under the new scheme but asked to send a nominated representative to National Council with voting rights. This was agreed at the A.G.M. in 1974 and in 1977 the Northern Ireland Region was approved.

The District Associations continued to grow, with several large ones sub-dividing. A total of 34 new D.A.s were formed between 1971 and 1980, although North-West Surrey D.A. foundered after less than a year.

By 1971 many D.A.s were producing their own newsletters. Roy Burnham, a former Club Chairman, presented a trophy in an annual competition for the best D.A. or Section newsletter. The first winner was Bucks, Herts and Middlesex D.A. for its magazine *Headlines*.

In the same year proposals and requests for a Boating Group were repeatedly made in the correspondence columns of the magazine. The Boating Group was approved in 1972, although it had to collect its own subscriptions and do its own administration. In 1979 it requested permission to send an observer to National Council meetings, and it was agreed to invite them to send a representative on the same basis as the non-voting sections.

The Motor Caravan Section reached 3,000 full members in September 1973 so became entitled to have full voting rights on the National Council. The Trailer Tent Group reached that figure three years later.

Backpacking was beginning to take off and lightweight camping was again booming after a long period of decline boosting the membership of the Association of Cycle and Lightweight Campers.

Several major camping equipment suppliers were again introducing lightweight tents to their ranges. At the Lightweight Section's 75th Birthday Celebration Rally at Wantage, in August 1976, more than 100 lightweight campers from all over Britain, including eleven guests from Holland, filled the large field almost to capacity. This was a record for a Lightweight Section event and to date it has not been equalled. Many members cycled to the Rally, and some took part in a commemorative ride from Reading to Wantage taking, as far as possible, the original route used by the first six cycle-campers in 1901.

The Club was very active internationally despite the high rise in costs of travel overseas. All the F.I.C.C. rallies were well attended, except for

Left: In 1972 the Club was the main sponsor of the rejuvenated Camping and Outdoor Life and Travel Exhibition. More than 122,000 people visited the show, and among them was ex-Prime Minister, now Leader of the Opposition, the Rt. Hon. Harold Wilson. On the Club's stand Mr Wilson revealed that he had been a lightweight cycle camper in his youth. Our picture shows Harold Wilson signing the visitor's book with Club Chairman, Roy Burnham. (Club Archive)

In 1972 Club Chairman Roy Burnham is interviewed by Dilys Morgan for the B.B.C. radio's ever popular Woman's Hour *programme. Roy Burnham always understood the value of publicity for the Club. He organised Club President Don Dewey being interviewed on Radio 4's* Today *programme, as well as countless local radio interviews around the Club-sponsored Camping and Outdoor Life and Travel Exhibition. Television items, filmed both at the show and at the Chertsey Club Site, appeared on* London This Week, *B.B.C.'s* 24 Hours *programme and the children's programme* Blue Peter. *Today, Roy's name is still remembered in the Burnham Trophy awarded each year for the best newsletter. (Club Archive)*

the Rally at Otranto, Italy in 1971, when only 92 Club members attended. The following year, over 1,000 went to Lechbruch and in the year after, 160 Club members, part of a British total of 585 campers, went to the Rally in Turkey.

The F.I.C.C. trophy for the largest number of participants from any one country was awarded to the British contingent. Other smaller rallies were held both in Europe and in the U.K., as well as International Youth Rallies, which were well attended. The Youth Rally at Oteppe, Belgium in 1975, was notable for the thick treacley mud left by constant rain and snow and on which the participants had to pitch. [As a parent who had to clean up all the gear after that particular event, the least said the better!]

Unfortunately very few Club tours were organised, apart from those taking participants to International Rallies, mainly because more and more members were looking to travel independently by car. The Social and Cultural Section arranged a Winter holiday in Mallorca in 1973, and also organised more tours to Turkey.

In 1974 a change in the Air Charter regulations meant that the *raison d'être* for the Section became invalid and was therefore wound up. Future tours would be arranged by committees of the Club and by Headquarters staff. In practice, most of the future tours were to the F.I.C.C. rallies. The development of the Club's travel services and the introduction of Carefree holidays – where ready-erected tents could be booked abroad through the Club – during this decade made it much easier for independent car travellers, although there is no doubt that the camerarderie experienced on the Club tours will never be forgotten by those who went on them.

Another new venture was Club rallies in Europe where Club volunteer stewards stayed on a specially-booked area of a commercial site, reserved for Club members. The area was run as a Club Meet and members had the advantage of an English-speaking steward with local knowledge and who was also often proficient in the local language.

The Club's attendance at national exhibitions faltered somewhat in the

1970s. The Camping and Outdoor Life Exhibition in 1971 was supported poorly by the camping trade. The large presence of the motor-cycle and cycle trade did not help those members specifically looking for camping equipment. The Club agreed to sponsor the 1972 show, although its stand was later criticised by the organiser, which would no longer offer free tickets to full members. Lacking a substantial change of attitude by the organiser in 1975, the Club announced it would no longer participate in the Camping and Outdoor Life Exhibitions. It did, however, continue to take stand space at various other caravan shows.

Television do-it-yourself guru, Barry Bucknall, teamed up with the Daily Mirror to produce kits of popular leisure items. Best-known of course is the Mirror dinghy but Barry also produced the Mirror trailer tent which was regularly advertised in the Club magazine. (Club Archive)

Do what we tell you

(and save a whole lot of new pence)

Just follow our simple illustrated instructions, which come with the set of kit parts—and you have a Mirror Tent Trailer.

Prices are from £180·23 (£180 4s 6d), depending on which version you want and you can save upwards of seven thousand new pence compared with the cost complete.

The parts are pre-cut and numbered for ease of construction. A few weekends and your Mirror Tent Trailer is ready.

From then on you can go where you like and stop where you like. Your holiday home is ready for you literally at a moment's notice.

Send for a brochure to Mirror Tent Trailers, Department CO, Daily Mirror, 33 Holborn, London EC1.

Mirror Tent Trailer

Caravans from the 1970s
by Andrew Jenkinson

Once inside the Sprite, life was a simple affair, extras could be added at a later date. The Sprite name was unfortunately dropped from the U.K. market on its 50th year in 1998.

Launched in 1977 was this Alpha Sport the shape of caravans to come? It certainly was ahead of its time.

Panther models were to become an overnight success, this is the 500 from 1973.

To many the 1970s will be the era that they first began caravanning. Many fondly remember some of those touring caravans that graced our sites and roads. It was a time when caravans could easily be identified from one make to the next and names such as Eccles, Knowsley, Sprite and Thomson were on most caravanners' wish lists.

Water pumps and 12V strip lamps were basic essentials. Double glazing didn't become widespread till the early 1980s nor did fridges or heaters for that matter – unless you bought one of the super clubman tourers. A typical towcar would have been a Ford Cortina – and if you were well-off you would have chosen the caravanner's dream tug – a Volvo 240. Sites in general were not well appointed, as most caravanners' needs were few.

In those days if you were a first-time caravanner chances are that you would have bought a 12ft Sprite Alpine (£438 in 1972) or maybe the 14ft Musketeer at a little over £480 in the same year. For that you got a basic caravan, with equipment consisting of a two-burner hob with grill and two gas lamps. You did get a super parts back-up though, a well-proven design and a caravan from the world's largest manufacturer.

The Sprite/Ci umbrella encompassed Eccles, Europa and Fairholme, all popular choices with caravan buyers. Ci was even to venture into that void of solus dealerships, copied years later by A.B.I.

Which brings us to Ace who, like Astral, Mardon, Silverline and Swift, expanded the Humberside area as a major caravan manufacturing centre. Ace joined with holiday-home maker Belmont to form A.B.I., a new force in the industry. For a time A.B.I. owned Elddis but by 1990 Elddis was independent again.

When A.B.I. launched the low cost Monza range for 1973 it hit Sprite sales straight away. Then Abbey, Astral, Bailey, and Thomson launched new budget ranges to capture Sprite's lucrative market.

Meanwhile luxury clubman tourer manufacturers such as Carlight, Castleton, Cotswold, Safari, Viking and Welton were making high quality, well-equipped caravans. Their heavy weights meant that towcars such as Jaguar and Rover were favourites to pull them.

New manufacturer Avondale scored well with its distinctive clubman tourers and spread into other market areas with its budget Perle and mid-market Leda. The latter were based on export models, and were also to sport layouts including the early end bathroom designs. Until the late 1970s the end-kitchen reigned supreme, and was classed as the elite of all layouts.

Boom time for the caravanning industry was the beginning of the 1970s. Manufacturers mushroomed. Most were from around the Hull area but some such as Fleetwind, Lunar, Trophy and Viscount started to put the north west firmly on the caravan makers' map.

In the mid-1970s the introduction of Value Added Tax, the oil crisis and inflation sent tourer sales tumbling. Clubman makers such as Cheltenham and Welton were forced out of business.

Manufacturers such as Forest, Mustang and Panther went into holiday-home production, as this market lay virtually unaffected, re-joining tourer manufacture as things picked up a year or so later.

Apart from full independent suspension being the norm by this decade, when it came to reversing your tourer it was a case of "unhitch and shove". Auto reverse systems weren't available until 1974. The Sigma unit was put into place on the B&B chassis (now Al-Ko), and this revolutionised this caravanning manoeuvre.

Caravan interiors, like now, were fairly conservative in design, but Lynton changed all that, with these rosewood and purple colour schemes. By 1977 Lynton had returned to conventional interiors.

Al-Ko was first used in the U.K. by Astral caravans in 1977 on its export Shadows, which it made available to U.K. buyers complete with polyplastic double glazing, heater, fridge, plus full polystyrene insulation. The slight upturn in tourer sales saw some new makers, such as Churchill, Compass, Elite, and Monolite introduced to the market. After a few years most went out of production, with the exception of the ex-Elddis founders Cooks with the Compass range.

Safari had become part of Cosalt, then makers of Abbey. Safaris were also classed as an elite tourer, and were definitely on the "made it list" in caravanning circles.

Bedtime in a 1975 Monza; as a child I loved having a bunk bed in the 'van.

Churchill were fine-looking clubman tourers and became popular in the 1970s – designed as a value-for-money luxury tourer.

Estuary's Cavalier 1200 S from 1972, again a very popular range of tourers, and many members will have owned one at some time.

1980–1989: Another move and a Royal site

The 1980s saw many new developments within the Club, not least of which was a change of name, a move to new specially-built premises in Coventry and the election of the first lady Chairman since World War One. It would also see another 20 new sites, including one on a Royal estate, and the further development of additional services for members. The General Secretary, George Cubitt, retired at the end of the decade after almost 33 years service, and the Club was to mourn the death of John Lloyd, elected Chairman in 1984, during the first year of his term of office.

The Club celebrated its 80th birthday with a reception at London's Guildhall where Sir John Cripps, former Chairman of the Countryside Commission and an eminent countryside expert, accepted the office of Club President. He made it clear that he intended to take an active part in Club affairs. Throughout the decade he attended many National Council meetings and all the N.F.O.L.s, where he made it his business to meet as many Club members as possible.

At the beginning of the Club's 80th year the Editor of *Camping and Caravanning* looked back to the Club's first 'Coming of Age' to find evidence of a remarkable continuity: "Although the D.A.s were far fewer and met less frequently, their activities were as varied as they are today and enthusiastically supported. The youthful caravan group was flexing its

Left: The Camping and Caravanning Club Patron, H.R.H. Prince Philip, Duke of Edinburgh. The Club celebrated 50 years of royal patronage in 1988. King George VI granted his patronage to the Club in 1948 and Prince Philip became Patron in 1952 after the King's death. This picture was taken in 1990 at the opening of the Club Site on the Sandringham Estate.
(Peter Frost)

In the wider world

South Atlantic War: 1982 was marked by the invasion of the Falkland Islands by Argentinian forces and the counter-offensive mounted from Britain, over 8,000 miles away. As an exercise in logistics it was an outstanding achievement but heavy losses were sustained on both sides before British rule was re-established.

Chips with everything: 1982 saw a rapid increase in the use of silicon micro-chips in new items such as pocket calculators, watches, word processors and many more devices. The technique by which complete electronic circuits can be imprinted onto tiny pieces of silicon gave rise to almost limitless possibilities in the future.

Olympic gold for Bolero: The young Nottingham pair of ice skaters, Jayne Torvill and Christopher Dean, captivated the audience and gained maximum points from all judges for their interpretation of Ravel's *Bolero* at the Olympic ice dancing event, which had previously been dominated by Russia.

Storm Havoc hits south-east: During the early hours of 16 October 1987, hurricane force winds left many thousands of trees devastated, much damage to property and a number of deaths, in a trail of destruction from Cornwall to East Anglia. Gusts up to 110mph caused greater havoc than any storm in the 20th century.

muscles, and the horse had not yet been superseded by the motor car as a means of traction. Foreign Touring, on an organised Club basis, was more popular than it is today. Fixed camps, of the type we now call Holiday Rallies, were a regular feature of Club life and Brittany was a favourite spot, just as it is today after the passing of nearly 60 years.

"If we exclude the inevitable development of camping and caravanning equipment, and the equally inevitable growth of a vast production and marketing industry, the main difference between the Club's early years and today is the expansion of the pastime from one with a small and predominantly middle-class appeal to one with a universal following. Many thousands of members had joined for strictly economic reasons, a reflection of the times.

"The Club should take pride in the fact that it can provide a home and a voice for all its varied membership and, as in the past, act as the 'impartial custodian of the pastime'."

The truth of the final paragraph was amply confirmed when a special meeting of the National Council was convened early in 1981 to consider the Minister's Conclusions to the Touring Caravanning and Tent Camping Consultation paper, produced after more than ten years of talking, writing and consideration.

One of the Civil Servants involved addressed the Council and answered questions from those present. It was clear from the start that restrictions on tent-camping, hitherto virtually non-existent, could be catastrophic, since the vast majority of tent-camping at popular holiday resorts in peak periods was on unlicensed sites. Indeed 75 per cent of tent camping and as much as 60 per cent of caravanning was accommodated on such sites.

If the proposals were implemented then only five units would be allowed on any one of these sites and it was suggested that eight units would be allowed on a site granted a certificate by an exempted organisation. It was not thought possible to devise a formula that would take account of tents according to size, and the term 'tents' would apply to tents of all sizes, including children's pup tents that would have to be counted as a separate unit. There would be no restrictions for lightweight tents if these were used in remote and wild country, not accessible by motor vehicles.

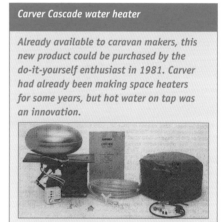

Carver Cascade water heater

Already available to caravan makers, this new product could be purchased by the do-it-yourself enthusiast in 1981. Carver had already been making space heaters for some years, but hot water on tap was an innovation.

The Association of District Councils and the Council for the Preservation of Rural England suggested that up to ten tents be allowed on an unlicensed site, and this was endorsed by some Club Regions and the British Caravanners' Club (B.C.C.). The Club's Management Committee felt that five units was far too

Fun and games at Stratfield Saye's National Feast of Lanterns, 1989. A team from the Association of Lightweight Campers takes the lead in the gun carriage race. (Graham Patterson)

drastic, and since many of these sites would be for caravans only so the reduction in tent pitches would be much more severe than it would first appear. It suggested ten units, but with not more than three, or possibly five of those to be caravans.

The Council felt the time to implement the proposals would be when it became clearly evident that "there will be adequate accommodation for members of the public who wish to camp and caravan". The Club also proposed that clubs authorised to establish certificated sites should be given the power to do so in respect of either caravans, tents or both caravans and tents, according to the make-up of their membership. At the time The Caravan Club had over 3,000 Certificated Locations as against The Camping Club's 250 Certificated Sites. If The Caravan Club were able to accept tents onto their sites The Camping Club would clearly be at a big disadvantage. It was impossible to forecast when the Bill would be introduced before Parliament, but it was unlikely to be before 1981 or 1982 and could possibly be later.

The fears of the Cambrian and Wyvern Region unfortunately proved founded when the Article Four Directive became operative in July 1981. The whole area of the Gower Area of Outstanding Natural Beauty was affected, not just small sensitive areas within its boundaries. The Club felt that the original intention of such directives was that they would only be applied to small areas. Certainly they were not intended as a blanket cover for the whole of an area.

The effect of the Directive was to stop all exempted camping both for individual Club members and for Club units. This loss of freedom to camp hit the West Wales District Association (D.A.) very severely, and it

Members of the National Council, 1981. Chairman Vic Sinden is in the centre front row, Vice-Chairman Molly Rayner to his right and Honorary Treasurer Vic Jones to his left. (Club Archive)

was also a heavy administrative burden on it. It was not always possible to specify the actual field to be used for a meet when applying for planning permission, and the arbitrary imposition of numerical limits on meets for which planning consent was granted caused even more problems. A member of Headquarters staff was detailed to accompany the D.A. officials on all meetings with the local authority and other bodies. This person would also be responsible for preparing and submitting planning applications on behalf of the D.A. The Club continued to oppose the making of Article Four Directives over large areas of land, so made great efforts to get Club Meets excluded from the Gower Article Four Directive, unfortunately without success. Meanwhile the D.A. was assured of the National Council's help and support in overcoming its difficulties.

It is when problems such as these occur that you realise the huge amount of work and responsibility that is taken on by ordinary people who volunteer to take office in the Club's Regions, D.A.s and Sections, simply because of their enjoyment of camping and without any monetary rewards.

The long-awaited new legislation on camping and caravanning suddenly appeared in 1983 when Peter Hubbard-Miles, the newly-elected M.P. for Bridgend, was successful in the ballot for Private Members' Bills to go before Parliament. His Caravan and Tents Sites Bill later became a victim of party political manoeuvring and was repeatedly objected to on Second Reading. It was eventually talked out in the House of Commons in July 1984. The Bill was now dead and its demise gave the Club an opportunity to reconsider the question of new legislation affecting camping and caravanning. Ron Harding said he hoped the opportunity would be taken to draw up positive proposals on matters which the Club would like to see in any new Bill but the Management Committee decided that no further action would be taken until fresh proposals for legislation were put forward.

The 1983 General Election caused many changes in Parliament during which the Club lost its staunchest parliamentary ally when James Wellbeloved, M.P., was narrowly defeated and lost his seat. The Club acknowledges the enormous debt of gratitude for the time and effort he gave freely in defending its interests over a long period of years. He succeeded in blocking many Bills to the Club's advantage. He was elected a Vice-President of the Club in 1984. Fortunately several other M.P.s rallied round to fill the gap left by his departure and helped to support the Club in its fight against Peter Hubbard-Miles' Bill.

JAMES WELLBELOVED, M.P. from 1965–1983, was Chairman of the All-Party Camping and Caravanning Group from 1967–1983. He was able to influence Ministers, government departments and civil servants in respect of proposals that might adversely affect camping and caravanning and played a leading role in scrutinising legislation which might affect camping. He is a Vice-President of the Club.

After yet another consultation paper on Caravan and Tent Site licensing appeared early in 1987, the Government decided to shelve its proposals to amend the licensing laws on camping and caravanning sites. The sense of urgency that was apparent when the proposed changes, first envisaged almost 20 years previously, were made was no longer relevant. Camp sites had increased in number more or less in step with the number of people wishing to use them. There had been no appreciative overcrowding,

West Kent District Association's entry in the Mardi Gras parade at the National Feast of Lanterns, Brands Hatch, 1982. (P.H. Constance)

The Fitzgerald family backpacking at Graffham Club Site, 1981. (P.H. Constance)

even in the most popular areas at the height of the season, and the vision of pitchless campers and caravanners filling lay-bys never materialised. Much of the credit for the establishment of satisfactory camp sites must be given both to this Club and to The Caravan Club, both of whom worked extremely hard to establish good quality sites over these years.

Another blow to camping of a different kind occurred in 1981 when there was an outbreak of Foot and Mouth disease. All camping was forbidden in affected areas and Club sites in other areas that were subject to restrictions were closed while the restraints were in force.

Towards the end of the decade, which had more than its fair share of poor summers, the hurricane in October 1987 severely affected meets, particularly in the Eastern and South-East Regions. Club sites in the path of the hurricane did not escape. Many trees were lost but damage to buildings and other property was comparatively slight. It took a four-man team the whole of the following winter to deal with tree clearance and repair work on Club sites.

The Club began to take on more and more professional services for the benefit of members. In 1981 a Club Insurance bureau was established to exploit the size and character of the Club membership in securing advantageous terms and rates for various types of insurance that could be offered as a benefit of Club membership. This would clearly be an excellent recruiting incentive. The Club already offered free kit insurance as well as third party cover for incidents that might happen when camping. However, the kit insurance was very limited. Problems often occurred as it was not always realised how limited the cover actually was until a claim was made.

Carefree services were expanded to include a Pitch Abroad reservation scheme where members could book their ferry crossings and reserve a pitch on selected sites in France. A vehicle recovery service was introduced at the same time. Arrangements were made for members to book caravan or tent-camping holidays further afield through a specialist company at reduced rates in 1984. At the same time the Club introduced a Special Finance Plan enabling members to obtain loans for camping equipment, cars and caravans, etc, at specially advantageous rates. This was yet another scheme that would hopefully attract more members.

Holidays in ready-erected tents with Eurocamp and bookings through Eurocamp Independent were later offered to members but these were not as popular as it was thought they would be. Eurocamp later pulled out of the scheme and Carefree reverted to the original Pitch Abroad scheme. It extended the network of sites available to members in countries other than France. By the end of the decade members were able to choose just any one of the services offered by Carefree – either a ferry booking, or the holiday insurance, or car recovery or take the whole package. Special terms were offered to Club members to join R.A.C. as Associate Members through the

Zippy Ashmore – now a veteran member and still canoeing – and his dog, Penny, at Kegworth Lock in 1984. (Ron Harding, Club Archive)

Lightweight tents were growing to family size in 1986. Frame tents were not so numerous and more families were beginning to appreciate the convenience of the smaller tents. Phoenix, well known for its mountain tents, introduced a new tent, the Phor 4 for families who wished to go what Phoenix described as "car boot-packing".

Club at reduced rates and considerably better benefits than those offered to other R.A.C. members. In 1989 a Club Credit Card was offered to members, carrying with it a number of useful benefits.

Problems with membership handling continued to occur. Several pleas were made for a rolling membership system that would allow a member to join at any time of the year and renew again in one year's time. Although the 18-month membership option for those joining in the main season was popular, the system of full-year, half-year and 18-month memberships was a nightmare for the volunteer members to explain to the public at the Club stands of various shows.

The explanation of the fees was so complicated and sometimes long-winded that people often lost interest and walked away. The idea of rolling membership was rejected in 1984 and 1985, largely because the operation of the membership records was outside the control of the Club but it would be considered again as and when the Club had sufficient accommodation and proper computer facilities to bring membership records handling back in-house. A system was finally installed at Club Headquarters in 1986, although membership records continued to be handled by an outside agency.

Club fees rose rather sharply during the decade, rising to £18 for a Full Member in 1990. Although some of the rises were rather high, the Club subscription was still considered good value for money. Rising costs had to be met and there was a need to improve and expand Club services to members.

A big recruiting drive was launched in 1986 after a bumper year when the membership figures increased by over 8,000. More members were needed for a variety of reasons, not least that the more members the Club had the stronger the its voice would be in defending campers' interests. The Club also needed the finances to expand, improve and extend services generally. Another reason was that the more active members there were in the D.A.s and Sections, the stronger the voluntary activity of the Club would be.

Recruitment was nevertheless a problem, especially with tent campers. Ron Harding said that not enough money was being spent on publicity. This was evident in that tent-campers were leaving the Club and new tent-campers were not being recruited because they felt the Club had become caravan-orientated. The Club also needed to emphasise that it was the only large Club catering for all forms of camping. A free weekend on a Club site was offered as a recruitment incentive, but Northern Ireland Region pointed out that this was no help to them as they had no Club sites in their Region, and members would need to come to the mainland to redeem their vouchers! It was suggested that special recruitment incentives involving some form of discount rather than vouchers redeemable at Club sites should be offered.

The free membership scheme for state pensioners with 25 years continuous membership of the Club was reviewed in 1983 in the light of a recommendation by the Management Committee that it be terminated. There were already over 800 members taking advantage of the offer and the numbers were growing larger each year. It was agreed to continue the scheme for a further three years and then introduce a reduced subscription for those members who qualified

Club Treasurer Vic Jones escorts Prince Philip around the new Sandringham Club Site, along with Club President Sir John Cripps (in the background), Club Chairman Terry Burchnall (behind Prince Philip), and Club Director General George Cubitt. (Peter Frost)

for it. Club sites were rapidly expanding, with the Club taking on the management of more local authority sites and purchasing the freehold of several others as well as developing new ones. Unfortunately Denham Court, which the Club had managed for 50 years, had to close in 1986. Operating difficulties and continuing financial losses were stated as the reasons, due mainly to the fact that the site did not accept trailer caravans and there was only chemical sanitation.

Emphasis had to be placed on upgrading and improving Club-operated sites to the standards of the Club's competitors. The Sites Management Committee proposed spending one and a quarter million pounds to do this. At least 27 Club sites were in urgent need of maintenance and upgrading in order to provide the facilities campers were beginning to ask for, and which were commonly available on sites owned by commercial operators and other organisations. The National Council agreed but said something also had to be done to attract more family campers to Club sites, possibly by adjusting the fees. Eventually special family deals were offered to families with more than one child, enabling some of the children to camp free of charge in the high season (they already camped free in early and late seasons).

The Club now had to look at the site network in a commercial way and compete on standards with commercial sites. The site fees had to be increased and there were quite a few objections to this. Increases were necessary to meet rising costs and to maintain the financial viability of the network so that it would not become a drain on the Club's income from other sources. Many members also felt that the Club should not open its sites to non-members, even though an extra charge was made. In many cases this had to be done to ensure sites were viable. At those sites which the Club managed for outside bodies, local authorities, etc, the Club was obliged to accept non-members. There were still a few Club-owned sites strictly for members only.

A new Sites Director, Ron Walker, was appointed to succeed the former Sites Manager early in 1985 and the Club was delighted when two of its sites – Great Shelford in Cambridge, and West Runton, near Cromer in

In the crypt of London's Guildhall on the occasion of the Chairman's Reception, 1980. (Back row, left to right) Stan Lowczowski, Sir John Cripps, George Cubitt, Valery Kelly, Peter Marsh, Iain Morris, Pa Cousins, ? and Bob Reynolds. (Front row, left to right) Josephine Franklin, Lillian Cura, Jessie Challis, Vic Sinden, Grace Sinden, Jean Reynolds, Margaret Cruickshank and Edith Cousins.

MRS MOLLY RAYNER, who joined the Club in 1947, was Secretary to West Essex District Association, North London and Eastern Counties and Chiltern Regions and Regional Representative to National Council. She had a season ticket at Balls Park and worked on the committees there. In 1982 she became the first lady Chairman of the Club since 1916.

Norfolk – won the prestigious Midland Camp Site of the Year award from the Automobile Association in 1986 and 1989 respectively.

Some 20 new Club sites were opened during the decade, although three others, Denham Court, Saltram and Byrness-in-Redesdale had to be closed. In 1989 Her Majesty the Queen granted a lease to the Club for its new camp site on the Royal Estate at Sandringham. This most prestigious of the new Club Sites was opened by the Club's Patron, H.R.H. Prince Philip, Duke of Edinburgh, in 1990.

Despite the generally poor weather throughout the decade there was a record occupancy of Club sites. Temporary Holiday Sites (T.H.S.s) grew in number and continued to flourish. Some complaints had been received about the use of Citizens' Band (C.B.) radios on Club sites and at D.A. Meets. These were at first prohibited by the Management Committee but the National Council lifted the ban because site rules relating to nuisance could, if necessary, be enforced. In some cases C.B. radios were helpful when an emergency occurred.

In 1982 Mrs Molly Rayner became the first lady Chairman of the Club since Mrs Elizabeth Lynn during World War One. An early resolution passed by the National Council under her Chairmanship was to give the Club's non-voting Sections the opportunity to nominate one of their members each year for a Certificate of Honour.

There were also changes to some of the Club committees, the main one being the T.H.S. Sub-committee, which became a main committee of the Club. A proposal that the Club should run T.H.S.s was to be actively pursued. In the end Club Headquarters did the work of applying for planning permission and made contacts with the relevant authorities, although Club units were responsible for the actual running of the T.H.S. An administration charge had to be added to the site fees to cover the expenses involved by Headquarters in doing this work. There was some objection to the charge but all meets had to be self-financing and it was felt that the Club's administrative work should be paid for by the units running the meets.

SIR JOHN CRIPPS had a great love of the countryside and was Editor of The Countryman magazine from 1947–1971. He was Chairman of Nature Conservancy from 1970–1973, Chairman of the Countryside Commission from 1970–1977 and President of the Club from 1981–1991. He and his wife, Lady Ann, enjoyed camping and much preferred their tent to the caravan which was often provided at official Club functions.

The lightweight area at the National Feast of Lanterns, Weston Park, Shropshire, 1990. (P.H. Constance)

The Public Relations Committee was divided into the Publicity Committee and a Publications Sub-committee, and the International Committee was abolished and an International Officer appointed instead.

Under Molly Rayner's Chairmanship, on 1 November 1983, the Club officially changed its name to The Camping and Caravanning Club Ltd. The camping trade responded by donating a new Chairman's Badge to the Club, the formal presentation being made to John Harris at the Camping and Outdoor Leisure Association's Annual Dinner at Harrogate in November 1985. A President's badge was also obtained and presented to Sir John Cripps, who declared himself proud to be its first wearer.

During the decade the Club suffered the loss of several well-known members. Capt. Frazer-Allen, without whose efforts in collecting archive material and researching into the history of the Holding family and the Club it would have lost much of its recorded history, died in February 1981.

Two Council members, former Chairman 'Dai' Evans and S.T.A. Rouse, who was President of the B.C.C. died in 1983, and 'Hicky' Liversidge, another former Chairman, died in 1984. The death of John Lloyd in 1985 during his term of office was most keenly felt. He had been elected Chairman in 1984. His death was a great and unexpected blow both to his family and to the Club. A fund to his memory was established and was used to help the development costs at the Club's newest site at

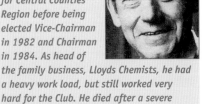

JOHN LLOYD originally joined the National Council as the Representative for Central Counties Region before being elected Vice-Chairman in 1982 and Chairman in 1984. As head of the family business, Lloyds Chemists, he had a heavy work load, but still worked very hard for the Club. He died after a severe heart attack in the Spring of 1985 after less than one year as Chairman.

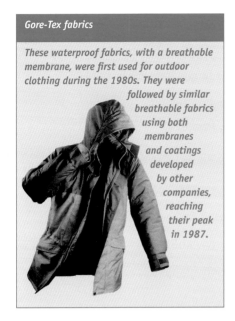

Gore-Tex fabrics

These waterproof fabrics, with a breathable membrane, were first used for outdoor clothing during the 1980s. They were followed by similar breathable fabrics using both membranes and coatings developed by other companies, reaching their peak in 1987.

the time, Rhandirmwyn, near Llandovery, which was designated The John Lloyd Memorial Site. Bill Whiteman, a Club Vice-President and well-respected caravan journalist, died at the end of 1989.

Because of the appointment of a new Sites Director, the Secretary-General was appointed Director General in 1985. Extra staff were employed at Headquarters to help improve services to members, and a Director of Administration, Lt. Col. Claude Smith, O.B.E., was appointed in 1987. Vic Jones, the Club's Honorary Treasurer was appointed an M.B.E. in the New Year Honours List of 1988. He was the first of the Club's Honorary Officers to receive such an award. He said it was an honour for the Club and to the many voluntary officers, their wives and husbands, who served it.

In December 1986 the Club magazine had a new look. Using better quality, but still lightweight paper, enabled superior colour reproduction of photographs to be used. Peter Frost, who was Art Editor at the time, was appointed Editor of the magazine at the end of 1987 when Iain Morris retired. In 1989 the April issue of the magazine went on sale on the bookstalls as a recruiting incentive. It was full of articles on the theme of "all you ever wanted to know about caravans and camping but were afraid to ask". It was well received. Another new move was to publish the

Club Chairman Mrs Molly Rayner, centre, at a Club Annual General Meeting.

Out & About pages in the magazine as a separate supplement.

The *Club Handbook and Sites List* was now published every two years and sported a full colour photograph on the cover. In 1987 a larger format was used in order to accommodate all the additional sites and in 1989 a more radical change took place when the format was changed again to A4 size. The Club sites were published annually in a separate book, *Your Place in the Country* and the listed sites were published biennially in *Your Big Sites Book*. With the help of Club members more than 1,000 Certificated Sites had been added to the sites list by June 1984, and by the end of the decade there were more than 1,500 such sites available to members. The *Handbook Section* was now published as a separate book and was issued free of charge to all current Full Members and all new Full Members. A new *Handbook* would only be issued when a major revision or a reprint was required.

A new *International Sites List*, based solely on recommendations from Club members, was published in 1983 and sold well, but there were considerable gaps in the information provided. In 1986 the Club

Aerial view of the International Federation of Camping and Caravanning Rally, Shepton Mallet, 1990. (Margaret Groves)

co-operated with R.A.C. to produce a first joint International Guide, but there were many complaints about the binding falling apart.

The Regions and D.A.s continued to play their important roles within the Club, particularly in the organisation of T.H.S.s and the National Feast of Lanterns (N.F.O.L.). The N.F.O.L organised by North West Region at Tatton Park was notable for the appalling weather. More than 3,500 units attended and many tents were damaged in high winds, causing

Today, most campers arrive by car, but it wasn't always so. Wilf and Doris Wilton always travelled by public transport to Club sites, carrying their kit on small trolleys. (P.H. Constance)

quite a few members to give up and go home early. Two marquees were flattened but there were no serious injuries and only the parachute drop had to be cancelled.

Those who braved the weather enjoyed themselves. The following year there was good weather when South West Region hosted the event at Shepton Mallet, although less than 3,000 units attended. In 1985 prolonged rain did not dampen the spirits of those who braved the Yorkshire weather at Castle Howard, even though some of the roadways were a sea of mud by the end of the weekend. The event at Silverstone in 1986 was blessed with beautiful weather after a lot of rain had soaked members of the working party the previous week. Almost 10,000 people were present and there were some fantastic interpretations of the 'Transport through the Ages' theme for the weekend. The N.F.O.L. for 1987 was held at Lincoln Showground with over 4,500 units, while in 1988 the venue was Lartington, near Barnard Castle, another event with somewhat mixed weather. Southern Region organised the 1989 N.F.O.L. at Stratfield Saye in Berkshire, and in 1990 Weston Park, in Shropshire, was the venue.

Three new D.A.s, Bangor (Northern Ireland), North Gloucestershire and Sarum were founded during the decade. Birmingham D.A., effectively the Club's oldest D.A., celebrated its 75th birthday with a grand meet at Stratford-on-Avon Racecourse in 1982. Section activity was generally

flourishing but the Mountaineering Section decided in 1987 that it could
not continue in its present form because numbers had dropped to below
100. The Management Committee considered ways and means of reviving it,
and in September it was announced that a Mountaineering and Activity
Section would replace the Mountaineering Section with a broader base of
activity. Derek Wood of the Yorkshire Region was thanked for his efforts in
getting the new Section going and by March 1988 it was fully operational
under the title of the Mountain Activity Section. In 1988 it was noted there
was a need to improve relations between the Regions and the Sections so
steps were taken to enable them to play a fuller part in the administration
of the Club at Regional level by enabling them to send a representative to
Regional Council meetings.

This was particularly important where the Sections did not have a
large group within a Region but needed their views to be heard. The Youth
Section was having problems with recruiting, despite the activities which
were on offer. At the beginning of 1981 there were more than 9,000
members, but by 1990 Youth Section membership had dropped to 1,798.
This was extremely worrying, for the Youth Members form the nucleus of
future Club membership.

It was decided that only members of the Club's Youth Section who had

The Camping and Caravanning Club's Headquarters in Coventry.

First in the field A Century of The Camping and Caravanning Club

passed the Youth Camping Test would in future be allowed to camp on Club-operated sites without supervision from the age of 14.

In former days when many sites had their own Youth Leader there was no problem. Now the sites were all Wardened and run on commercial lines it was necessary to ensure that Youth members were

The Club danced into the pages of the Guinness Book of Records at the National Feast of Lanterns, Brands Hatch, 1982. 8,659 people linked up for the conga around the racing circuit to take the world record. It's still a British record, but sadly, 119,986 people just pipped the Club in Miami, Florida, 1988. (M. Winnell, Club Archive)

proficient before being allowed to camp on such sites on their own. International Youth Rallies were still very popular and one amusing incident occurred in France in 1989 when the Club Youth were runners-up in the football competition. Subsequently it was discovered that the winning team were in fact a local football team and were not participants in the Rally! As a result, the Camping Club Youth (C.C.Y.) team were declared to be the winners.

Endeavours were made to rekindle interest in the Club's Countryside Care scheme in 1985 with the appointment of a National Countryside Care Officer. In July of the following year the Club was rewarded by the presentation of a Certificate of Commendation by the Keep Britain Tidy Group under their Beautiful Britain award scheme for the efforts made under the Club's Countryside Care Schemes.

Interest in International Federation of Camping and Caravanning (F.I.C.C.) Rallies was maintained with many members making the long trip to Finland in 1981, the Costa Brava, Spain in 1982 and a much shorter journey to Paris in 1983. Other venues included Poland, Portugal, Hungary, Denmark, and Ireland. The Rally in Austria in 1989 was a disaster. The host country was completely unprepared for the vast numbers participating. Many British Club members had travelled a long way at some considerable expense and were very disappointed. The Rally in 1990 at Shepton Mallet, organised by the Club, restored much of the damage done by the fiasco of the 1989 Rally and fulsome tributes to the organising skills of the British appeared in publications and letters from many countries.

In 1989 it was announced that the Club would revert to its former practice of rotating the Annual General Meetings (A.G.M.s) around the country and in future the appropriate Region would be responsible for the organisation of the event. The Club A.G.M.s are attended by many more people than would have been able to attend in London. Overall attendances are also very much greater.

The most notable event of the decade was the decision to move Club Headquarters out of London so in 1988 a site on the outskirts of Coventry was inspected. The Club's Executive was authorised to proceed with negotiations, as there would be considerable savings on outgoings in the future. The rising costs of real estate in London were phenomenal and the Club could no longer afford to have premises there. By the end of January 1989 contracts were drawn up and it was hoped the premises would be ready for occupation by the end of the year. The National Council met in Coventry in July and was taken to see the site. Although the foundations had been laid it was by now obvious that the building – Greenfields House – would not be ready for occupation until January or February 1990. Claude Smith was appointed Deputy Director-General to oversee the move to the new premises, and he would succeed George Cubitt when he retired, which would not be later than April 1991.

By February 1990, the Club had decided on the name Greenfields House for the new Headquarters, and this was confirmed as the Registered Office of the Club. The move from London was accomplished smoothly in March 1990, with many new staff, recruited locally, settling in well. The lease on Lower Grosvenor Place in London was sold in August, although that on the additional premises used by the Club in Grosvenor Gardens was proving much more difficult to dispose of. In September 1990 David Welsford was welcomed as Director of Administration (designate) and it was announced that George Cubitt would retire as Director General at the end of December. With new computers installed and a specialist in charge, the membership handling was brought back in-house in November 1990. By the end of 1990, the membership was a little short of 200,000.

Left: The Club Patron, H.R.H. Prince Philip, Duke of Edinburgh, takes time out at the opening of Sandringham Club Site to look inside a member's awning and caravan.
(Peter Frost)

1991–2001:
From strength to strength and into the future

D espite a generally gloomy economic situation when many businesses experienced great difficulties, the Club thrived during the next ten years. Its 90th birthday was marked with a special pennon and a souvenir issue of *Camping and Caravanning*, and the Association of Lightweight Campers held its 90th Birthday Meet at Wantage, near the site of the first Official Camp of the Association of Cycle Campers in 1901.

The Canoe-Camping Club's Diamond Jubilee in 1993 was celebrated with an International Tour of the Thames, the first-ever event in the U.K. with official International Canoe Federation status. It also won the Federation's Trophy for the best organised international event of the year. Special meets marked the Golden Jubilees of the Club's original Regions and the Yorkshire Region, the Silver Jubilees of the younger Regions and the 21st birthday of Northern Ireland Region.

Birmingham District Association (D.A.) had two notable anniversaries, its 90th birthday and 40 years of its Temporary Holiday Sites (T.H.S.s) at Harlyn Bay, Cornwall, believed to be the first ever T.H.S. run by a D.A. The Boating Group celebrated its 21st birthday and the Mountain Activity Section its 10th birthday. Members were challenged to climb Britain's three highest peaks, many managed at least one, but

In the wider world
A woman in space: International co-operation in space exploration took a further step forward when a British woman scientist, Helen Sharman, joined Russian astronauts in a space mission on board a Russian spacecraft. On her safe return to Earth, Helen made a number of visits to schools, describing her experience and encouraging pupils, especially girls, to take up science as a career.

War in the Gulf: The invasion of oil-rich Kuwait by Iraq led to massive retaliation by Anglo-American air, ground and naval forces in Operation Desert Storm. Despite fears of the possible use by Iraq of chemical or biological weapons, the invading forces were defeated, although many think that political rather than military decisions left the job uncompleted.

Happy birthday, Ma'am: In August 2000 the whole nation rejoiced in the 100th birthday of Queen Elizabeth the Queen Mother who, from the early days of World War One, the unexpected accession to the throne of her husband, his passing away after World War Two and her subsequent appearances in public life, retained a place in the affections of everyone.

Global warming: The oft-repeated predictions of global warming seem at odds with the weather experienced during much of 1999 and 2000, when the cold and wet conditions, with flooding in many areas, were not conducive to good camping weather. Maybe the experts have got it wrong after all?

Left: The Camping and Caravanning Club Site at Luss. (Club Archive)

several made it up all three. Another highlight was the formation of The Camping and Caravanning Club Band in 1994.

Notable awards to Club members included the award in 1991 of the Gold Medal of the Féderation Française de Camping et de Caravaning to Eric Stride, the Club's International Officer, and the award of the

OLIVE REAY, M.B.E. joined the Club in 1969 and was Club Chairman from 1993–1995. Right from the start she has been active in the Club at local and national levels. She received the M.B.E. for services to camping in 1995. She is President of Durham District Association and a Vice-President of the Club.

M.B.E. to Olive Reay in June 1995 and Ralph Lee in January 1999.

Sir John Cripps retired in March 1991 due to ill-health, after serving ten years as Club President, and sadly died in the Autumn of 1993. George Cubitt, who had recently retired as Director General, was appointed a Vice-President in 1991. In the following year Lord Robert Baden-Powell, grandson of Lord Baden-Powell of Gilwell, was appointed President of the Club. In 1995 Claude Smith, the Director General, retired and was succeeded by David Welsford, the present incumbent.

RALPH LEE, M.B.E., awarded the M.B.E. in 1999 for services to caravanning, joined the Club in 1922 and built his first caravan in 1931. Well-known for his articles on caravanning, he also advises the Club's Technical Committee. He was President of the British Caravanners Club from 1966–78 and is a Vice-President of the Club.

LORD ROBERT BADEN-POWELL, 3rd Baron. The grandson of Lord Baden-Powell of Gilwell, Lord Robert was born in Africa and came to England as a child. He was Chief Scout's Commissioner from 1963–1982, and is now a Vice-President of the Scout Association. He became President of the Club in 1992.

In the first full year after its move to Coventry the Club began to expand and improve the services it provided for members. Specialists from the marketing and travel industries were appointed to oversee the new marketing department and a greatly enlarged Carefree Travel Service department. There were huge increases in Club membership, business activities, turnover, number of sites and sites usage. Computer support increased and was further developed in-house, with new systems in the accounts and travel departments. The membership system was changed to a rolling membership, enabling members to join for a full twelve months at any time of the year. The business was much less costly to run than the old smaller London organisation although the number of staff increased considerably, so much so that the offices in Coventry had to be extended in 1998.

The Annual Report of 1991 stated: "In every area, from Club sites to Club services, we have concentrated upon improving the quality and have begun – following the expense of relocation – laying firm foundations for the future."

It is quite clear that the move to Coventry set in motion several record-breaking years for the Club. With more cost-effective premises and – one has to say it – far better working conditions for the staff, the Club continued to grow and grow.

There was great potential for increasing the Club's income by adding to the services offered to members. By 1992 the number of members using those services grew rapidly, as its value-for-money ethos became more widely appreciated.

"As the Club grows and the volume of business increases so does our negotiating power and our ability to achieve better value for money for members," the Report continued.

Donated by Roy Burnham, this award is presented to the unit producing the best newsletter each year, the latest winner was Hampshire District Association for its newsletter Guyline. *The Lord Baden-Powell hands the trophy to* Guyline *Editor Peter Burton.* (Nick Harding)

Roy Burnham, who died in July 1992, originally suggested that the Club should engage in commission-earning activities. He was regarded as the founding father of the Club's Carefree Travel Service, and his idea led to similar earnings possibilities in other fields that eventually reaped huge benefits for members. Apart from Carefree, these activities involve virtually no outlay for the Club but offer either better facilities or more attractive rates than similar services available to the general public. Carefree and those activities contributed £700,000 in 1999 ensuring that Club subscriptions could remain at a reasonable level.

The new Marketing Department soon showed benefits from its work, with a full-time Press and Publicity Officer dealing with the media. The benefits of joining the Club were publicised via advertisements in the commercial press, at trade shows both at home and abroad. The Marketing Department also produced foreign language brochures explaining the value of temporary membership for visitors to the U.K. A new video, new exhibition stands and a new dealership scheme, supported by Headquarters, freed the voluntary Public Relations Officers (P.R.O.s) from routine visits to dealers and from holding large stocks of materials in their homes. These efforts led to a massive increase in membership, which passed the 200,000 mark in 1991. The Club also retained more of its existing membership than ever before.

Membership grew every year, reaching 268,632 by 1995, an increase of over 10,000 on the previous year. Ninety-five per cent of members surveyed said they would renew their membership, the main reason given for dropping out was stated as a change in family circumstances. Marketing strategies worked well and another promotional video was produced. Better designs of stands for use at the major shows attracted favourable comments. Some 50 per cent of new members were recruited through an improved dealer scheme and at Club sites. By 1999 dealers were able to offer instant membership where the new member received a full membership pack immediately on joining. This was a great success.

In recent years the Club has introduced Instant Membership – membership in a box – sold by caravan and motorhome dealers, suppliers of camping equipment and other retail outlets. It's now possible to buy Club membership over the counter and use the benefits straight away.

By the end of 1999 the magical 300,000 membership figure was surpassed with a total of 301,849 members – 100,000 more had been recruited in just eight years. Those members were also making increasing use of Club sites and more were also attending the Club Annual General Meetings (A.G.M.s) following the decision in 1990 to move the A.G.M. around the country. Over 300 members attended the A.G.M. at Huddersfield in 1991. At every venue since then there has been a packed house – it is sometimes hard to find a location large enough for all who wish to attend. Members' Meetings continued to be held after the A.G.M. and at other venues around the country. In 1997 a new style of presentation by the Management Committee and senior members of staff was introduced at these Meetings, leading to stimulating and well-informed debate about the Club and its activities.

Over 1,000 camping and caravanning dealers, shops and other outlets help the Club with its recruiting. Colourful dispensers, like the one below, offer free leaflets and sites guides outlining the benefits of Club membership.

In 1991 the Club's insurance services were completely revised under the new Club Care scheme and business doubled within the following year. A variety of high quality insurance services were made available to members at competitive prices so that by the end of 1992 Club Care was the U.K.'s second largest caravan insurer. In 1998 the Club's insurance providers signed an exclusive deal with another organisation so a new provider had to be found. After much negotiation even better value-for-money insurance facilities, offering members all types of cover (not just for caravans and camping equipment), were offered by the new provider, with whom the Club signed an exclusive contract. Another service to members was the installation at Headquarters in 1993 of a minicom system enabling deaf enquirers to communicate and receive information.

A new financial service, Club Direct, was launched in 1994. Over 10,000 members belonged to R.A.C. through the Club's associated scheme. In 1996 a completely new recovery and rescue service exclusive to Club members – Arrival – was launched by the Club, again in conjunction with R.A.C. This offered even better facilities. In 2000, when the laws regarding commercial caravan transport were changed, members

Security devices

The unfortunate rise in the theft of caravans and motor caravans led to the development of a number of good security devices, including wheel clamps and security posts which were difficult for unauthorised persons to remove. Another innovation was the Caravan Registration and Identification Scheme, a security marking system which meant that new caravans so marked were easily traceable.

who belonged to the Arrival scheme were relieved to find that, unlike some other organisations, they were still covered for the recovery of their caravans and motor caravans. Other new services launched during the 1990s included a Weathercall service and Legal Call, offering a telephone helpline to those members with legal problems.

The Club was able to sustain its volume of business so that in 1993 the surplus from normal trading before tax exceeded the £1million mark for the first time, but even that figure was insufficient to meet the rising costs of site acquisition and development and to improve services to members.

The income from Club sites, which had previously been the major source of additional revenue began to be overtaken by the income from other Club services. These, as already stated, are basically commission-earning. For example, every time a member uses their Club Credit Card, the card provider Bank of Scotland makes a contribution back to the Club. From the time they were first introduced to the end of 1993, the cards had been used by nearly 10,000 members, enabling the Club to raise over £80,000 in revenue to help buy new sites, upgrade others and provide play areas for children. Other play areas were sponsored by Club Direct and Club Care. One was provided at Moffat Club Site by a fund set up in memory of

Celebrating 90 years of camping, two members of the Association of Lightweight Campers in modern and 1900s cycling dress at the site of the former Wantage Road station, preparing to cycle to Wantage for the 90th Birthday Meet in 1991. (P.H. Constance)

Ron Harding, a former Club Chairman and Vice-President of the Club, who died in September 1991.

Then, despite some very difficult years, the Club's turnover still continued to grow rising from £5million in 1990 to over £17million in 1999, but a careful watch was kept on expenditure to keep it within budget. In 1995 there was an increase in operating costs for the first time since the Club's move to Coventry, due to the additional resources required to maintain service standards to members following ever-increasing membership levels. Capital development programmes continued, improving Club sites and Headquarters' systems to raise the level of services provided, but the major extra costs were incurred through servicing the new members, in particular telephone, postage and stationery.

In 1999 Government legislation (the Minimum Wage and the new Working Time Directive) caused expenditure to increase by more than the rise in income, although the expanded Headquarters building also had an effect on costs. One problem during these years was the difficulty, because of the depressed London property market, to dispose of the lease on the Grosvenor Gardens premises. This was a severe drain on Club finances. Fortunately in 1999 the Club were able to relinquish the lease on the premises, which had been empty for ten years.

In 1992 following a member's suggestion, a Policy Advisory Committee was set up with wide terms of reference. In 1996 the Committee recommended that National Councillors should not be eligible to serve after their 70th birthday. Accordingly, a proposal to amend the Club's Articles of Association was put to the A.G.M. in 1997 but after much debate both for and against the proposal the motion was declared not

Supplement for disabled campers

Published in 1998, this supplement showed how, with the right gear, camping could be enjoyed by disabled people.

As well as the monthly magazine, Camping and Caravanning, *the Publications Department produces site books and brochures.*

carried as the majority in favour did not reach the required 75 per cent. In 1999 changes to the electoral system to encourage more members to use their vote resulted in a greatly increased number of votes being cast in 2000, leading to some new faces on the Council.

The Club magazine, *Camping and Caravanning*, continued to improve, with colour being used in the *Out & About* supplement for the first time in 1991. A special 90th anniversary issue was published in August and other special editions covering camping for disabled people and boating were well received by members.

In 1992 official Audit Bureau of Circulation (A.B.C.) figures showed that *Camping and Caravanning* was the largest monthly magazine in the world devoted to the pastime. During that year the full range of caravans, tents, motor caravans and trailer tents was featured over several issues, although some concern was expressed over the amount of advertising which was becoming over-intrusive and tended to spoil the enjoyment of its readers. The number of advertisements were reduced the following year and only those which had relevance were accepted. More regular features were instigated and a Technical Information Officer was appointed, who not only provided an information service for members but also technical features for the magazine. Although there were fewer advertisements the revenue from them actually increased so that, by 1994, the rising cost of providing the magazine and other publications to members was contained.

New technology and a major investment in computer hardware enabled the typesetting of the magazine to be brought in-house, resulting in major financial savings.

By 1996 the Publications Department was producing all the Club's major publications in-house, including *Your Place in the Country*, *Your Big Sites Book* and the *Carefree* holiday and travel brochures. The magazine was now even more colourful, with new product giveaways being an added attraction to readers. The contents provoked interest and debate in the wider field, especially when the Club Chairman raised the question of new caravan design and quality. Data Sheets were produced dealing with the most common queries.

In 1998 more informative articles were published, later reproduced as Data Sheets, covering many aspects of buying, maintenance and safety issues for all types of camping units. These have enhanced the Club's reputation as a source of authoritative technical information, with some being handed out by police forces during roadside safety checks. A new supplement with information for disabled campers, *Camping and Caravanning for All*, was well received both by Club members and disabled persons' organisations outside the Club. The biggest-ever editions of the *Carefree* brochure and *Your Place in the Country* were produced, major prizes were offered to competition winners and *Out & About* was improved again.

In the following year a full-colour *Your Big Sites Book* was issued and for the first time advertising revenue derived from it outstripped the cost of production, a huge bonus for the Club. *Out & About* turned to full-colour printing in April 1999 at no extra cost. It now includes more information and features on some of the Special Interest Sections, Regions and D.A.s.

All this encourages members to look through the pages in search of holiday and weekend breaks. The Club also contributed to and produced a revised edition of the *Caravan Towing Code* for the National Caravan Council. Another record-breaking *Carefree* brochure and *Your Place in the Country* were produced for the year 2000.

Camping and Caravanning magazine has gone from strength to strength, from a tiny two-page leaflet in 1906 to an 80-plus page monthly magazine with a 30-plus page supplement in the year 2000.

In 1996 a new Technical Sub-committee, made up of Club members, was appointed – it was very busy during its first year of operation. The Club was represented on a number of bodies discussing standards for all types of unit and instigated an amendment to a British Standard on electrical installations to cover safe supplies to trailer tents and tents on site.

Caravan manoeuvring courses, which the Club had been running for some years, increased in popularity. In 1997 the Club doubled the number of courses and invested in six caravans with Club livery for use on the courses. A book and video were produced for course participants, general sale and to Club members.

The Club is represented on a number of British and International Technical Committees, including a European Committee reviewing camp site safety.

By far the greatest activities took place in the Sites Department and on Club sites. These were responsible for the largest amount of

Club President Lord Robert Baden-Powell opens the new Barnard Castle Club Site in 1996. (Club Archive)

expenditure ever undertaken by the Club. The quality of Club sites needed improving and new ones had to be found. Major redevelopment began at Horsley, which had been purchased in the 1930s, and other sites were modernised and improved. An ambitious development programme costing nearly £1million was envisaged for 1992 and over 300 electric hook-ups were installed on Club sites. A reluctant decision was made not to

continue with the Club sites at Kilkerran and Polesden Lacey. The Club could not accept the long-term losses forecast for these sites without changes in the conditions of the leases to make them viable and it was unable to negotiate with the landlords for this.

Rhandirmwyn Club Site was declared the best site in Wales by the A.A. in 1992 and major development work was begun at Clent Hills and at Oldbury Hill. Unfortunately much of the planned work could not be completed because of delays in planning permission and by the requirements of the National Rivers Authority. The cost of running sites was rising rapidly, in particular the cost of disposal of waste liquids which in some cases had increased tenfold.

The leasehold of Blackmore Club Site was purchased by the Club in 1993, thus securing the site for 125 years. Redevelopment was envisaged but had to be put on hold and it would not be until July 2000 that it was completed. The Club-managed site in Roundhay Park, Leeds, was given up because of vandalism and theft. The Club also felt it could

From the Club magazine

Awnings (November 1991): "All awnings should have clearly marked entrances – preferably wide open. Camping and caravanning, after all, is supposed to be the outdoor life."

Early start to the silly season (September 1995): "The silly season has started early for The Sports Council, who have decided to remove The Camping and Caravanning Club from their list of recognised activities. Amazingly, they have ruled that camping is no longer a sport."

no longer guarantee its members secure camping at that location. Over £2million was spent in 1993 on improvements to Club sites.

In the following year three more sites were refurbished and full facilities were installed at Cannock Chase. Sandringham Club Site was extended to provide 250 pitches in 1995, but another site, Chard, was given up. Major works at Inverewe, Speyside and Woodhall Spa were undertaken during the year, and the freehold of Chipping Norton site was purchased. Cardigan Bay and Oban Club Sites won A.A. awards for the best site in Wales and Scotland respectively.

The year 1996 was a record one for sites use mainly because of the fine Summer weather. It also saw the largest capital sites development and redevelopment programme in the Club's history. The redevelopment of Hertford Club Site and the development of a new green field site at Barnard Castle fell behind schedule and building work was not completed on time.

Lord Baden-Powell re-opened Hertford Club Site – originally purchased as a memorial to his grandfather – in July, although the final works were not completed until August. Barnard Castle opened after many delays and difficulties just before the August Bank Holiday.

At both sites the Club's continuing commitment to the environment can be seen. A lake was created at Hertford to encourage wildlife by channelling water from the new land drainage scheme to the lake without adding any extra water except the rain. Over 11,000 trees were planted at Barnard Castle, providing shelter belts to help screen the site from prevailing winds illustrating the Club's commitment to using environmentally-friendly materials in all its site activities. Three other sites were refurbished and extra facilities and camping space were created at Chipping Norton. The freehold of Kendal site was acquired and a lease purchased at Minehead.

In all respects 1997 was a record year. The Club had more of its own sites than ever before, more of them were open all year and more

The Chairman of the local authority plants a tree in the rain at Barnard Castle Club Site, 1996. (Club Archive)

members used them than ever before. More than £3million a year was being spent on improving Club sites and adding new ones.

By 1998 ten new sites had been added to the network. Five more were added that year, including another new green-field site at Devizes, alongside the Kennet and Avon Canal. When proposals for the restoration of the then derelict canal were formulated in the 1950s it was suggested

that there should be camp sites at regular intervals along the canal and that "the Camping Club might run them". Although the Club did not get a chain of them, at least it did get one. Three more sites saw major improvements and Salisbury Council, for whom the Club manages the site near Old Sarum, enlarged and redeveloped its site.

Freak floods at Easter made 1998 one of the wettest years on record. St Neots Club Site was completely flooded and other sites had to operate at reduced capacity

West Sussex District Association Temporary Holiday Site in the grounds of Lancing College, near Worthing. **(Norman Taylor)**

because of waterlogged pitches and flooding. Three more sites were added to the network in 1999 and in July 2000 the Blackmore Club Site, now completely redeveloped and in all but name a new site, was officially opened by the Mayor of Great Malvern and the Chairman of the Heart of England Tourist Board.

In 1994 proposals were made to improve the quality of Certificated Sites and by 1999 the number available to members had been considerably reduced, reflecting the standards now required by the health authorities for water and waste disposal. An additional factor was the Uniform Business Rate, which was being levied on many Certificated Sites and a lot of owners felt that their sites would no longer be viable.

In 1988 a record 300 T.H.S.s were held. These Meets are always popular with Club members and provide a valuable source of new members to the Club.

The Parliamentary scene was reasonably quiet during the 1990s.

New Age Travellers were creating problems and in 1992 the Club was consulted on Government proposals for the reform of the Caravan Sites Act of 1968 and put forward its views to ensure members' interests were safeguarded. The following year Parliament was able to gain increased control over New Age Travellers without any detailed reform of the Act. The Club became closely involved with the review of the Caravan Sites and Control of Development Act 1960, which it was monitoring carefully.

In 1995 the Club took action to protect members' interests with the possible changes to vehicle excise duty. Papers were submitted opposing some of the proposals that would affect members who lay up their vehicles during the winter months. The Club was delighted when the Chancellor of the Exchequer listened to its views and members are now able to make a sworn declaration if they wish to keep their vehicle off the road which normally lasts twelve months. If they want to use the vehicle before the twelve-month period is up the vehicle must be relicensed.

The Management Committee of the Club held a reception for members of both Houses of Parliament at the House of Lords later that year, hosted

Caravan manoeuvring course

Proper training is always the first step towards safety. The Club organises manoeuvring courses all over the country to train members in the safe use of their caravans. Today more than 500 members a year take part in these courses. (Peter Frost)

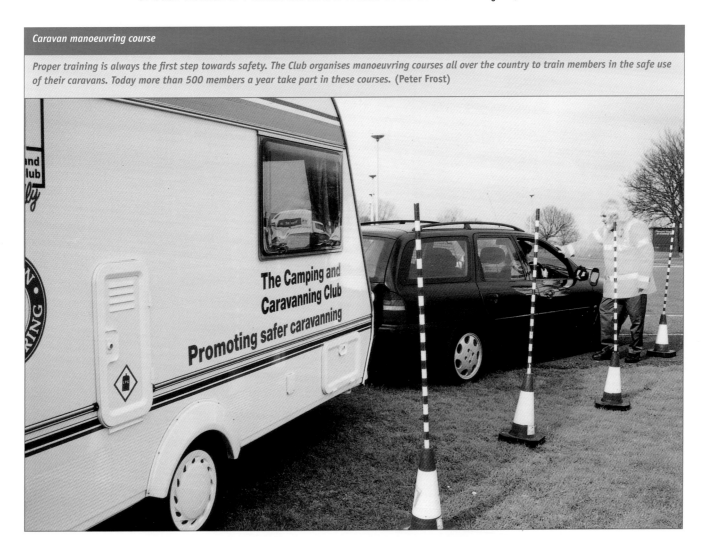

by the Club's President, Lord Baden-Powell. Those who attended were impressed by the breadth and depth of the Club and by the commitment shown by it to the countryside.

In 1996 it was announced that no major changes were envisaged to the Caravan Sites and Control of Development Act 1960. The Club was complimented on the responsible manner in which it administered its exemptions under the Act. The Club was active, together with other members of the motor caravan industry, in drawing the Government's attention to the classification of motor caravans over 3.5 tonnes and the levying of an increased tax rate on these vehicles. It was successful in getting a number of questions asked in Parliament but has not yet succeeded in getting the tax reduced on these vehicles.

The General Election meant that matters concerning camping and caravanning were not brought to the fore in 1997. With a new Government in place in 1998 new legislation and consultation papers began to arrive thick and fast at Greenfields House. The Club responded to a number of these papers, in particular those relating to transport, the impact of which, if ever fully implemented, would have severe implications on the Club's activities. Two recent major pieces of legislation, namely the Minimum Wage and the Working Time Directive, have adversely affected the management and working of Club sites. The Club continues to work with others on areas that affect its activities and contacts with M.P.s, civil servants and Members of European Parliament (M.E.P.s) have been strengthened to ensure the Club's points of view are known.

In 1991 the Club left the British Federation of Camping and Caravanning and became an independent member of the International Federation of Camping and Caravanning (F.I.C.C.). An International Sub-committee was appointed to revitalise the Club's participation in and influence on the F.I.C.C. and the Alliance Internationale de Tourisme and to monitor the development of the

Association of Lightweight Campers' members entered these Mighty Giants in the Mardi Gras Parade at the National Feast of Lanterns, Cholmondeley Castle, 1994, and won the Avon Shield for the best small entry. (P.H. Constance)

Carefree Travel Service, undoubtedly the most popular of the Club's services. Now an Association of British Travel Agents-bonded agency, the department has grown beyond all recognition since the move to Coventry, when the Carefree operations were serviced by just three members of staff. Now there are more than 30 staff, at least four of whom are multi-lingual.

The number of Continental Rallies has increased over the years and they have been well-supported, particularly the D-Day 50-year celebrations in 1994 and the winter sun rallies. There was only one disappointing year in 1996, when there was a reduction in the number of holiday bookings because of the weakness of Sterling at the time and the fine weather at home. Carefree, however, fared very well compared with other travel companies, who were experiencing a very difficult time.

In 1999 more than 60,000 members made use of the Carefree Travel Service, some travelling on escorted tours to Europe or on fly-drive motor caravan escorted tours to Canada, New Zealand and North America. Some tried the Freedom of Europe go-as-you-please scheme, which proved very popular while others booked fully-inclusive holidays in Europe. Still more members simply made use of the ferry booking, site booking, or travel insurance services. Carefree receipts were almost £6million and there was a net surplus of over £500,000, which all goes to help develop or purchase Club sites and other services.

The F.I.C.C. Rallies remained popular with a small contingent travelling

The Camping and Caravanning Club Brass Band – founded in 1994 – after a performance at the Saddleworth Whit Friday competition. (Les Cottrell)

First in the field A Century of The Camping and Caravanning Club

to Czechoslovakia in 1991. Fifty-two members travelled to Canada for the Rally in 1992 where they received a warm welcome and great support from their North American friends when the weather turned against them. An extra Rally was held in Japan in 1994, which 13 Club members attended. In 1997 many Club members crossed the Irish Sea for the event. The Rally was in England in 1999 and although it was organised by The Caravan Club many members of the Club helped with tasks.

The Youth Section membership again fluctuated during the 1990s and has unfortunately remained pretty static since. The Club's youth members are often praised for their good behaviour, especially when they represent the Club at international events, and they do enjoy themselves, so it is a pity that more young people do not take advantage of Youth Membership. The Club's hard working voluntary Youth Leaders provide a wide range of interesting activities and are much appreciated by the Club. The Children Act, which became law at the beginning of the decade, virtually prevents the participation of children under the age of eight in Camping Club Youth Junior activities.

The restrictions of the Act have also affected the number of those volunteering to be Youth Leaders. Many are wary of the implications of the legislation when opting to work with young people but the Club tries to encourage suitable members to offer their services because in some areas there are no active youth groups.

International Youth Rallies were attended by many young people – who must pass their Camping Club Youth Test before being allowed to take part. Nearly 200 Youth members went to Poland for the International Rally in 1991 and in 1994 over 300 went to Holland, where they were the largest overseas contingent. With appalling weather and a very exposed site, much damage was done to tents but the local people came to the rescue and all seemed to enjoy themselves. Youth members braved the snows in Switzerland in 1995 and were again the largest contingent. In the Club's Centenary year the International Youth Rally was hosted by the Club in York.

Vis-a-vis dome and tunnel tents

Following the trend towards lightweight family tents, continental and British makers introduced larger tents built on lightweight principles, but with standing headroom and two or more bedrooms. The poles and canvas were much lighter and packed down to a more manageable size. They took less time to erect than a frame tent, and once up most of them had just as much room inside.

Each year the Club organises the largest camping and caravanning rally in the world – the National Feast of Lanterns. Attendance varies but averages between 4,500 and 5,000 units – around 12,000 campers. This picture shows the 1999 N.F.O.L. at Stanford Hall, in the heart of England.

Conditions were of the worst possible kind at a British Caravanners' Club Meet, Carsington Water, at Easter, 2000.

Regions, Sections and D.A.s all worked hard to establish activities in their own areas, although many were affected by poor weather conditions. This was most apparent in 1998 when atrocious conditions at Easter affected many meets. A large number had to be cancelled or scaled down at the last minute. Yorkshire Region was particularly badly hit, with large numbers of fixtures being cancelled for several weeks running. Many of their early meets had to be cancelled again the following year due to poor ground conditions. Easter 2000 was again affected by atrocious weather with more meets being cancelled, especially in the south of the country.

All Regions had significant anniversaries but in 1998 Northern Ireland celebrated its 21st birthday with a rally in the grounds of Stormont Castle, the first-ever outside body to be allowed to hold an event on the estate. In the same year over 80 units crossed the Irish Sea to attend the N.F.O.L. in Edinburgh, the largest ever group from the Province to visit the event.

The D.A.s are the backbone of the Club, providing from their ranks the many thousands of volunteers that keep the Club going forward. Many of them organise large events that are considered national events within the Club. Since 1965 South Lincs D.A. has organised the Tulip Rally, which takes place the same weekend as the famous Tulip Parade at Spalding: it organised a very successful 30th Rally in 1995. The Goose Fair Meet, organised by Notts D.A. and a popular annual event, was seriously affected by a major fire at Walesby Scout Camp in the same year, with 700 bookings having to be returned. The Club's Countryside Care team played a major role in helping to restore the site for future use. The Countryside Care team received two special mentions in the 1998 Tidy Britain Queen Mother's Birthday Awards for work done at Ferry Meadows Country Park, Peterborough, and the Stowmarket Rural Life Museum. It has also received many other local awards.

In 1993 Fife D.A. was formed, the first new D.A. for some years. Yorkshire Region also had a new D.A. – Danum – formed in 1994. In 1996 a Boundary Working Party review of D.A. and Region Boundaries was completed and its recommendations were accepted.

Section membership generally decreased during the decade with the exception of the Boating Group, Mountain Activity Section and the Folk Dance and Song Group, the latter being the fourth largest Section within the Club. Its annual Easter Meet attracts so many members that it is often difficult to find a suitable venue. Despite the drop in numbers of the other Sections, its activities are as strong as ever. At its 31st Birthday Meet in 1998 the Trailer Tent Group made a presentation to Barry Bucknall, the designer of the popular Mirror trailer tent.

N.F.O.L.s are held in a different Region each year and are so popular that a new booking system had to be instituted so that everyone has a fair chance of attending. All bookings now go through Club Headquarters with

The Club's award-winning Countryside Care team in action. Pictured here, the group is creating a riverside viewing point and picnic area at Ferry Meadows Country Park, Peterborough. **(Club Archive)**

provisional bookings are no longer accepted. Once again it is becoming increasingly difficult to find suitable sites for such large meets.

The North West Region was looking for a suitable band to lead the Mardi Gras Parade at Cholmondeley Castle in 1994, when Club member Les Cottrell pointed out that with such a large membership there were bound to be enough musicians within the Club to form a band. He put a notice in the Club magazine and 38 members turned up. They played for the Mardi Gras and gave a concert on Sunday morning, without rehearsal, and were an instant success. The band now has more than 70 players, including some retired principal players from the forces and some who play for championship bands as well as a number of very talented young players. It now plays on the march, has its own signature tune *Out and About*, and has produced a compact disc and tape recording. For a band whose players come from all parts of the U.K., including Northern Ireland, and who rarely have a chance for long rehearsals, it is exceptional and is very popular whenever they appear.

The Club adopted a new logo for use during the Centenary Year. As well as being used in publications and advertising it featured on a number of souvenir Centenary items sold by the Club.

The first N.F.O.L. to be held in Scotland took place in Edinburgh in 1998 when 3,000 units attended. The new booking system worked well, although some members were somewhat put out to find themselves sited between the main runway of Edinburgh International Airport and the main A8 road! In 1999 Central Counties Region organised the N.F.O.L. at Stanford Hall, Leicestershire. It was fully booked and 4,500 units attended in glorious weather. The only disappointment was that there was so much entertainment laid on that very few members bothered to decorate their units and the usual crowds of people walking around the site to view the decorations just did not happen. Southern Region, organiser of the Centenary N.F.O.L. in Hampshire in 2001, witnessed a reversal of the trend when nearly every unit lit up like N.F.O.L.s of long ago.

The Club's Centenary year began with a Centenary Dinner at the Guildhall, London and National Camping Week starting with the Spring Bank Holiday weekend when it was hoped that every Club member would be out camping. A service in Coventry Cathedral followed by a garden party in September rounded up the celebrations. In addition, there were a number of events organised by the Regions and Sections, as well as an exhibition about the Club's history at Wantage Museum coinciding with National Camping Week.

A quote from the 1995 Annual Report really sums up the success of the Club and what it is all about: "The success of the Club must be attributed to the unique relationship between the Club's Honorary Officers and the staff, both at headquarters and on the sites, who work so closely together to improve and promote the Club. The Camping and Caravanning Club's reputation as The Friendly Club sets us apart from the rest and focuses everyone's efforts on that hard-earned reputation handed down to us from those that have gone before."

In 1999 the Chairman, Barry Rook, finished his Annual Report with these words: "We go forward into the next century and look forward to our Centenary with confidence, in the knowledge that those who have gone before would be proud of what the Club has become, and would still recognise the warmth and friendliness they knew in the early days."

The Club's Centenary Year celebrations started with the Annual General Meeting and Centenary Dinner held in London's prestigious Guildhall. Over 500 Club members and their guests enjoyed the celebrations, with the keynote speech being made by Dr David Bellamy. (Nick Harding)

Club Presidents

1901-06	Thomas H. Holding
1907-08	Capt. Sir Edmund Verney, R.N., F.R.G.S.
1909-11	Capt. Robert Falcon Scott, R.N., C.V.O.,D.Sc., F.R.G.S.
1912-18	Vacant
1919-40	Lord Baden-Powell of Gilwell, O.M., G.C.M.G., G.C.V.O., K.C.B.
1941-49	Vacant
1950-59	Stephen Hilhouse
1960-70	John A.C. Champion, O.B.E
1971-80	Donald Dewey
1981-91	Sir John Cripps, C.B.E
1992-	The Lord Baden-Powell

Club Chairmen

1901-06	T.H. Holding		1958-60	D. Dewey
1906-07	S. Hilhouse		1960-62	F.A. Cousins
1907-08	H. Biden-Steele		1962-64	E.H. Evans
1908-10	G.J. Gill		1964-66	D. Dewey
1910-11	D.B.L. Hopkins, R.N., M.V.O.		1966-68	H. Liversedge
1911-12	R.B. Searle		1968-70	L.G. Goodwin
1912-14	S. Hilhouse		1970-72	A.R. Burnham
1914-15	R.B. Searle		1972-74	W.V. Jones, M.B.E.
1915-16	G.J. Gill		1974-76	R.E. Cripps
1916-17	Mrs F.A. Lynn		1976-78	F.A. Hyde
1917-19	H.J. Lewis		1978-80	A.R. Harding
1919-20	P.J. Maddock		1980-82	V.C. Sinden
1920-22	S. Hilhouse		1982-84	Mrs M. Rayner
1922-23	R.T. Phillips		1984-85	J.E. Lloyd
1923-26	S. Hilhouse		1985-87	K.J. Harris
1926-27	R.J. Hunt		1987-89	F.H. Grant
1927-29	R.T. Phillips		1989-91	T.D. Burchnall
1929-31	S. Hilhouse		1991-93	W.J. Garner
1931-41	J.A.C. Champion, O.B.E.		1993-95	Mrs O.M. Reay, M.B.E.
1941-49	M.P. Lindsey		1995-97	Capt. D.J. Barrett
1949-51	W. Rankin		1997-99	L.W. French
1951-53	D.S. Langridge		1999-01	B. Rook
1953-56	W.L. Austin		2001-	D. Stubbs
1956-58	E.H. Evans			

Club Sites

Sites owned, leased or managed by the Club. Sites marked * are currently open and listed in *Your Place in the Country*, 2002 edition. Other sites are no longer owned, managed or leased by the Club but are mentioned in the text.

	Opened	Relinquished
Adgestone, Isle of Wight*	2000	
Ardgartan, Dunbartonshire*	1936	
Bakewell, Hopping Farm, (Youlgreave), Derbyshire*	1970	
Bala, Gwynedd*	1985	
Bangor-on-Dee, Clwyd*	1978	
Barnard Castle, County Durham*	1996	
Barns Ness, Lothian*	1969	
Beadnell Bay, Northumberland*	1977	
Blackmore, Worcestershire*	1969	
Blair Atholl, Perth and Kinross	1971	1987
Bodmin, Cornwall*	1972	
Boroughbridge, North Yorkshire*	1994	
Boswinger, Cornwall	1967	1988
Box Hill, Surrey	1939	1950
Bracklesham Bay, Sussex	1935	1939
Brandesburton, East Yorkshire	1985	1992
Bude, Cornwall*	1998	
Byrness-in-Redesdale, Northumberland	1970	1987
Caernarfon, Gwynedd	1987	1991
California Cross, Devon*	1982	
Cambridge, Cambridgeshire*	1975	
Cannock Chase, Staffordshire*	1982	
Canterbury, Kent*	1993	
Carbeth, Stirling	1940	1952
Cardigan Bay, Ceredigion*	1980	
Castle Semple, Renfrewshire	1947	1957
Chard, Somerset	1990	1995
Charmouth (Monkton Wylde Farm), Dorset*	1997	
Charmouth, Dorset	1961	1971

	Opened	Relinquished
Chertsey, Surrey*	1927	
Chichester, West Sussex*	1996	
Chipping Norton, Oxfordshire*	1985	
Clent Hills, West Midlands*	1937	
Clitheroe, Lancashire*	1984	
Clumber Park, Nottinghamshire*	1983	
Crowborough, East Sussex*	1985	
Crowden, Cheshire*	1977	
Croyde Bay, Devon	1976	1978
Cuffley (Tylers' Causeway), Hertfordshire	1939	1948
Culzean Castle, Strathclyde*	1961	
Dalavan Bay	1937	1940
Damage Barton, Devon*	1962	
Delamont Country Park, Northern Ireland*	2001	
Denham, Buckinghamshire	1924	1925
Denham Court, Buckinghamshire	1938	1986
Derwentwater, Cumbria*	2000	
Devizes, Wiltshire*	1997	
Dingwall, Highlands*	1977	
Dunstan Hill, Northumberland*	1964	
Ebury Hill, Shropshire*	1977	
Edinburgh, Redhall	1948	1952
Folkestone, Kent*	1965	
Foots Cray, Kent	1948	1963
Freshwater East	1976	1978
Godrevey	1972	1975
Graffham, West Sussex*	1944	
Grim's Dyke, Middlesex	1938	1939
Grizedale Hall, Cumbria	1962	2000
Haldon Racecourse, Devon	1979	1982
Haltwhistle, Northumberland*	1989	
Hayfield, Derbyshire*	1979	
Hereford Racecourse, Herefordshire	1976	1982
Hereford Racecourse, Herefordshire	1997	2000
Hertford, Hertfordshire*	1953	

	Opened	Relinquished
Honiton, Devon*	1985	
Horsley, Surrey*	1930	
Hurley, Berkshire	1938	1940
Huntsmoor Park, Buckinghamshire	1922	1924
Inverewe Gardens, Highlands*	1994	
Isle of Man	1954	1970
Jedburgh, Borders*	1977	
Kelvedon Hatch, Essex*	1936	
Kendal, Cumbria*	1990	
Kessingland, Suffolk*	1989	
Keswick, Cumbria*	1969	
Kingsbury Water Park, West Midlands*	1982	
Kilkerran	1971	1992
Lake of Menteith	1939	1940
Laleham, Middlesex	1951	1973
Largs, Inverclyde	1959	1963
Lauder, Borders*	1999	
Leek, Staffordshire*	1996	
Leysdown, Kent	1939	1948
Lingfield, Surrey	1979	1980
Little Berkhampstead, Hertfordshire	1938	1939
Llanystumdwy, Gwynedd*	1967	
Looe (Tencreek), Cornwall	1964	1978
Lower Burleigh	1950	1952
Ludlow, Shropshire	1978	1982
Luss, Argyll and Bute*	1977	
Lydford, Devon*	1991	
Lynton, Devon*	1988	
Mablethorpe, Lincolnshire*	1981	
Machrihanish, Strathclyde*	1979	
Milarrochy Bay, Stirling*	1934	
Minehead, Somerset*	1970	
Moffat, Borders*	1973	
Moreton, Dorset*	1998	
Nairn, Morayshire*	1999	

	Opened	Relinquished
Newmarket, Cambridgeshire	1995	2001
Newperran, Cornwall	1967	1988
Norman's Bay, East Sussex*	1959	
Norwich, Norfolk*	1988	
Oban, Argyll and Bute*	1991	
Oldbury Hill, Kent*	1946	
Oxford, Oxfordshire*	1998	
Pax Hill, Hampshire	1942	1953
Perranporth, Cornwall	1961	1967
Polesden Lacey, Surrey	1946	1992
Rhandirmwyn, Carmarthenshire*	1981	
Rhyl, Denbighshire	1985	1989
Rickmansworth, Hertfordshire	1924	1961
Rosemarkie, Highlands*	1987	
Roundhay Park, West Yorkshire	1986	1993
St David's (Red Wharf Bay), Pembrokeshire	1958	1970
St David's (Berea), Pembrokeshire*	1985	
St Neots, Cambridgeshire*	1979	
Salisbury, Wiltshire*	1971	
Saltram, Devon	1972	1987
Sandown, Isle of Wight	1997	2000
Sandringham, Norfolk*	1989	
Scone, Tayside*	1975	
Scoughall, Berwick	1939	1941
Sennen Cove, Cornwall*	1967	
Shanklin, Isle of Wight	1993	1996
Sherriff Hutton, North Yorkshire*	1980	
Slapton Sands, Devon*	1960	
Slindon, West Sussex*	1972	
Slingsby, North Yorkshire*	1976	
Southwell Racecourse, Nottinghamshire	1977	1989
Speyside, Grampian*	1992	
Stratford-upon-Avon Racecourse, Warwickshire	1976	1995
Sutton Hill, Dorset*	1968	
Tarland, Aberdeenshire*	1998	

	Opened	Relinquished
Theobalds Park, Hertfordshire*	1938	
Towcester Racecourse, Northamptonshire	1983	1986
Tregurrian, Cornwall*	1967	
Trelowarren, Cornwall	1970	1992
Trewan Hall, Cornwall*	1965	
Ulrome, Yorkshire	1938	1940
Umberleigh, Devon*	1993	
Veryan, Cornwall*	1996	
Walton on Thames, Surrey*	1913	
Ware, Hertfordshire	1937	1937
West Runton, Norfolk*	1961	
Weston-super-Mare, Somerset*	1984	
Weybridge, Surrey	1905	1908
Winchcombe, Gloucestershire*	1997	
Wolverley, Worcestershire*	1974	
Woodhall Spa, Lincolnshire*	1971	
Worcester Racecourse, Worcestershire	1979	1986

District Associations

Until 1970 the year of formation is given as the year before the first entry appears in the Club *Yearbook*. These are as accurate as possible, as a few yearbooks are missing and not all dates are recorded. After 1970 the dates have been taken from the Annual Reports of the Club. Details of some new D.A.s were not recorded when they were formed from splitting up older D.A.s.

1907	Metropolitan D.A. (Middlesex, Essex, Kent and Surrey dissolved 1910)
	Birmingham D.A.
1908	North Midlands D.A. (Leicester, Nottinghamshire, Derby, Lincoln and Rutland)
1909	Glasgow and West of Scotland D.A.
1910	Nottinghamshire D.A.
	East Midlands D.A. (replacing North Midlands D.A.)
	Northumberland and Durham D.A.
1911	Manchester D.A. (dissolved 1914)
	Yorkshire D.A.
1914	Lancashire, Cheshire and North Wales D.A. (replacing Manchester)
1916	Nottingham and East Midlands D.A. (replacing two separate D.A.s)
1921	Hampshire, Dorset and Wiltshire D.A.
	Liverpool D.A.
	London D.A.
	Surrey D.A.
1923	Derbyshire D.A. (later absorbed into Leicester and Nottinghamshire)
1925	Bucks, Herts and Middlesex D.A.
	Leicester and Notts. D.A. (from Notts and East Midlands)
1927	Essex D.A.
1930	North Lancashire D.A.
1931	Berkshire and Oxfordshire D.A.
	East Kent D.A.
1933	Bristol, Gloucester and Somerset D.A.
	Edinburgh and East of Scotland D.A.
	Wessex D.A.
	West Kent D.A.

1934	Sheffield D.A.
	Teesside D.A.
1938	East Yorkshire D.A.
1940	North London and East Hertfordshire D.A. (later re-named Hertfordshire and North London D.A.)
1947	Bristol D.A (replacing Bristol, Gloucester and Somerset D.A)
	Hampshire D.A.
1949	Renfrew D.A.
1950	Bedfordshire, Cambridgeshire and Hunts D.A.
	Gloucester and Monmouth D.A.
	Lincolnshire D.A.
1951	East Kent and Sussex D.A. (replacing East Kent D.A.)
	Somerset and Wiltshire D.A.
	South Wales D.A.
1952	Devon and Cornwall D.A.
	Dorset D.A.
	Sussex D.A. (now independent of East Kent)
1953	Norfolk and Suffolk D.A.
1953	Shropshire D.A.
1954	Coventry D.A.
	Northamptonshire D.A.
1955	Central Yorkshire D.A.
1956	Liverpool and North Wales D.A.
	Lancashire and Cheshire D.A. (replacing Lancashire, Cheshire and North Wales D.A.)
1957	Derby D.A.
1958	Bristol and Gloucestershire (replacing Bristol D.A. and Gloucester and Monmouth D.A.)
	Staffordshire D.A.
1959	Leicestershire D.A.
	Nottinghamshire D.A. (replacing Leicester and Notts D.A.)
1961	East Essex D.A.
	South Yorkshire D.A.
	West Essex D.A.
1962	West Sussex D.A.
	East Sussex D.A. (replacing Sussex D.A.)

1963	Bristol D.A. (subsequently known as Avon (Bristol) D.A.)
	Gloucester D.A. (replacing Bristol and Gloucestershire D.A.)
1964	North East Cheshire D.A.
	West Wales D.A.
1965	Central Lancashire D.A.
1965	Northern Ireland D.A.
1966	South Lincolnshire D.A
	Lindum D.A. (replacing Lincolnshire D.A.)
1967	Leinster D.A.
	Liverpool and South-West Lancs D.A.
	Wirral and North Wales D.A. (replacing Liverpool and North Wales D.A.)
	Worcestershire and Herefordshire D.A.
1968	Durham D.A. (replacing Northumberland and Durham D.A.)
	Huddersfield D.A.
1969	Berkshire D.A.
	Oxfordshire D.A. (replacing Berkshire and Oxfordshire D.A.)
	Solent D.A.
	Northumbrian D.A
	Lakeland D.A.
1970	Leeds D.A.
	Grampians and North East Scotland D.A.
1971	North Warwickshire D.A.
	New Forest D.A.
	West Midlands D.A.
1971	Devon D.A.
	Cornwall D.A. (replacing Devon and Cornwall D.A.)
1972	North Staffordshire D.A.
	South Lancs D.A.
1973	Wiltshire D.A.
	Loddon D.A.
	Mid Anglia D.A.
1974	Chesterfield D.A.
	County Down D.A.
	North-East Lancashire D.A.
1974	Bedfordshire D.A.
	Spen Valley D.A.

	Yorkshire Derwent D.A.
	Fenland D.A.
1975	Nene Valley D.A.
	Perth and Angus D.A.
	Trent Valley D.A.
1976	South Suffolk D.A.
	Roch Valley D.A.
	North Cumbria D.A.
	North Gloucestershire D.A.
	Aylesbury Vale D.A.
	Tamar D.A.
1977	Waterside D.A.
1977	East Worcestershire D.A.
	Gwent D.A.
1978	Isle of Wight D.A.
	North West Surrey D.A. (wound up in November 1979)
	South Downs D.A.
1979	Dyfed D.A.
1979	Lune Valley D.A.
1980	Chase D.A.
1981	Bangor (Northern Ireland) D.A.
1985	Sarum D.A.
	North Gloucestershire D.A.
1993	Fife D.A.
1995	Danum D.A.
	Snowdonia D.A.

Club Regions

1947	Scottish Region
1948	North London and Eastern Counties Region
	South Eastern Region
	South West Region
	Central Counties Region
	North East Region
	North West Region
1949	Yorkshire Region

1973	Cambrian and Wyvern Region
	Chiltern Region
	Eastern Region
	North Central Region
	Southern Region
	North London and Eastern Counties Region wound up
1977	Northern Ireland Region

Club Specialist Sections and Special Interest Groups

1901	Association of Cycle Campers
	1935 section status refused by National Council
	1944 reconstituted as a specialist Section of the Club
	1965 changed name to Association of Cycle and Lightweight Campers
	1984 simplified name to Association of Lightweight Campers
1932	Folk Dance Group formed, but did not survive World War Two
1962	Folk Dance and Song Group revived
1932	Mountaineering Section formed
1987	Mountaineering Section wound up
1933	British Canoe Association became the Canoe Section of the Club, and adopted the title Canoe-Camping Club
1933	Caravan Section formed
1937	Caravan Section adopted the name British Caravanners' Club
1935	Photo Group formed
1939	Artists Group formed
1960	Artists Group ceased to exist
1942	Youth Camping Association formed
1951	Youth Camping Association withdrew from Club umbrella
1952	Camping Club Youth formed
1963	Motor Caravan Section formed
1967	Social and Cultural Section formed
1974	Social and Cultural Section wound up
1967	Trailer Tent Group formed
1972	Boating Group formed
1988	Mountain Activity Section formed (replacing Mountaineering Section)
2001	Trailer Tent Group re-named Trailer Tent and Folding Camper Group

National Feasts of Lanterns

1921	Deepdene, near Dorking, Surrey
1922	Walton Club Site, Surrey
1923	Walton Club Site, Surrey
1924	Walton Club Site, Surrey
1925	Rickmansworth, Hertfordshire
1926	Hatfield Park, Hertfordshire
1927	Hatfield Park, Hertfordshire
1928	Gorhambury, St. Albans, Hertfordshire
1929	Knole Park, Sevenoaks, Kent
1930	Shardloes Park, Amersham, Buckinghamshire
1931	Knole Park, Sevenoaks, Kent
1932	Horsley Club Site, Surrey
1933	Shardloes Park, Amersham, Buckinghamshire
1934	Bagden Farm, Polesden Lacey, Great Bookham, Surrey
1935	Aldenham Park, Elstree, Hertfordshire
1936	Ewood, near Newdigate, Surrey
1937	Aldenham Park, Elstree, Hertfordshire
1938	Gatton Park, Merstham, Surrey
1939	Planned for Grim's Dyke, near Harrow & Wealdstone, but not held
1940-45	No N.F.O.L.s during World War Two
1946	Aldenham Park, Elstree, Hertfordshire
1947	Lullingstone Castle, Kent
1948	Theobalds Park Club Site, Waltham Cross, Hertfordshire
1949	Polesden Lacey Estate, Great Bookham, Surrey
1950	Debden Green, Essex
1951	Trent Park, Cockfosters, Greater London
1952	Debden Green, Essex
1953	Mapledurham, Oxfordshire
1954	Balls Park Club Site, Hertford
1955	Stratford-upon-Avon, Warwickshire
1956	Gorhambury, St. Albans, Hertfordshire
1957	Mentmore Park, Buckinghamshire
1958	Manton Forest, Clumber, Worksop, Nottinghamshire
1959	Bourley Camp, Crookham, Hampshire
1960	Rood Ashton, Wiltshire

1961	Friday Wood, Colchester, Essex
1962	Wynyard Park, County Durham
1963	Teddesley Park, Staffordshire
1964	Bourley Camp, Crookham, Hampshire
1965	Stanley Park, Blackpool, Lancashire
1966	Longleat, Wiltshire
1967	Newby Hall, Ripon, Yorkshire
1968	Woburn Abbey, Bedfordshire
1969	Wynyard Park, County Durham
1970	Mallory Park, Leicestershire
1971	Lingfield Park, Surrey
1972	Ribby Hall, Lancashire (cancelled due to County Council objection)
1973	Sixpenny Handley, Salisbury, Wiltshire
1974	Newby Hall, Ripon, Yorkshire
1975	Marsh Gibbon, Bicester, Oxfordshire
1976	National Agricultural Centre, Stoneleigh, Warwickshire
1977	Raby Castle, County Durham
1978	Northington Down Farm, Hampshire
1979	Alton Towers, Staffordshire
1980	Peterborough Showground, Cambridgeshire
1981	Cheltenham Racecourse, Gloucestershire
1982	Brands Hatch Motor Racing Circuit, Kent
1983	Tatton Park, Cheshire
1984	West of England Showground, Shepton Mallet, Somerset
1985	Castle Howard, Yorkshire
1986	Silverstone Motor Racing Circuit, Northamptonshire
1987	Lincoln Showground, Lincolnshire
1988	Lartington South Park, near Barnard Castle, County Durham
1989	Stratfield Saye, Berkshire
1990	Weston Park, Shropshire
1991	Ipswich Showground, Suffolk
1992	Cheltenham Racecourse, Gloucestershire
1993	Agricultural College, Hadlow, Kent
1994	Cholmondeley Castle, Cheshire

1995	West of England Showground, Shepton Mallet, Somerset
1996	Carlton Towers, Yorkshire
1997	Otmoor Park, Oxfordshire
1998	Royal Highland Showground, Ingliston, Edinburgh
1999	Stanford Hall, Leicestershire
2000	Greystone Farm, near Winston, County Durham
2001	Broadlands Estate, Romsey, Hampshire

Index